# Fighting Through
## to Anzio

By the same author:

*Scattered Under the Rising Sun: The Gordon Highlanders in the Far East 1941–1945* (Pen & Sword Military, Barnsley, 2012)

*St Valéry and Its Aftermath: The Gordon Highlanders Captured in France in 1940* (Pen & Sword Military, Barnsley, 2017)

# Fighting Through to Anzio

## The Gordon Highlanders in the Second World War (6th Battalion and 1st London Scottish)

Stewart Mitchell

Pen & Sword
**MILITARY**

First published in Great Britain in 2023 by
Pen & Sword Military
An imprint of Pen & Sword Books Limited
Yorkshire – Philadelphia

ISBN 978 1 39905 821 6

A CIP catalogue record for this book is
available from the British Library

Typeset by Mac Style
Printed in the UK by CPI Group (UK) Ltd, Croydon, CR0 4YY.

Pen & Sword Books Limited incorporates the imprints of After
the Battle, Atlas, Archaeology, Aviation, Discovery, Family History,
Fiction, History, Maritime, Military, Military Classics, Politics,
Select, Transport, True Crime, Air World, Frontline Publishing, Leo
Cooper, Remember When, Seaforth Publishing, The Praetorian Press,
Wharncliffe Local History, Wharncliffe Transport, Wharncliffe True
Crime and White Owl.

For a complete list of Pen & Sword titles please contact

PEN & SWORD BOOKS LIMITED
47 Church Street, Barnsley, South Yorkshire, S70 2AS, England
E-mail: enquiries@pen-and-sword.co.uk
Website: www.pen-and-sword.co.uk
or
PEN AND SWORD BOOKS
1950 Lawrence Rd, Havertown, PA 19083, USA
E-mail: Uspen-and-sword@casematepublishers.com
Website: www.penandswordbooks.com

# Contents

# Maps

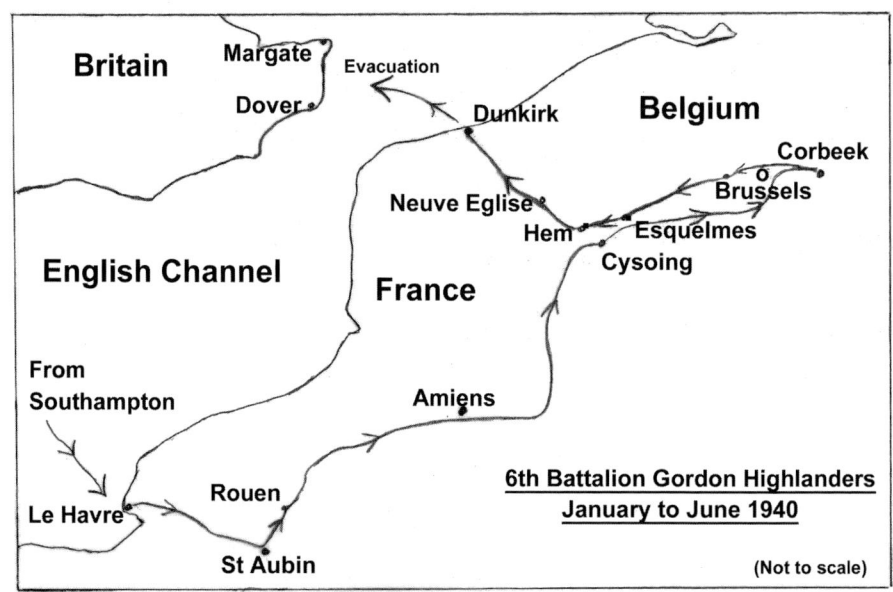

Britain

Margate

Evacuation

Dover

Dunkirk

Belgium

Corbeek

Brussels

Neuve Eglise

Esquelmes

Hem

Cysoing

English Channel

France

From Southampton

Amiens

Rouen

Le Havre

St Aubin

6th Battalion Gordon Highlanders
January to June 1940

(Not to scale)

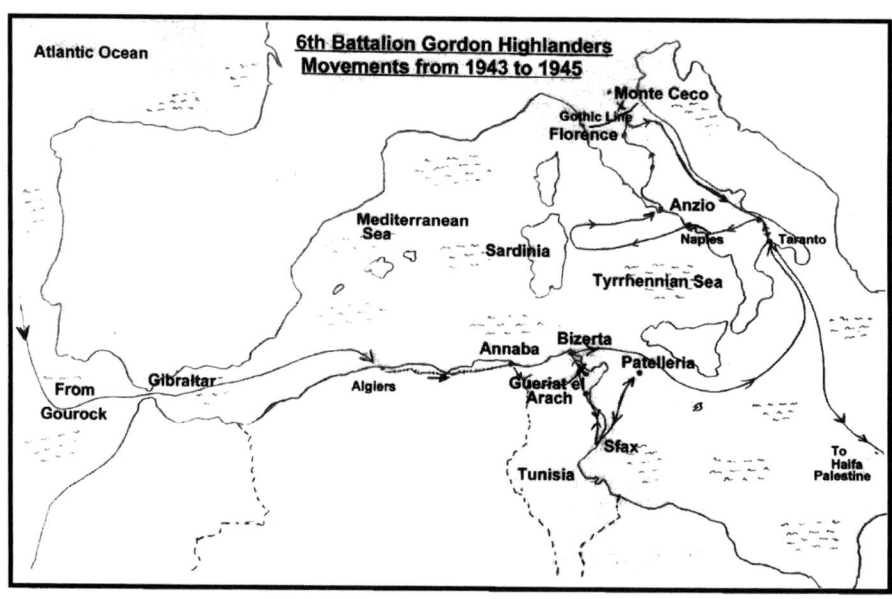

Atlantic Ocean

6th Battalion Gordon Highlanders
Movements from 1943 to 1945

Monte Ceco

Gothic Line

Florence

Mediterranean Sea

Sardinia

Anzio

Naples

Taranto

Tyrrhennian Sea

Gibraltar

From Gourock

Algiers

Annaba

Bizerta

Gueriat el Arach

Patelleria

Sfax

Tunisia

To Haifa Palestine

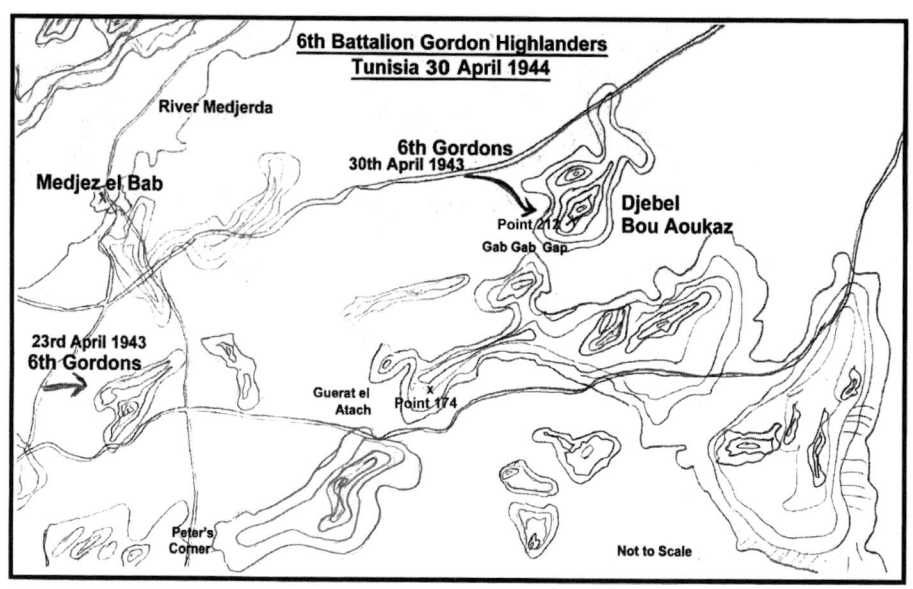

6th Battalion Gordon Highlanders
Tunisia 30 April 1944

River Medjerda

Medjez el Bab

6th Gordons
30th April 1943

Point 212
Gab Gab Gap

Djebel
Bou Aoukaz

23rd April 1943
6th Gordons

Guerat el
Atach

Point 174

Peter's
Corner

Not to Scale

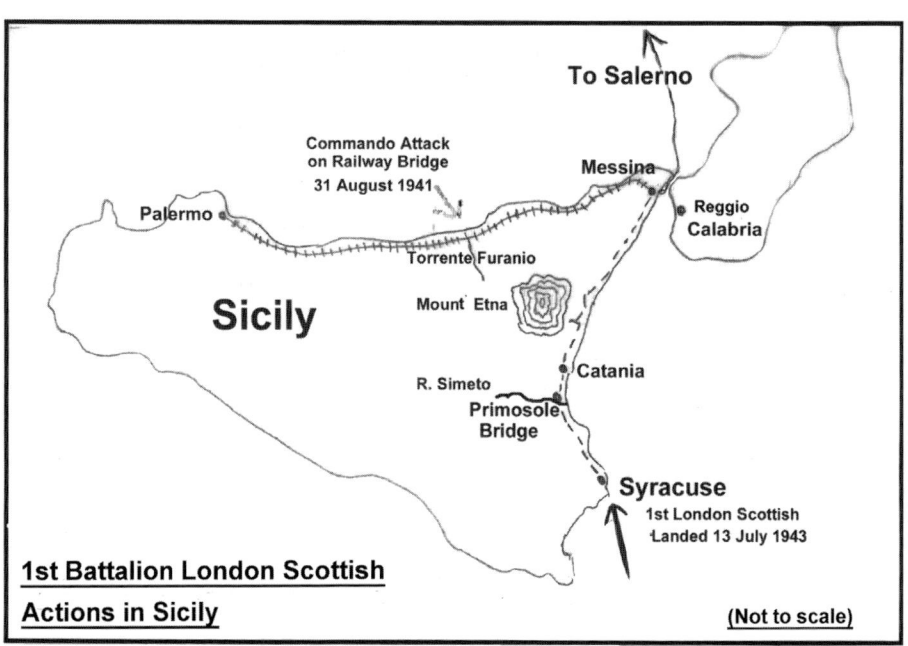

To Salerno

Commando Attack
on Railway Bridge
31 August 1941

Messina

Palermo

Reggio
Calabria

Torrente Furanio

Sicily

Mount Etna

Catania

R. Simeto

Primosole
Bridge

Syracuse
1st London Scottish
Landed 13 July 1943

1st Battalion London Scottish

Actions in Sicily

(Not to scale)

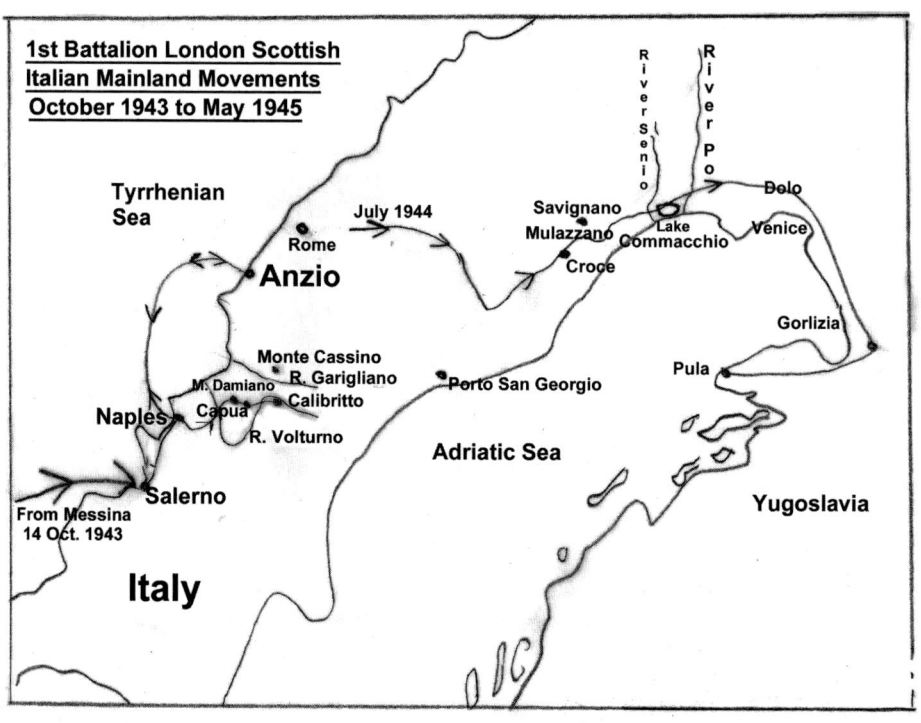

## 1st Battalion London Scottish Italian Mainland Movements October 1943 to May 1945

Tyrrhenian Sea

July 1944

Rome

**Anzio**

Monte Cassino
R. Garigliano
M. Damiano    Calibritto
Capua
R. Volturno

**Naples**

Salerno

From Messina
14 Oct. 1943

**Italy**

Savignano
Mulazzano    Lake
Croce    Commacchio

River Senio

River Po

Dolo

Venice

Gorlizia

Pula

Porto San Georgio

**Adriatic Sea**

**Yugoslavia**

---

## Capoleone Salient ANZIO 1944

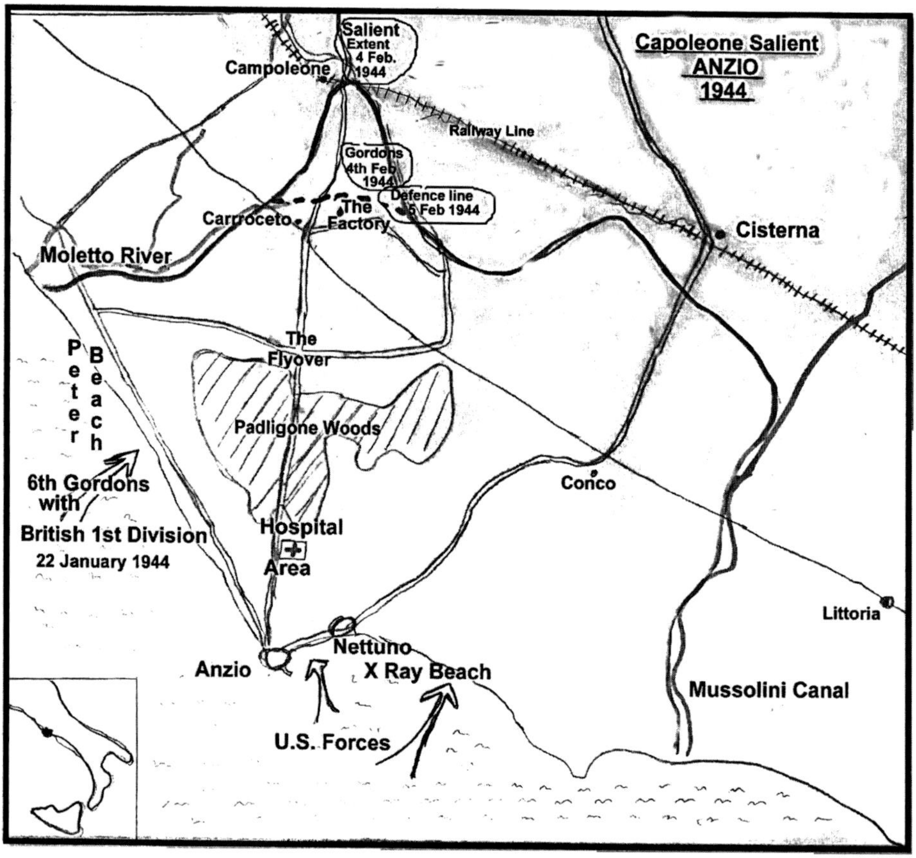

Salient
Extent
4 Feb.
1944

Campoleone

Railway Line

Gordons
4th Feb
1944

Carroceto    The
Factory

Defence line
5 Feb 1944

Cisterna

Moletto River

The
Flyover

Padligone Woods

Peter Beach

6th Gordons
with
British 1st Division
22 January 1944

Hospital
Area

Conco

Littoria

Anzio

Nettuno
X Ray Beach

U.S. Forces

Mussolini Canal

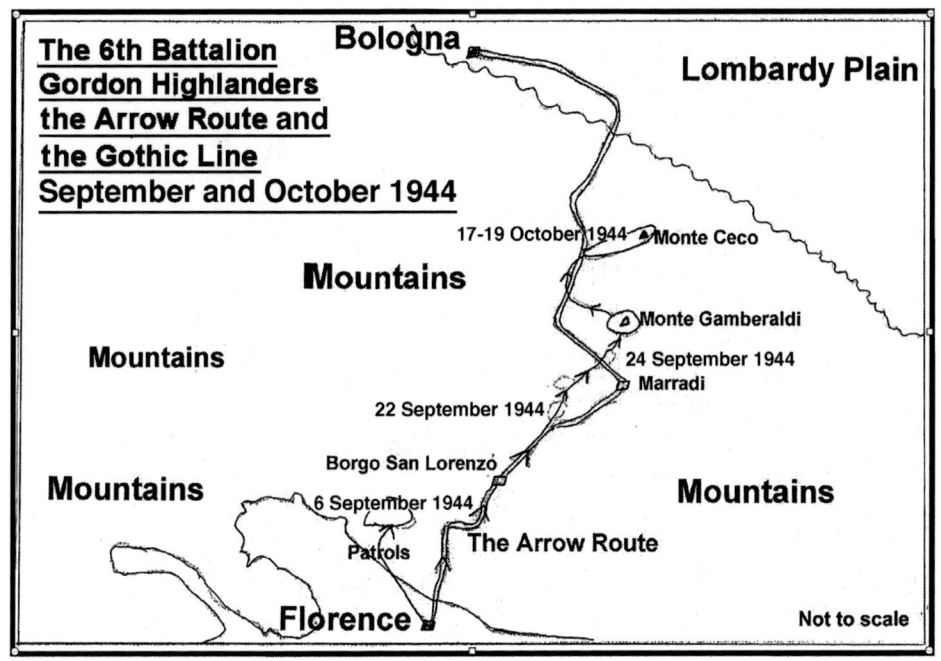

The 6th Battalion
Gordon Highlanders
the Arrow Route and
the Gothic Line
September and October 1944

Bologna

Lombardy Plain

Mountains

17-19 October 1944 — Monte Ceco

Monte Gamberaldi

Mountains

24 September 1944
Marradi

22 September 1944

Borgo San Lorenzo

Mountains

6 September 1944

Mountains

Patrols

The Arrow Route

Florence

Not to scale

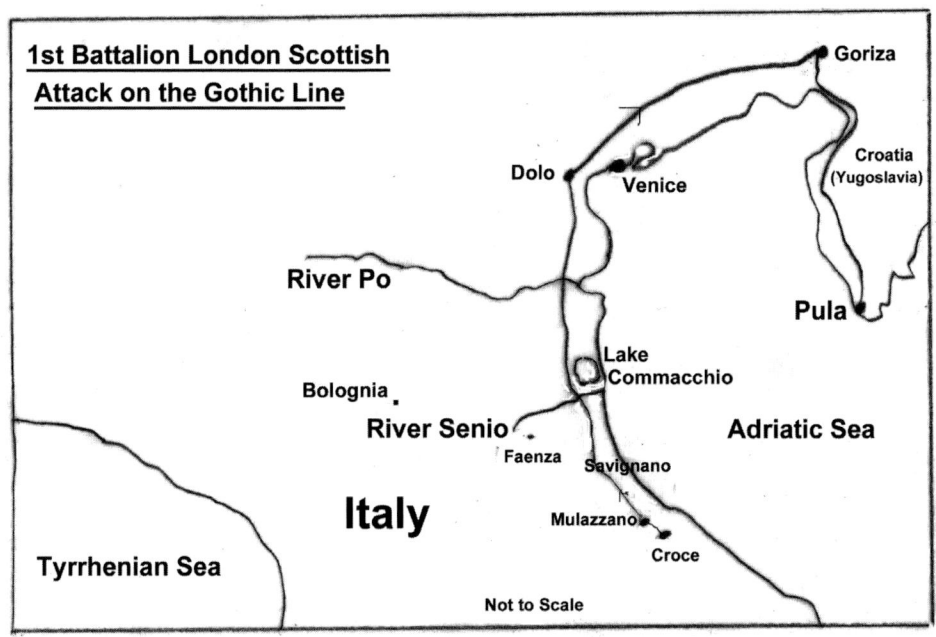

1st Battalion London Scottish
Attack on the Gothic Line

Goriza

Dolo

Venice

Croatia
(Yugoslavia)

River Po

Pula

Lake
Commacchio

Bolognia

River Senio

Adriatic Sea

Faenza

Savignano

Italy

Mulazzano

Croce

Tyrrhenian Sea

Not to Scale

# Acknowledgements

This book could not have been produced without the support and assistance of many people. I wish to thank Colonel (Rtd.) Charles Sloan, OBE, the Chairman of the Gordon Highlanders Regimental Trust and the Gordon Highlanders Museum in Aberdeen, and Executive Director, John McLeish, Curator, Ruth Cox, and other Museum staff (Ian Pithie, Darren Sharp and Lewis Gibbon). Special thanks are also due to Lieutenant General (Rtd.) Sir Peter Graham, the last Colonel of the regiment, and the Regimental Secretary, (Major (Rtd.) Grenville Irvine-Fortescue). In addition, I wish to thank the Gordon Highlanders Museum Research Team, particularly Major (Rtd.) Malcom Ross, Gordon Third and Anne Clark and Oral History Co-ordinator, Arlene Foreman. I gratefully acknowledge access to the archives and photographic records of the Gordon Highlanders Museum and permission to use them. I was also greatly assisted by the Curator of the London Scottish Museum, Andrew Parsons, who was very helpful in identifying photographs of the 1st Battalion London Scottish, and to the Trustees of the London Scottish Regiment for allowing their reproduction.

I wish also to thank family members of the men who had served with the regiment who provided information about their loved ones: in particular, Squadron Leader (Rtd.) Leslie Fellows, who allowed extracts from his book, *An English Gordon – A Tribute to the Short Life of Leslie Tromans*, and Anne Hunter, who gave permission to use extracts and photos from her book, *Robert's Story*, which tells the tragic story of Robert Frame. I am also indebted to Michael Lobban, who shared his father's diary and to Donald Dallas, whose family archive was of enormous interest. There were many others who provided family photographs, documents and personal accounts. These included James Shand, Phyllis Reid, Margaret Russell, Eileen McIntosh, Alex Paterson Jnr, Major Sam Hughes, Frances Gillespie, Leslie Sudderick, Dennis Jones, Graham Robertson, Emma Stevens, Paul Feder, David Howie, Gillian Murphy, Major (Rtd.) Hervé Savary, Peter Lowden, Dennis Jones, James McGarrity and many others.

Every effort has been made to ensure that facts presented in this book are wholly accurate. However, if any discrepancy or inaccuracy has occurred, I apologize in advance.

## Photograph Acknowledgments

The captions of some of the photographs have been given the shortened acknowledgement of the 'Gordon Highlanders Museum' or the 'London Scottish Regiment's Trustees'. These images have been reproduced with the permission of the Trustees and Curator of the Gordon Highlanders Museum, Viewfield Road, Aberdeen and the Trustees and the Curator of the London Scottish Museum, Horseferry Road, London, together with the Trustees of the London Scottish Regiment. The remaining photos are reproduced with the permission of individual members of the families of the soldiers involved and their names noted in full. The generous permission given to use these photographs is fully appreciated as they assist considerably in illustrating the story of these two battalions of the Gordon Highlanders during the Second World War.

# Foreword

## By Lieutenant General Sir Peter Graham, KCB, CBE
## Last Colonel of The Gordon Highlanders

Stewart Mitchell is a long-serving volunteer researcher at the Gordon Highlanders Museum in Aberdeen and this is his third book recounting the story of individual Gordon Highlander battalions during the Second World War. A debt is owed to Stewart Mitchell for his considerable research and work in producing these books. The Gordons fought in almost every theatre of that conflict and upheld the proud tradition of the regiment fighting some of the fiercest battles. This work tells the story of two Territorial Army battalions, the 6th (Banffshire) Battalion and the 1st Battalion London Scottish. (The London Scottish became part of the Gordon Highlanders in 1937, when the London Regiment was broken up.)

Although the main theme of this book is the Italian Campaign, these two battalions had very different journeys to the Italian theatre of the war. The 6th Battalion Gordons served with the British Expeditionary Force (BEF) in France and Belgium. Four battalions of Gordon Highlanders served in this ill-fated episode. The 6th Battalion were evacuated from Dunkirk with the 4th Battalion but the 1st and 5th Battalions, part of the 51st (Highland) Division and under French command, were trapped, unable to get away from St Valery-en-Caux. My father-in-law, Captain David Morren, 153 Brigade's Anti-Tank Officer, like virtually the whole division, was captured there and spent the next five years as a prisoner of war in Germany.

In 1943, the 6th Gordons fought in Tunisia. It was in an action here that Bobby Smith, who later commanded the 1st Battalion while I was his adjutant, was apparently seriously wounded. He was saved by his steel helmet, which is now an exhibit in the Regimental Museum in Aberdeen and displays the large hole made by German mortar bomb shrapnel.

The first invasion of Europe began with the amphibious landings on Sicily in July 1943. The Gordon Highlanders were represented by the reformed 1st and 5/7th battalions – veterans of the North African campaign, including the epic turning point battle of El Alamein – and the London Scottish, who, in contrast, were going into their first action. It was a bloody introduction to the war for them but they distinguished themselves. The London Scottish went on to fight at Monte Cassino, a notorious location as the Germans chose to block the Allied route to Rome there. Here the fighting was intense, with the Germans skilfully using the mountainous terrain and fast-flowing rivers to enhance their defensive positions. It was during the battles to break through that on the night of 23 January 1944, Private George Mitchell successfully led an attack on strong enemy positions on Damiano Ridge. With total disregard for his own safety, he succeeded in taking them, resulting in many Germans being killed or captured. Tragically he was shot by one of the German prisoners, but he was posthumously awarded the Victoria Cross, Britain's highest gallantry award. This was the only VC awarded to the regiment during the war and one of only 181 awarded during the entire war. As in the case of George Mitchell's VC, half of these were awarded posthumously.

With the stalemate at Anzio, an outflanking operation was planned which resulted in the amphibious landings at Anzio in January 1944. The 6th Battalion Gordon Highlanders were the first British battalion ashore. After the failed attempt to break out of the bridgehead, the 6th Gordons were holding a strategic position defending the salient created by the earlier advance. When the German counterattack came, the 6th Battalion were virtually surrounded, but held on when joined by the 1st London Scottish. Using the sound platform of the 6th Battalion's position, the London Scottish advanced and the counterattack was beaten off. Both battalions paid a heavy price for this success, with the 6th Battalion losing almost 3 entire companies while the London Scottish took over 120 casualties, but together they had held the line.

At Anzio, both officers and men of both battalions were recipients of many gallantry awards. In my early career I knew James (Jim) Williamson and Edward (Ted) Grace both very well and both were awarded the Military Cross for their courageous leadership in the bridgehead, with Ted Grace being seriously wounded and subsequently having to be evacuated back to Britain. Both men subsequently wrote moving accounts of the battle. The 80th anniversary of the Anzio landings occurs in January 2024. It would be a fitting tribute to these men and the regiment to ensure their actions are fully known.

Another Gordon Highlander who was seriously wounded at Anzio was Major Malcolm Munthe, who had earlier joined the Special Forces. Munthe and his Special Operations Executive (SOE) team rescued Senator Croce, Italy's leading anti-fascist, as German troops surrounded his house. For his work with the Resistance, Munthe was presented with a seventeenth-century broad sword with an engraved inscription, 'With the true thanks of the Italians to the British officers and men who saved them at Sorrento, led by Major

Malcolm Munthe of the Gordon Highlanders.'This sword is also now part of the collection of the Gordon Highlanders Museum.

The 6th Battalion continued to fight in the bridgehead, but very occasionally there were calmer moments. The combined drums and pipes of both battalions performed among the tented Anzio hospital area to raise the morale of the patients. After the breakout from the bridgehead and the liberation of Rome, the 6th Battalion's drums and pipes had the honour of leading the victory parade through the streets of Rome. The Gordon Highlander's Museum has a painting depicting the scene with the colosseum as the backdrop. Wherever the drums and pipes played, they received a rapturous welcome with the spectacle of the swagger of the men in their kilts and the skirl of the pipes thrilling Scots and Italians alike.

In the latter part of 1944 both battalions continued to fight in Italy. They were engaged in attacking the formidable German defences north of Florence, known as the Gothic Line, where both battalions again distinguished themselves, but at a high cost. At the end of 1944, the 6th Gordons moved to quell the trouble spot of Palestine while the 1st London Scottish finished the war in Trieste, but both battalions had suffered enormous losses during the war.

As a result of MOD (Army) reorganizations, the London Scottish exist today as a company of the household division but also retain informal links with the Gordon Highlanders. The close-knit feeling between the 6th Gordon officers was such that in 1924 they formed their own 6th Battalion (Great War) Dinner Club. Their annual dinner had one or two special customs such as 'The Memory' and that wherever they as individuals were at 21:00 hours on the day of the annual dinner, they would drink a toast of 'The Memory'.

In 2012, there were no 6th Battalion Gordon officers left that could travel to the dinner but they wanted to continue the annual dinner in some form. Could I, as colonel of the regiment, help? I advised they form a new dining club from the old and it would be called the Bydand Dinner Club open to all Gordon Highlander officers and to a few local people who were supportive of the museum. The customs of the 6th Great War Dinner Club would be retained. This was agreed by all concerned and the Bydand Dinner Club continues to use those customs so that the 6th Battalion is not forgotten and continues to be remembered with pride and affection.

Bydand,
*Peter Graham*
2023

# Chapter 1

# An Uneasy Peace

The Gordon Highlanders have a proud 200-year record of service. From 1794 to 1994, the regiment served kings, queens, and country all over the British Empire and fought in virtually every major conflict during their long and distinguished history. Among the many gallantry medals awarded throughout this period are nineteen Victoria Crosses. After the reorganization of the British Army in 1921, when the Territorial Force was reconstituted as the Territorial Army (TA), the Gordon Highlanders comprised a regimental headquarters or 'depot' (Aberdeen), two Regular Army battalions and four TA battalions for part-time soldiers. At any particular time only one of the Regular Army battalions (1st or 2nd) would serve at 'home' (i.e., somewhere in the UK), whilst the other was overseas (i.e., somewhere in the British Empire). The TA battalions were distributed throughout the regimental recruiting area, which for the Gordons was north-east Scotland. The TA battalions were the 4th (Aberdeen City) Battalion, the 5th/7th (Buchan, Mar & Mearns) Battalion and the 6th (Banff & Donside) Battalion, which were joined in 1937 by the London Scottish when the London Regiment was broken up. However, the association of the London Scottish and the Gordon Highlanders goes much further back in time than 1937. The London Scottish earned their first battle honour 'South Africa 1900–02' while serving with service companies of the Gordon Highlanders in the Boer War. A total of four officers and eighty-six other ranks of the London Scottish served with the Gordons in South Africa. The first draft met the 2nd Battalion Gordon Highlanders in Ladysmith on 24 March 1900 and in 1901 a second detachment relieved the first contingent; in total more than 200 London Scots served in the South African War. In addition, during the First World War, a royal warrant was issued, on 12 July 1916, which officially 'associated' the London Scottish and the Gordon Highlanders.

With the long association with north-east Scotland, their glorious military history and the long list of local noble families who have served in the regiment, the Gordon Highlanders were highly regarded and respected; for example, Colonel Sir George William Abercromby DSO, 8th Baronet of Birkenbog, who had served with distinction during the Great War, was the 6th Battalion's Honorary Colonel. The TA battalions were firmly rooted in their own geographic areas and so developed strong links and bonds with their whole community generating local pride, goodwill and affection. This meant that the battalion pipe bands would often be called on to perform at civic functions. TA soldiers were part-time volunteers, so in addition to their soldiering activities, they were also engaged in full-time occupations working in their communities. For example, in Keith, the location of the 6th Battalion's headquarters, Major A. G. Innes Fleming was a local solicitor in the family legal firm started by his father, Colonel J.G. Fleming, and also served the burgh council as the town clerk. He had two older brothers who had both died in the First World War. Captain Duncan S. Annand owned the local ironmongery, Captain Robert (Robin) Rae was the Assistant Manager of Seafield Wool Mills and Captain (Doctor) James Lennel Taylor, a local GP, was the battalion's Medical Officer. The other ranks were filled by men from every walk of life engaged in the local distilleries, wool mills, agriculture, etc. For example, Sergeant William Ogg had previously worked at Kynoch's Isla Bank Wool Mills, but with fifteen years of service in the TA was appointed as the Orderly Clerk at the Keith Drill Hall just before the outbreak of the Second World War. Sergeant (Piper) Tom Bruce was a spinner, Sergeant William Stables worked in his family's grocery shop in Keith, Corporal John Spence was a Banffshire County Council roadman, Corporal Douglas Harrower was a stone mason, Private James Carmichael was a woodman, Private Keith Boardman was a bank clerk and Private Robert Milton was a farm worker. This pattern was mirrored throughout the other towns in the area such as Buckie, Huntly and Turriff. Events organized by the Gordons would not only attract the attention of the local population but command the support of the prominent members of society who wished to be seen at these functions. In February 1939, before the cares of the Second World War, the annual C Company Ball at Huntly was attended by numerous couples from far and wide and included not only officers and men of the battalion and RAF officers from Aberdeen, but also various dignitaries, local clergy, doctors and businessmen, all accompanied by their wives and girlfriends.

This is the story of two of the Gordon Highlanders TA battalions during the Second World War: the 6th Battalion (Banff & Donside) and the 1st Battalion London Scottish. Although the two battalions were in different divisions, fate threw them together at Anzio, where they fought side by side. Both units had already distinguished themselves in the First World War. The 6th Battalion was mobilized in August 1914 and crossed to France in November. They were the first TA battalion of the famous 51st (Highland) Division ('the Ladies from Hell') to take their place in the Front and were involved in the Christmas truce of 1914, when British and German soldiers left their trenches to meet in no man's land to wish each other Merry Christmas. Private George McIntosh, from Buckie, Banffshire, who was serving with the 1st/6th Battalion, was awarded the Victoria Cross for an action in July 1917 at Ypres, Belgium. During the Great War, the London Scottish was a part of the 14th London Regiment (London Scottish). The 1st/14th Battalion was mobilized on the outbreak of war and landed in France in mid-September 1914. Only six weeks later the battalion was the first TA unit to encounter German forces at Messines in Belgium. The 2/14th Battalion did not land in France until the summer of 1916, but was then transferred to Palestine, where Charles Train and Robert Cruikshank were both awarded the Victoria Cross in separate incidents in December 1917 and May 1918. Charles Train was born in Finsbury Park, London but traced his Scottish ancestry through his father, who was from Loanhead, Midlothian. Robert Cruickshank was born in Winnipeg, Canada and owed his Scottish heritage to his father, who was from Aberdeen.

As the titles of each of the TA battalions of the Gordon Highlanders suggests, each had a defined geographical area for recruitment with a regimental HQ located within their district and various companies and also individual platoons distributed around their area. In each location, the men would meet in local drill halls for training, parades and administration, although some social aspects around the battalion, such as sports, dinners and dances, were also important cohesive forces in developing a strong esprit de corps.

Despite the horrors of the Great War from 1914 to 1918, in the deeply patriotic society which prevailed, recruitment into the Regular Army and the TA was still positively admired in the 1930s, particularly in the rural areas of Aberdeenshire, Kincardine and Banffshire, but was also seen favourably in the city of Aberdeen. At this time unemployment was high and for those engaged in agriculture their wages were low, so the small annual bounty provided by the TA, augmented by receipt of the same wage as a Regular Army soldier for the two-week annual summer camp, was a welcome addition to tight household budgets of the married men. For the young men, the appeal of the uniform to the young lasses of the district was no doubt also a factor. The additional attraction of the annual camp for most men was as good as a holiday they could not otherwise afford. The TA also gave an opportunity to experience army life for young men who were contemplating a career in the Regular Army and was often a stepping stone to that change in lifestyle.

The 1930s were a politically turbulent decade of the twentieth century with the rise of fascism in Europe, particularly in Germany, Spain and Italy. Britain had no stomach for a repeat of the carnage of the First World War and the growing military strength of Hitler's Germany went unchallenged. Ultimately, the incorporation of Austria into the Third Reich (Anschluss) in March 1938 and Hitler's demands to incorporate the Sudetenland, a largely German-speaking area which was part of Czechoslovakia, prompted some action. There was a strong element within the British Government which favoured the appeasement of Hitler in the hope that another war could be avoided. The Munich Conference was convened to discuss the matter and after German assurances this was the final demand for an expansion in Europe, Hitler's demands were accepted by both Britain and France, with Prime Minister Neville Chamberlain returning to London brandishing the agreement which he claimed guaranteed peace. German forces occupied the Sudetenland in October 1938 without a shot being fired.

In 1939, with a deteriorating international situation, the continued rise of Nazi Germany and the increasingly belligerent approach of Adolf Hitler, the government decided that the British Army should be enlarged and in the spring ordered that the TA be doubled. Additionally, Leslie Hore-Belisha, Secretary of State for War, persuaded Neville Chamberlain's government to introduce a limited form of conscription. As a result, Parliament passed The Military Training Act on 26 May 1939. This Act applied to males aged 20 and 21 years old who were to be called up for six months full-time military training, and then to be transferred to the Army Reserve and return to their civilian employment. This was the UK's first act of peacetime conscription and was intended to be temporary in nature. Men called up were to be known as 'Militiamen' to distinguish them from the Regular Army. To emphasize this distinction, each man was issued with a suit in addition to a uniform. There was one registration date under the Act, on Saturday, 3 June 1939. Understandably, but significantly, registration under this Act was not required for men who had already enlisted into the TA, which in some minds was an incentive to join the part-time TA rather than spend a compulsory full-time six months in the army.

This national mood, coupled with the government's desire to double the size of the TA, prompted the TA battalions to mount recruiting drives within their areas. These took the form of exhibitions in village and town halls where there were parades, lectures and weapons displays. For example, the 6th Battalion carried out a recruiting exercise in their whole battalion area from 13–20 February 1939. The local drill halls were thrown open to the public during the normal training sessions which began with short introductory speeches being made by the Commanding Officer, the Provost, and any other local influential person. Weapon demonstrations were given and in general these proved a popular attraction and sixty new recruits signed up during the week.

These events had proved so successful that a demonstration unit was formed by the 6th Battalion, which became known as the 'circus'. The circus held public demonstrations at weekends in virtually every town and village in Banffshire and western Aberdeenshire throughout April 1939. The programme included the drums and pipes playing in full dress, under Pipe Major Willie Geddes, and a demonstration by the PT squad led by Captain Innes Flemming. In addition, there were weapon demonstrations of the Bren gun and the Bren gun carrier (a newly acquired versatile half-tracked vehicle ably demonstrated by Lieutenant David Morren), while Lieutenant A. J. Lockhart led a demonstration of their 2-inch mortars. The squad also demonstrated the defence for a gas attack and taking on of an aeroplane attack. The 'circus' was led by Captain Duncan S. Annand, of whom it was joked that he would qualify for a BBC announcer after all his practice with a loudspeaker. Under the slogan 'Double Up and Double the Size of the Sixth', this whole exercise was very successful with enough recruits signing up to double the size of the Battalion. A measure of their success was that a waiting list had to be drawn up as the 6th Battalion and its new sister battalion (the 9th Battalion) were both up to war strength.

Similar activities were going on for the other TA battalions. Michael Burge was working in a shipping office in London and despite his family having a naval background, having no Scottish ancestry or ever having been to Scotland, he was attracted to the posters he saw around London which proclaimed, *Join the London Scottish.*' He decided to take the matter into his own hands so, with a friend, went to a local recruiting office and volunteered for the London Scottish. He was subsequently posted to the Gordon Highlanders Regimental Headquarters (the Depot), which had become No. 9 Infantry Training Centre, Aberdeen, where he carried out his basic training. Two years later he was commissioned into the reformed 2nd Battalion Gordon Highlanders and served with them in north-west Europe and Tripoli. Incidentally, the poster seen by Michael Burge was almost certainly the recruitment poster designed by Robert Souter, who was a prolific artist and pre-war London Scottish Territorial.

Traditionally each year, for four days at the beginning of August, the local TA units and others assembled at the rifle ranges at Blackdog, just north of Aberdeen, for the annual 'wapenshaw'. This had a long tradition, being first inaugurated in 1911, and the word 'wapenshaw' was a Scots corruption of 'weapon show'. It was originally an event, formerly widely held all over Scotland, to review local troops. Competition at the event was fierce and in 1939 the 6th Gordons shone, taking much of the silverware but, just as in the previous year, they were pipped for the King's Cup by CSM Moultrie of their sister battalion, the 5th/7th Gordon Highlanders. A testament to the high standard of the 6th Battalion's musketry throughout all of the ranks was highlighted by Private Basil Ricketts, who had volunteered to join the 6th Battalion only a few months earlier, winning the Recruit's Cup, while Commanding Officer Lieutenant Colonel Ledingham won the Bruce Cup.

# Chapter 2

# The Road to War

After Adolf Hitler became Chancellor, i.e., the head of the German Government, in 1933, he spread Nazi propaganda within Europe. He especially targeted German-speaking people in the region to consider themselves part of a 'Greater Germany'. With his eyes on Austria's natural resources, needed for the expansion of the German war machine, Hitler pursued a prolonged, but largely unsuccessful courtship of the Austrian people. After some political manoeuvring, German soldiers boldly crossed the Austria Frontier in March 1938, where they were welcomed unopposed. This emboldened Hitler, who turned his attention to the Sudetenland, a largely German-speaking area of Czechoslovakia. This eventually sparked an international crisis and the British Army were put on alert with the 1st Battalion Gordon Highlanders, then based in Aldershot, being mobilised and getting as far as boarding a ship in Southampton in preparation to defend the integrity of Czechoslovakia's borders.

A meeting was convened in Munich between Britain, France and Germany to resolve the issue of sovereignty of the Sudetenland and once again Hitler achieved his goal with the area ceded to Germany, without the consent of the Czech Government. The Munich agreement was signed on 30 September 1938. When Adolf Hitler and Neville Chamberlain settled the Sudetenland question, there was an understanding that this was an end to all of Germany's territorial claims. However, Hitler did not keep his word on this. Only six months later, Germany seized the whole of Czechoslovakia and pressed for the inclusion of the city of Danzig (modern day Gdansk), Poland into the Third Reich. This issue had been a source of discord between Germany and the Polish state for many years. After the end of the First World War, the borders of Poland were the subject of intense discussion as part of the Treaty of Versailles. It was agreed that access to the sea, without dependence on access through Germany, was an imperative for the viability of the Polish state and to enable this, a 'corridor' was created, along with making Danzig a 'free city' administered by the League of Nations. This corridor effectively separated German East Prussia from the rest of Germany, which created tension between Germany and Poland. Given Hitler's previous actions, the Polish Government were extremely concerned by the increasingly aggressive behaviour of the

German Government, but with Britain and France guaranteeing the integrity of the Polish borders, they were largely reassured.

On the morning of Friday, 1 September 1939, there was a meeting in 10 Downing Street of the cabinet, chaired by Neville Chamberlain. The unfolding and confused reports that Germany had invaded Poland were discussed and agreement reached on the wording of an ultimatum to be delivered to the German Government. The wording was unambiguous. This required that the German Government give a satisfactory assurance that all aggressive action against Poland would cease and German forces be withdrawn promptly from Polish territory, otherwise the United Kingdom would, without hesitation, fulfil their obligations to Poland. This, in effect, warned Germany that unless their actions in Poland ceased, Britain and France would declare war, although the British Government desperately hoped this could still be avoided. The cabinet also agreed that the British Army, including the Territorial Army (TA) should be mobilized immediately, together with a general call-up of the reservists. The government also introduced 'the National Service (Armed Forces) Act of 1939 which introduced conscription for all men aged between 18 and 41 years old. Very few were exempt, but excluded were men working in essential industries, i.e., jobs such as baking, farming, medicine, police and other emergency services.

In common with regimental and battalion headquarters all over the country, a telegram, with the word 'Priority' emblazoned in large letters across the bright red envelope, was delivered to the headquarters of the 6th Battalion Gordon Highlanders in Keith, Banffshire. The duty officer opened this to find it was short and to the point instructing the mobilization of the battalion. This was followed two days later by another telegram which was equally brief, stating 'War has broken out with Germany. Acknowledge.'

In faraway Westminster, London, at the HQ of the London Scottish, 59 Buckingham Gate, a similar message was received by Captain Hill, the adjutant of the 1st Battalion London Scottish. This was the trigger for the assembly of some 300 men who made their way to Chelsea Barracks where their numbers were swelled to twenty-six officers and almost 600 other ranks. To have a degree of influence in the training of conscripts bound for the London Scottish, a group of experienced men were dispatched to the Gordon Barracks, Bridge of Don, Aberdeen which was where all Gordons were now being trained. The battalion remained in Chelsea until the end of October 1939, when they moved to Broome Park in the Canterbury area of Kent. On 22 October, before their move, they received a special guest in the form of Sir Ian Hamilton GCB, GCMG, DSO, TD, who was the Honorary Colonel of the Gordon Highlanders – a largely ceremonial role. Sir Ian was a very distinguished Gordon Highlander with a long and illustrious career. Sir Ian was not the most important visitor, however. Queen Consort Elizabeth, who was the Honorary Colonel of the London Scottish, paid them a visit in April 1940.

Back in Aberdeen, at Gordon Barracks, the Militiamen called up in mid-July were partway through their intended six-month training, but this was now compressed and there was now no prospect they would return to their civilian lives until the war was over. With general conscription now in place the demands for training became more pressing. Men being conscripted and destined for both the 6th Battalion Gordon Highlanders and the London Scottish were trained at Gordon Barracks, Aberdeen. This included men from all over Britain, such as John Menzies from Brighton, Sussex, and Harold Chandler from Newport, Monmouthshire and it was the first time many had been this far from home. This was not the case however for Private Robert Taylor, as the Gordon Barracks was just at the end of the street where he lived. After his training was completed, he was posted to the 1st Battalion London Scottish as the traditional regimental recruitment areas were now disregarded.

In addition to Gordon Barracks, men were accommodated at various public buildings around Aberdeen. These included Linksfield and Sunnybank Schools and the Beach Ballroom. The ballroom was a large art deco building on the seafront which was a popular pre-war entertainment venue which could accommodate 1,000 dancers on the floor with a restaurant and tea lounge seating 350 people at one time. In addition to this being a training venue, the recruits guarded and patrolled the long sandy beach which was in close proximity. Training used the open spaces to the north of Aberdeen, on Scotstown Moor and the sand dunes just south of Balmedie, where firearms practice at the Blackdog firing range meant a 16-mile march for the round trip.

After the 1st Battalion London Scottish arrived in Kent, their training began in earnest and a further draft of almost 150 recruits was received from Gordon Barracks, Aberdeen in October. During their time in Kent, they provided a response to invasion threats. All of the alarms were false, but the situation was not unexpected with tensions in the county closest to Nazi-occupied France running high. On 2 December 1939, Colour Sergeant R.L.H. (Lindsay) Bridgman, who had held that rank in the battalion for seven years, was commissioned into the 6th Battalion Gordon Highlanders and he would go on to play a decisive role with his new battalion.

When the 6th Battalion was mobilized, this involved men from the wide surrounding area of Banffshire and west Aberdeenshire assembling at the battalion headquarters at the Drill Hall in Keith. At towns and villages large and small, the men were given an emotional send-off. This was a huge logistical undertaking as men had to travel from a wide area. In the larger towns, men assembled and marched to the railway station. In the small village of Garmond, home to just a few hundred people, friends and relatives gathered round to see off the young men of the village as they boarded their army transport bound for Keith. Among them was James Hadden, who had joined up only four months earlier. At Keith there was a requirement to find accommodation and meals for the hundreds of men flooding into the headquarters, providing a gigantic headache for Quartermaster Lieutenant Charles Munro, MM, who was a veteran of the First World War. The 6th Battalion were part of the 51st (Highland) Division so destined for France. On 7 October, they prepared to leave for Hampshire. The battalion formed up, paraded on the local football pitch and were bade farewell and good luck by Provost of Keith and Honorary Battalion Colonel Sir George Abercromby Bt., DSO. As they marched the mile to Keith Railway Station, bound for Aldershot, they had formed up into their platoons, with each one receiving a rousing send-off from the townsfolk. One of the women waving her husband off was Isabella Milton (neé Mackie), a bride of only seventeen days, having married Private Francis Milton, who was born in Australia where his family remained. His father had emigrated from Moray over twenty-five years earlier. Isabella had two brothers, William and George, who were also serving with the Gordon Highlanders; unlike her husband, they had joined the Regular Army.

Before the 6th Battalion could go overseas, they required additional training. They were posted to the Farnborough area and stationed at Delville Barracks, Hampshire, arriving there on 7 October 1939. Their brand-new barracks was among a group all named after First World War battles, constructed in the Aldershot area to house the rapid expansion of the British Army. The battalion was brought up to their war establishment by 104 Cameronian Militiamen newly trained at Number 3 Infantry Training Centre, Hamilton, and 124 men transferred from the recently formed 9th Battalion Gordon Highlanders. The next ten weeks were spent in training to bring the units up to scratch, including lectures on various topics, such as their duty to escape if captured, etc. Mechanized movement exercises, etc. were also undertaken. Around the end of December there was a move to Aldershot, where the 6th Battalion was based at Maida and Corunna Barracks. The men were granted leave back home and it was a great opportunity to celebrate Christmas with their families, knowing their future was uncertain with the impending move to France in the New Year. Lieutenant Leslie Hatt was married at the end of October, while Corporal Henry Garioch chose to get married on his home leave shortly after New Year. The declaration of war had a profound effect on many men who were already in a romantic relationship. In the first few days after war was declared (4–14 September 1939) there was, in the experience of Aberdeen District Registrars, 'a situation, without parallel'. There was a threefold increase in the number of marriages registered in Aberdeen, rising from a pre-war average of thirty-five per week to one hundred and ten. One telling feature told it all: most of the men who brought their brides before a minister or sheriff were in uniform. The unexpected mobilization also meant that those men who were posted away had to await their first home leave to tie the knot and Henry was not alone in marrying at this time.

The 6th Battalion Gordon Highlanders, together with the 5th Battalion Gordon Highlanders and the 4th Battalion Black Watch (Royal Highland Regiment), made up 153 Brigade of the 51st (Highland) Division. There were a few ceremonial duties to perform before embarkation to join the British Expeditionary Force (BEF) in France. King George VI and Queen Elizabeth visited the 51st (Highland) Division on 18 January 1940. The 5th and 6th Battalions Gordon Highlanders, together with other units of the division, lined Wellington Avenue, Aldershot, along which Their Majesties walked and reportedly remarked how impressed they were with how well the men were turned out, particularly bearing in mind the short service of many of them. The visit by the royal couple was a great surprise and morale boost for the soldiers as the visit had been kept secret for security reasons.

The next day there was another historic occasion when both battalions paraded together again on the parade square of Corunna Barracks, Aldershot. They were joined by the 1st Canadian Division, including the 48th Highlanders of Canada that were allied to the Gordons and the 75th Toronto Scottish whose affiliation to the London Scottish also made them a part of the Gordons family. The London Scottish was also physically represented at this parade, as a number of their officers had been posted to the 6th Battalion. The 48th Highlanders were stationed in barracks close to the 6th Gordons, and with both wearing the same tartan, the officers and men of the two units instantly became close comrades. At the joint parade, they were inspected by the Colonel of the Regiment (Sir James L.G. Burnett of Leys Bart, CB, CMG, DSO & Bar) who was himself a Gordon Highlander, commissioned into the Regiment in 1899. Subsequently he commanded the 1st Battalion, and then a brigade during the First World War. His distinguished career did not finish with the end of the First World War and he rose to the rank of major general commanding the famous 51st (Highland) Division during the inter-war period. He took the salute as they marched past to the massed drums and pipes of 153 Brigade. This was the first time that an "Allied" regiment had paraded with the Gordon Highlanders, but it was the last time that these units would officially be seen wearing the kilt until the end of the war.

The Highland Division was now ready for action and the 6th Gordons embarked for France. On 29 January 1940, they left Aldershot in heavy blowing snow and travelled to Southampton. The next morning, they were ferried across the Channel on the RMS *Lady of Mann* and the RMS *Ben-my-Chree*, both owned by the Isle of Man Steam Packet Company but repainted grey and pressed into naval service as personnel carriers. (Both these vessels later saw service at Dunkirk and on D-Day.) The daylight crossing of the convoy had an escort of two destroyers but there was no threat. The 6th Battalion arrived at Le Havre on 30 January but were advised that they would not disembark until the following day, so spent another night crammed aboard ship. Snow fell during the night and the battalion disembarked to a snowbound France, immediately boarding a train for Yvetot. They eventually arrived at the billets in the villages of Touffreville and Louvetot. After a 5-mile march, Jimmy Scott and some others were billeted at a farm. On exploring their surroundings, they discovered the farm had an orchard; in one outbuilding, the thirsty soldiers found several vats brewing cider, where upon they got absolutely 'sozzled' on the scrumpy. Unsurprisingly, the Commanding Officer immediately made this building out of bounds.

The cold was so extreme that it affected the vehicles. If there was a heavy frost, the engines were left to run all night to prevent them from freezing as there was no anti-freeze available. Despite it being the coldest winter in living memory, they were warmly welcomed by the locals. To maintain good relations with the local people, the pipe band played in the square. This was quite an ordeal with the slippery conditions underfoot, making it difficult for the pipers and drummers to keep their feet. Fortunately, there were no mishaps. When off-duty, the Gordons could shop and visit local cafés and bars. Their custom was very much welcomed by the local shopkeepers. Favourite items to send home were the novelty embroidered French postcards. Married men with families or those with sweethearts would use them to write home with something more special than an ordinary letter.

In considering the standard of training of the Territorial Divisions in France, General Lord Gort's command decided it would be beneficial if each brigade exchanged one Territorial Army battalion for a battalion of Regulars. Since the 51st (Highland) Division comprised all Territorial Army units, it was one of the divisions affected by this decision. In 153 Brigade of the 51st (Highland) Division this was accomplished by exchanging the 6th Battalion Gordon Highlanders for the 1st Battalion Gordon Highlanders from 2 Brigade of the 1st Division, who were expected to bring some additional experience and professionalism. The substitution took place at the beginning of March 1940. This event was not allowed to pass without some ceremony. The 1st Battalion paraded at Cysoing on 6 March. General Harold Alexander, the divisional commander, came and said his farewell while Brigadier Charles Hudson VC intimated how sorry he was to lose them from 2nd Infantry Brigade. The next day they departed, marching off to strains of the band of the 2nd Battalion Staffordshire Regiment.

As they prepared to leave the 51st (Highland) Division fold, the men of the 6th Battalion had no real idea where they were bound. After six months of the phoney war, many individuals believed they were headed for home. Corporal Jim Nicol was in the 5th Battalion but had originally enlisted into the 6th Battalion, in which his father also served. He grew up in Insch, Aberdeenshire and when he left school became an apprentice blacksmith there. Following in his father's footsteps he enlisted into the local 6th Battalion Gordon Highlanders. When he was offered a new position working in Hatton of Cruden, near Peterhead, he transferred to the 5th Battalion, which was based locally. His previous service meant he knew a lot of the 6th Battalion men well so when they heard of their move, with the rumour being this was back to the UK, his old friends started to pull his leg, saying he was 'in the wrong battalion now'! As events eventually unfolded, this friendly taunt was, ironically, an ominous prophecy as he was captured at St Valery-en-Caux just three months later. There were, however, a number of other 6th Battalion men who remained with the 51st (Highland) Division. They had been attached to 153 Brigade Headquarters and were required to continue in that role. Among others, they included the Brigade's Anti-Tank Officer, Captain David Morren, and Sergeant William Ogg and Privates Charles Morrison, Walter Philips and William Donald. When the 51st (Highland) Division were forced to surrender at St Valery-en-Caux, their war took a different turn from their former comrades in the 6th Battalion, with which Walter's brother, George, was still serving, so the two brothers parted company and would not be reunited until after the war. Although Walter successfully escaped back to Britain, George was captured at Anzio.

After a march of 3 miles, the 1st and 6th Battalions met at Seclin, where old friends had a chance to exchange news. In this all-Gordons affair, Brigadier George Burney, a Gordon Highlander himself, welcomed the 1st Battalion as part of 153 Brigade and bade farewell to the 6th. (George Burney was a Gordon through and through, a 'son of the regiment', his father being Brigadier General Herbert Henry Burney.)

The first man to die while the 6th Battalion was in France was long before the start of hostilities. Private Andrew Clark fell seriously ill and died on 9 March 1940. He had enlisted into the 6th Battalion Gordon Highlanders at the end of May 1939 as he fell into the age group of 20- and 21-year-olds who were required to enlist in the TA or await conscription for a full six months of military training from July 1939. He had opted to volunteer for the TA and tragically died, aged twenty-one years, after only nine months of service. He was buried in Douai Communal Cemetery, France.

In April, the battalion moved to Pas-en-Artois, near Amiens, where they continued their training and building defences. It was not all work and to relieve the boredom there were opportunities to go to hear the famous entertainers George Formby and Gracie Fields, who were performing under the auspices of ENSA (the Entertainments National Service Association) at Lille. With the warmer weather in the spring, the battalion were also able to put together a fairly good football team, playing other regiments in the area. Within the battalion there was a challenge match between the sergeants and the officers. The first match ended in a draw, so a deciding match was arranged. At half-time, things looked desperate for the NCOs, who were trailing 5–1, and the officers were feeling pretty smug. Not wishing to be humiliated by such a score line, and fearing more of the same in the second half, a pep talk changed the sergeants' tactics and determination so when the final whistle blew, the score was 7–5 in favour of the sergeants and respect was restored.

# Chapter 3

# The Battle for France

After a period when intelligence sources were warning that German forces were massing on the Dutch and Belgian frontiers, early on the morning of 10 May 1940 the battalion signaller took down a message which filled him with great excitement. Within minutes he had delivered it to the Adjutant, Captain Lindsay Bridgman. The message advised that the German Army had crossed the frontiers and arrangements had to be made immediately to move forward into Belgium to counter the Nazi advance. The first headache for Captain Bridgman was that the commanding officer, Lieutenant Colonel Taldo Pirie, and his second in command, Major Humphrey Bradshaw, were both in Britain on leave. In their absence, arrangements were made to move the battalion while these senior officers were urgently flown to France by the Royal Air Force to resume command. They arrived in time to lead the battalion over the frontier into Belgium on 11 May. Taldo Pirie had assumed command of the 6th Battalion at the beginning of the war and was an experienced Regular Army officer, with much of his service having been with the 1st Battalion. On 4 August 1914, aged just seventeen years, he was in the House of Commons with his father, Colonel D. V. Pirie, who was at that time the member of parliament for North Aberdeen. On this momentous day, Lord Grey had informed the House that a state of war existed between Britain and Germany. The young Taldo Pirie was introduced to the foreign secretary by his father, who said, 'Here is your first recruit,' and so it transpired his commission bore the date 4 August 1914. He went to France in May 1916 and was awarded a Military Cross at the end of the war. Major Bradshaw was also a 'Regular' officer who had served with the 1st Battalion Gordon Highlanders in the latter part of the First World War and in India. He was one of only a few Gordons who were awarded the Mohmand Clasp to his General Service Medal for operations against the Upper Mohmands in 1933 on the North-West Frontier. A small detachment of the 1st Battalion, which coincidentally also included Taldo Pirie, took part in this campaign, which was under the command of then-Brigadier Claude Auchinleck.

The 6th Gordons left Lille at 6.00 pm 11 May 1940 on a fleet of buses. They travelled along the roads choked by fleeing refugees, passing through Cysoing, Tournai, Renaix and Ninove. They travelled through the night. Most were silent, trying to get some sleep, but restless with the thought of what lay in store. Naturally, the married men worried if they would see their wives and young children again, while many of the young men were nervous but excited by the prospect of action. A few of the older men had seen action in the Great War. They arrived at their destination, a few miles outside Brussels, early in the morning and set off on foot to cover the last few miles to the front line. While marching through the city, led by the drums and pipes, they received a rapturous welcome from the local population. In the words of George Simpson, 'oranges, packets of fags [cigarettes], sweets and flowers were pelted at us from all angles'. On they marched eastwards until they finally took up a defensive position in their allotted sector on the River Dyle, just south of Corbeek, arriving in position in the evening of 12 May. Here, it was initially quiet, but it was known that the Germans were closing on their position as there was a steady stream of refugees coming towards them and over the river towards the Belgian capital. The next day passed quietly for the Gordons, observing the roads that were still very busy with refugees. Their first sight of the Germans came on 14 May when advance parties of infantry were seen on the opposite side of the Dyle valley; but at this stage, they made no attempt to cross the river. The Dyle was a moderate-sized river, navigable only by small ships. However, it flowed in a broad, shallow valley, so did not provide a very formidable obstacle to the Nazi advance, but the wooded areas provided some cover, allowing infiltration of the Gordons' forward lines.

The Germans started attacking across the river on 15 May and the 6th Gordons' first action came in the evening. A small party of Germans stumbled into one of their forward positions, where Lieutenant Victor Reid saw them off sharply with rifle fire. However, there was a strong German attack some 5 miles to the north at Louvain, which was beaten off, but around 15 miles to the south, near Warve, the French Army were forced back.

On 16 May, the Gordons held their position on the Dyle, where they were pummelled by enemy artillery and mortars. Sadly, when a shell landed in one of the Gordons' trench mortar positions, Corporal Douglas Harrower and Private James Carmichael, both from Keith, Banffshire, the home of the battalion headquarters, were killed. These two men were the battalion's first casualties killed in action. Lieutenant Ian Farquharson, an accountant from Edinburgh in civilian life, was also killed that evening. He was fatally wounded by a sniper as the 6th Battalion were withdrawing from their position on the River Dyle. When his men saw he had been hit, they rushed to his aid, but bravely he waved them away, saying, 'Don't worry about me, get the men out before there are more casualties.' These proved to be the last words spoken to his comrades before he died. Private George Thomson was posted missing.

The Battalion got away at dusk without further casualties under the cover of darkness. They withdrew through Tervueren, the small Flemish town which gave its name to the dog breed often confused with a long-haired German shepherd, and on to Brussels. The enthusiastic scenes which greeted their arrival only a few days before were not repeated as the locals considered they were being abandoned. Much to the surprise of the Gordons, many of the citizens were calmly going about their business, apparently indifferent to the Nazi tide approaching their city. Many of the older inhabitants had lived through the Great War, which had ended only just some twenty years earlier, when almost their entire country was overrun by the Germans. They appeared to be coolly accepting the nightmare of another occupation of their ancient city. However, this was not a universal feeling, and not all were prepared to accept the inevitable. Many were fleeing with all their worldly possessions, merging with the retreating armed forces and choking the roads to the south and east of the city.

The 6th Gordons continued their steady withdrawal, arriving at Ninove on the River Dendre in the late afternoon of Sunday, 18 May, where they had a welcome rest after marching some 15 miles in the sweltering heat. There was, however, no respite, with a further withdrawal taking place the next day to Esquelmes, a distance of almost 40 miles. This was much too far to travel on foot, but the air raids by the Luftwaffe had reduced the motorized transport available to a level where not all of the men could be accommodated. Lieutenant David Hutcheon found some seventy volunteers who were willing to attempt to march. However, their luck was in when enough abandoned bicycles were found to continue the journey by pedal power.

On 20 May, the 6th Gordons were in a defensive position covering just under a mile of the west bank of the River Scheldt (known by the French as the River Escaut) at Esquelmes, just north of Tournai, Belgium. The next two days were quiet, but the battalion were heavily shelled on 22 May. Major Duncan S. Annand, who commanded D Company, was concerned the men were not keeping their heads down; he was wounded while going around checking them when a shell exploded near him. He was immediately evacuated to the forward aid post where he was treated by Medical Officer Captain Lennel Taylor, who was amazed that, despite the serious nature of his injuries, he was able to sit up and talk to him. However, with his arm blown off in the blast, he required more intensive medical aid. He was evacuated, but tragically killed by a bomb on the journey to the casualty clearing station. Lance Corporal Walter Seivwright was hit by shrapnel and died of his wounds at the forward aid post while three others were wounded. On paper, the River Dendre did afford a defensible obstacle against the German advance, but its meandering course in its wide, partly wooded valley, combined with the low summer river flow, made it less than ideal. The position was further undermined with the surprise German blitzkrieg attack and rapid advance through the Ardennes, outflanking the Maginot Line. Their armoured units poured down the valley of the River Somme, the area of great battles in 1916, and on 20 May, approached the coast through Abbeville to St Valery sur Somme, cutting the British supply lines back to the Channel ports and threatening their rear. With this new development, the British High Command ordered a full-scale orderly withdrawal towards Dunkirk.

The 6th Gordons started their withdrawal at midnight. Marching due west, they arrived at Hem, France, where they occupied the Belgian-French frontier defences. German shelling affected the nearby town of Roubaix and there was an exodus of civilian refugees. The battalion were running low on rations, so this provided a golden opportunity for the Lieutenant Charles Munro, the Quartermaster, to replenish his stores as the deserted shops provided a welcome supply of foodstuffs, etc. He deduced it was likely to fall into German hands if left and concluded he had the moral right to deprive the enemy. Sporadic shelling continued which intensified on 25 May.

Active patrolling was undertaken to establish the German positions and Lieutenant Harry Shand was ordered to lead one of these. Volunteering to go with him were Corporal Robert Frame and his friend Jimmy Frew, who had enlisted and trained with him at Hamilton Barracks before they were both transferred from the Cameronians into the Gordon Highlanders in October 1939. On 25 May the patrol set off, in the pitch black of the night, crossing an embankment of the Roubaix-Lille railway line into 'no man's land'. As they left, their comrades in the front line watched them disappear as shadowy figures in the blackness of the night. Lieutenant Shand led the way. Unknown to the Germans, the Gordons had already spied them preparing mortar positions for a surprise attack on the Gordons' position. The area was open ground with a wooded copse and a farm in front and a sanatorium building on a small hill to the left of their position. They were some considerable distance from their own front line when a sudden burst of rifle fire alerted the Gordons to the fact that they had been spotted, but the patrol rushed forward and drove the Germans out of their forward post in the farm buildings. At that point a machine gun opened up from the direction of the sanatorium on their left and Harry Shand decided that his patrol would surround that position and silence the machine gun. He divided his small force into three parts: one to take the left side while one took the right, and a section was to remain and provide covering fire for the others' advances. As they started to make their move forward, they took rifle fire from the wood and Harry was wounded. Robert Frame tried to reach him, but he was also wounded by a bullet to his hip and then, when the German mortars opened up, he was hit in the stomach by shrapnel.

The rest of the patrol then came under accurate rifle fire, with bullets whizzing past them and thudding into the ground around them; it was clear that the enemy had sighted them and was not just firing blindly at sounds in the darkness. Realising the dangerous situation, Lieutenant Harry Shand shouted to his men to go back and that he would be all right. The patrol withdrew back over the railway line. Jimmy Frew and Alistair Clark hurriedly explained the situation to Lieutenant David Hutcheon, who was ordered by their Company HQ to organize a rescue party for the casualties. With dawn breaking soon, it was realized that this was a matter of urgency if the casualties were to be recovered, as their only chance was under the cover of darkness.

The rescue patrol, including stretcher bearers Privates Clark, Grant, Armit and Runcie, together with members of the original patrol to show the way, headed back over the railway and quickly retraced the steps of Lieutenant Shand's patrol. They found Harry Shand's revolver and steel helmet but no trace of him or Robert Frame, which could only mean they had been captured. Two rifles were also found, which suggested other men had either been captured or wounded and in hiding. A search discovered Private James Webster badly wounded in a ditch where he had crawled for cover after being injured, but there was no sign of William McHattie. They lifted Private Webster onto a stretcher and started back using the deep ditch to cover their movement. With the light improving, the Germans could see more easily, and Corporal Alex Taylor received a gunshot wound to his hand. The machine gun which had not been silenced then opened up and Donald Armit, who had just returned from home leave, was hit in the head and killed. As progression along the ditch proved difficult, they were forced to come into more open ground; the German snipers homed in on the little band and their casualties mounted. Alister Clark, the stretcher bearer, was hit in the knee, Robert Milton was hit in the hip and James Dingwall was killed. The rescue patrol was now effectively pinned down.

Watching from the Gordons' front line and assessing the situation with an experienced eye was Lieutenant Hutcheon. He was an experienced Regular soldier with eighteen years' service, having reached the rank of Regimental Sergeant Major in 1938 and promoted from the ranks, being commissioned in October 1939. He had served with the 1st Battalion in India and Palestine before the war. He readily appreciated the serious situation his men were in and sent the company runner back to the Battalion HQ to request a mortar smoke screen be laid down to conceal the patrol's movements from the Germans. When the smoke screen was established, David Hutcheon rushed out to assist his men, and the patrol was able to make their way back to their own line. He hung back and provided covering fire to keep the Germans' heads down until the patrol reached safety.

As the patrol withdrew, Harry Shand, Robert Frame and William McHattie had to be left to their fate and it was hoped the Germans would provide any necessary medical treatment. Also left behind were the dead men. James Dingwall was buried in the local cemetery at Hem. Donald Armit's body was not identified and he has no known grave, so was subsequently commemorated on the Dunkirk memorial. William McHattie was posted missing and was in fact taken prisoner, but died two days later and was also buried at Hem. James Webster was evacuated for treatment, but his injuries were so serious that he died the following day at Wormhoundt, where he was buried. Robert Milton and Peter McIntosh were also evacuated; after treatment, they survived. However, they and Alister Clark were discharged from the army soon afterwards, as they were declared medically unfit for further military service. Tom Gray's situation was also unknown and he was posted as missing, which was a concern to his twin brother Leslie, who was also serving with the 6th Battalion at Hem.

The next day an observation post was developed on the top storey of a factory which gave a commanding view over the approaches to their position. When Germans were seen emerging from the sanatorium buildings and mustering in a hollow a few hundred metres away, the observers alerted Captain Baucher, who organized his defences to counter the impending attack. Sergeant Major Riddell was ordered to take up a position on the factory tower armed with a Bren gun, while the rest of the company took up positions to reply to any attack with sustained and accurate rifle fire.

Suddenly, in the late afternoon, the Germans made their move and rushed the Gordons' position. The wave was met with a fusillade of rifle and Bren gun bullets, killing some of the enemy and dispersing the others. A group of Germans armed with machine guns did, however, manage to establish a forward position. They returned fire with such ferocity that, with bullets whistling though the windows and just missing his head, Sergeant Major Riddell was forced to climb down from his 'eyrie'. This meant the position's defence depended on the sharpshooters who had dug in, one of whom was Private William Stewart, renowned for his ability to hit a distant target. He was partnered with 2nd Lieutenant Thomas Lyall-Wilson, a London Scottish officer who was attached to the 6th Battalion. As soon as they detected any movement, Willie fired at the target with great effect. Lieutenant Lyall-Wilson was spotting with the aid of binoculars, but Willie could see his target just as well with the naked eye.

The situation became a standoff, with neither side giving ground. The situation changed when the Gordons received orders to withdraw again. The German breakthrough to the south, coupled with the capitulation of the Belgian Army, created a dangerous situation for the British. The decision to fall back on Dunkirk and await evacuation was taken as the only way to avoid complete encirclement and defeat. The 6th Gordons left Hem around midnight 26 May and marched through the night in the pouring rain as a thunderstorm raged around them. Withdrawing from their forward position without alerting the enemy was a difficult manoeuvre and had to be accomplished in near silence. To cover the withdrawal, Lieutenant Robert Rae was ordered to set up his Bren gun platoon in the front line where they sat in silence in the full darkness of the night, with their ears pricked and eyes straining for any enemy movement. When the Germans edged forward and cut the wire protecting the Gordon's position, Lieutenant Rae decided discretion was the better part of valour and moved back to a reserve line, where they awaited a further advance by the Germans that never came. The Germans had entered Hem, but chose not to chance any further advance in the darkness, not realising what a small force stood between them and the withdrawing main body of the British. At midnight, Lieutenant Rae and his Bren gunners left their positions and followed the battalion to Neuve-Eglise.

When the battalion reached Neuve-Eglise early in the morning, the men just flopped down on the pavements. They were soaked and utterly exhausted, having had little sleep for days on end. Captain Lennel Taylor, the Gordons Medical Officer, was having breakfast at the battalion HQ, which had been set up behind the church. In civilian life he was a GP in Keith, having taken over the medical practice from his father. Dr James Taylor was an eminent local dignitary as a former deputy lord lieutenant of Banffshire and had also served as a major in the Royal Army Medical Corps. Captain Taylor had received the sad news of his father's death only two months earlier while he was already in France with the 6th Battalion.

The Germans became aware that there was a concentration of British and French units stopping over in the town. Although they must also have known the town was packed with civilian refugees, they mounted a heavy attack with artillery and aircraft. Carnage ensued with heavy casualties among both the military and civilian personnel. As soon as the attack began, Captain Taylor immediately ran to help and treated some wounded men from the East Lancashire Regiment. He was in the process of returning to the battalion HQ when the *Mairie* was hit. Captain Taylor witnessed 19-year-old Lance Corporal Alex McCulloch, who was sitting in a truck in front of the building, being struck by shrapnel. Captain Taylor rushed to his aid and pulled him out of the vehicle and into the doorway of the *Mairie*, which afforded some shelter. The Captain dressed McCulloch's wounds, but unfortunately, his injuries were too severe to save him.

Captain Taylor's work was far from over. He and his stretcher bearers were hard-pressed to tend injured men in the streets as bombs and artillery shells rained down on the centre of the town. He set up a field aid post in a butcher's shop in the town square and calmly saw to the wounded men while mayhem reigned outside. Seeing the danger, Lieutenant Colonel Taldo Pirie ordered his men out of the town to escape the bombing. Just then, a blast demolished the house next to the butcher's shop, which caused a number of horses to go berserk. They stampeded wildly around the square, preventing evacuation of the wounded and the military unit's escape. The stretcher bearers tackled the dangerous task of capturing the terrified animals while bombs and shells continued to fall around them. Further tragedy struck just as the Gordons were marching out of the town. A shell fell directly on Number 12 Platoon of B Company, killing two men and wounding several others.

The short stop in Neuve-Eglise (known as Nieuwkerke in Flemish) on 27 May had cost the lives of three men and wounded eight. Among the wounded was Private Robert Jack, a conscripted Militiaman who had trained at Hamilton Barracks, Motherwell. He was a stretcher case and was evacuated in an ambulance, with Captain Taylor accompanying them to Dunkirk. Robert Jack recalled that, at Dunkirk, they were waiting on the beach for some time, but remembered embarking on a ship from the mole. On arrival back in Britain, he was taken to a Whitchurch emergency hospital in the north of Cardiff. During the war, part of the hospital was turned over to the military, becoming the largest emergency service hospital in South Wales and treating Allied and German personnel. He was admitted on 31 May 1940 and discharged to Aberdeen on 30 November 1940. Also wounded in this incident was Corporal John Spence, who was evacuated back to England, but sadly died of his wounds, leaving three young children. His remains were returned to his family and he is buried in his hometown of Keith, Banffshire.

The battalion moved on along the roads choked with refugees and mixed army units – many of the men had become detached from their own units and were just heading for the coast and the hope of evacuation. After a 10-mile march, that evening they took up a defensive position in Poperinge. Although there was an air raid on the town, it did not result in any more casualties for the Gordons. That night, the battalion received an order to put all the vehicles out of action and dump all equipment and supplies that could not be carried by the men. This was a straightforward and understandable order since the evacuation intended to rescue as many men as possible and there would be no time or facilities to load equipment onto the ships. The engines of the trucks were smashed and disabled in any way to make them permanently useless and mortar bombs were dumped into the river to make them inaccessible. While almost all of the military paraphernalia was expendable, dumping their instruments was a bitter blow for the pipe band. They were then to make their way to the village of Bray Dunes on the north-east perimeter of Dunkirk. This was a hard march of about 17 miles. Marching in single file, with their commanding officer in front, they took the path of a railway line and arrived at Bray Dunes on 29 May. Although exhausted from their journey and lack of sleep, they were ordered to occupy the seaward end of the French frontier defences. Here, the beaches were crowded with both British and French soldiers. The Gordons were in a relatively quiet area which allowed the men to get some much-needed rest, having covered almost 150 miles, much of it on foot, from their initial positions on the Dyle only 13 days earlier. Fortunately, when the 6th Gordons arrived at Dunkirk, the weather was overcast. This limited the operations of the German Luftwaffe, but there was still the danger posed by artillery shelling.

On 31 May, the evacuation operation suffered badly, as the cloud cover had dispersed and a number of the evacuating Royal Navy ships were hit and sunk. Consequently, Captain William Tennant, the senior naval officer ashore at Dunkirk in charge of the evacuation, decided to halt daylight evacuations. William Tennant was later to command the heavy cruiser HMS *Repulse* which had a special relationship with the regiment of the Gordon Highlanders. Before the war, in 1936, HMS *Repulse* had transported the 2nd Battalion Gordon Highlanders from Gibraltar to Egypt to quell a revolt in Palestine. Later, while HMS *Repulse* was commanded by William Tennant, she was stationed in Singapore where the 2nd Battalion were also. The battalion watched HMS *Repulse*, accompanied by HMS *The Prince of Wales*, sail past their battle station at Pengerang in December 1941, on the way to suppress the Japanese invasion in northern Malaya. Tragically, both ships were located by Japanese bombers and sunk on 10 December, but Captain Bill Tennant survived.

With no daylight evacuations taking place, it was therefore on the evening of 31 May when the battalion were relieved by North African Zouves, a French Army unit, and received the very welcome order to march into Dunkirk and assemble along the east mole to be evacuated back to Britain. The 7-mile march along the beach was hard going; running the gauntlet of enemy artillery fire was a constant hazard, but darkness was the battalion's friend. By dawn they had achieved their objective with only one man slightly wounded by shrapnel; he obviously did not wish to be left behind and managed to keep up with the help of his comrades and a walking stick. At Dunkirk Harbour, the battalion had to pick their way along the mole, which was badly damaged in places from air attacks, and wait their turn to be evacuated. Colour Sergeant George Murdoch was an old and experienced soldier, and he walked along the mole giving encouragement to steady the younger soldiers. When a man fell into the water, George Murdoch instinctively reached out to help him; another eager man behind also tried to help, but only succeeded in pushing George into the harbour as well. This was a dangerous moment, as the close proximity of the ship's propellers was a real danger, but ironically, the wash from the upward stroke of the propeller blades propelled him up and helped him scramble back to safety.

Just after dawn on the morning of 1 June, the Battalion boarded the Royal Navy destroyers HMS *Icarus* and HMS *Harvester* with Lieutenant Colonel Pirie taking charge of boarding arrangements. The Gordons had formed up on the pier with a number of French soldiers. Colonel Pirie sent them forward two by two, i.e., two Jocks followed by two Frenchmen and so on. The Colonel spent much of his early life living in France with his French grandparents, so his fluency in French was a great asset in this situation. Colonel Pirie, with his second in command, Major Bradshaw, were the last to board the ship. As they boarded, the Luftwaffe mounted another raid on the beaches and harbour, but this was seen off by concentrated anti-aircraft fire from the naval ships. HMS *Icarus* was able to get away safely; out to sea, HMS *Harvester* was targeted again by enemy aircraft which strafed the ship and dropped bombs. Jimmy Scott hid under some pipes on the deck with his hands over his head, but a piece of shrapnel hit him in the left armpit and he passed out. Meanwhile, the ship's anti-aircraft guns brought down a German Stuka dive bomber to great cheering on board. HMS *Icarus* carried on to Dover where, on arrival, the soldiers were surprised to be greeted as heroes. Although a little embarrassed by this, they were, nevertheless, relieved and delighted to be safely back in Britain. Jimmy Scott regained consciousness in the bowels of a ship surrounded by wounded men and felt quite disorientated. A medical orderly was standing over him holding a large syringe. Jimmy asked what had happened and where he was, only to be told he had been wounded and had been transferred to a hospital ship heading for 'Blighty'. He was then injected with a sedative. When he woke up, the ship had docked in Hull; he was transferred to Leeds City Hospital, where he remained for seven weeks before being given two weeks home leave, then was told to report to the Gordon Barracks, Aberdeen.

# Chapter 4

# Back in Blighty

Once back on British soil, the 6th Gordons were moved to Rotherham, Yorkshire. The pressing question worrying everyone in the country was: Would there now be an invasion? While the Battalion reorganized and were re-equipped, groups of men were given well-deserved home leave in rotation while the men left behind assisted with building defensive measures in preparation against any invasion force. The return home of a loved one was a great relief to the families of the men who had been evacuated, as the news from the Continent was so bad, many had feared the worst. At Halfway Village, Cambuslang, Glasgow, Henry Beadie returned home totally unexpectedly. He had returned with his friend William Graham, who lived nearby. The two had been called up together and trained together in Hamilton Barracks before transferring to the Gordon Highlanders. They had both sent word home two weeks earlier that they had been evacuated safely from France and were in South Wales. Willie Graham did send a telegram to his parents to say he was coming home for some leave; Henry didn't know until the last minute that he was getting leave, so didn't have time to send a message. As things turned out, it was a wonderful surprise for his family. For those families for whom there was no happy reunion, some of their comrades would visit the family and convey the fate of their relative, which brought some comfort and closure. When Henry and Willie left home to return to the Battalion, they were given a rousing send-off by their family, friends and neighbours.

Waiting for them in Rotherham was a draft of men from Aberdeen who were on a train bound for the Channel ports and France to reinforce the Battalion. Their train came to a halt between York and Doncaster, where they were told that the Dunkirk evacuation was already underway, so their posting to join the Battalion in France had been cancelled. The train was diverted to Rotherham, where they would now join the Battalion.

After his evacuation from Dunkirk, Robert Jack recovered from his wounds in Whitchurch Hospital, Cardiff. On 10 July 1940, he exchanged letters with Major George Anderson, who commanded B Company, asking if he had any news about his friend Private David Irvine. He explained that he had received a letter from David Irvine's mother, who had been informed that he had been posted missing and was hoping for some positive news about him. Major

Anderson was unable to give any information on the fate of David Irvine, only that he had fallen behind and out of the line near Neuve-Eglise. Following the order to withdraw to Dunkirk on 13 May, they travelled about 145 miles, mostly on foot; some men were not able to keep up and were left behind in the hope that rear transport would pick them up. It was later discovered that David Irvine had been captured and spent the next 5 years as a prisoner of war. In his reply to Robert Jack, Major Anderson asked if he could supply any news about Private James Green, as he had received a letter from his mother. Unfortunately, although not known to either man at that time, James Green died from wounds he received. This was typical of the situation after Dunkirk, where many of the men evacuated had become separated from their units and had difficulty in finding out where their own unit was. For example, the 6th Gordons had no connection with Rotherham, so none of the stragglers would have thought to journey there and so went back to the Regimental Headquarters in Aberdeen. The wounded were particularly liable to be 'lost' as they had been taken to hospitals all over the country, depending on the availability of beds.

The 6th Battalion Gordon Highlanders were severely depleted by their experiences in France and Belgium and their strength was only twenty-two officers and 326 other ranks. To bring up their numbers, 144 men transferred in from the Border Regiment together with a large draft of over forty men from the Infantry Training Centre in Aberdeen. These were almost all newly trained conscripts; in little more than a year later, over half of these men were reassigned to other regiments, mainly through a lack of fitness for the infantry role. Of the remainder, such was the casualty rate suffered by the 6th Battalion that, by the end of the war, almost half of this group had either been killed, wounded or captured to become prisoners of war.

Once the men had returned from leave, the retraining began in earnest, but the lack of weapons and equipment was a hindrance. Sir George Abercromby, their Honorary Colonel, became aware of the loss of the drums and pipes and knew the importance of functioning instruments to a Highland infantry battalion such as the 6th Gordons. He donated a bass drum and launched an appeal for other items. His appeal was successful and shortly afterwards, the desired items arrived.

The disaster of losing so many experienced soldiers in France and Belgium in 1940 meant that the army was short of experienced soldiers, especially NCOs, to assist in training conscripted men for the rapidly expanding British Army. However, there were many experienced men who were perfect for this role spread across the British Empire, in India, Malaya, Singapore and the Middle East. It was disadvantageous to deplete the overseas garrisons, so bringing these men back to train recruits meant they had to be replaced. The obvious answer was to use less experienced soldiers who had completed their basic training or had already seen some combat. As a result, a number of 6th Battalion men were posted to Singapore to the 2nd Battalion. James Scott, Robert Anderson and Peter Taylor (who had all been wounded in 1940), William Mackie, Robert Prise, William Davidson and Alan Greig were joined by a draft of men from the depot in Aberdeen and sent to Liverpool. On 4 August 1940, the MV *Batory* left Liverpool with Convoy WS 2, evacuating 300 children from the large industrial cities in Britain, which were the target of Nazi bombers, to Sydney, Australia, until the war was over. Some Gordons were asked to keep the children amused and played games with them, such as hide and seek. The ship's route was via Sierra Leone and Cape Town, South Africa. Here, the men were given shore leave, where they found the welcome and hospitality given by the local population overwhelming, with many families taking soldiers home for a meal. It was the first time that most had ever seen rice being offered as a savoury part of the meal and not the familiar rice pudding they had at home. Little did they realize that in quite a short time they would have to survive on little else. On leaving Cape Town, the convoy split up, with the larger part going on to the Middle East. The MV *Batory*'s voyage continued eastwards, calling at Bombay and Colombo en-route and arriving into Singapore. It was a fairly slow journey of three and a half months, partly as they were often zigzagging to avoid submarine attack. On arrival at Singapore, good-byes were said to the children, with many tears being shed on both sides. The journey had been a happy one, with so much music and laughter that the *Batory* was dubbed the 'Singing Ship'.

The 6th Battalion moved south to Lincolnshire at the end of June 1940, where they spent their time assisting the Home Guard, conducting coastal defence and fairly intensive training. It was during one of these training exercises that a tragic accident occurred in darkness during the night of 1 February 1941. The manoeuvres involved the men crossing the Foss Dyke Canal in collapsible boats while wearing a full battle pack of equipment weighing 30 pounds. The canal connected the River Trent to Lincoln. Each boat carried nine men; when one of the boats capsized, five men managed to scramble to the bank, but the four men who couldn't swim drowned as the weight of their packs pulled them down. Two of the men who died were Corporal Donald Duff, from Accrington, Lancashire, who was one of the men from the Border Regiment who transferred to the 6th Battalion in June 1940 and Private William Stewart, from Keith, Banffshire, who was one of the sharpshooters holding back the Germans at Hem. The others were Privates Ebenezer Anderson from Glasgow and James Knowles from Brechin. An enquiry heard from Private Victor Stanley who had also been in the boat but survived the incident; he stated there were men moving about in the boat which he thought had caused it to capsize but he was adamant there was no clowning about. The Coroner recorded a verdict of death by misadventure. On 28 May 1942, the 1st Battalion London Scottish had their first casualty with the accidental death of Private Vincent Vyner by drowning while on a cross-country exercise in Suffolk. In civilian life, he was the manager of a shoe shop in Barnstaple, Devon, and was married with three young children. Fatalities during training were not very common but the exposure to risk was part and parcel of the exercise.

On 1 July 1941, the 6th Battalion welcomed a new commanding officer: Lieutenant Colonel James Peddie. He was a Territorial Army officer from the London Scottish, posted to the 6th Battalion Gordon Highlanders, a Territorial Army Battalion, to replace Patrick Taldo Pirie. Taldo Pirie had been an inspiring example to the men of the 6th Battalion during the operations in France and Belgium. He had a strong personality, intensely disliking bad manners, vulgarity or unfairness, which he expressed with an old world courtesy. Medical Officer Captain Lennel Taylor recalled that he was surprised to have received a dressing down by him for leaving the battalion after Neuve-Eglise to accompany the wounded to Dunkirk. Lieutenant Colonel Pirie was displeased, as this had left the whole battalion without a medical officer. However, with his sense of duty towards looking after his men, he was the last man to board a Royal Navy destroyer after seeing all his men got aboard safely at Dunkirk. He was mentioned in dispatches for his 'distinguished service' in 1940.

As time went on, the training became more arduous. On the last three days of December 1941, the 6th Gordons spent the entire time in the open during a bitterly cold spell, enduring exposure and intense physical exertion. There was great relief when the exercise ended at dusk on 31 December (Hogmanay) and that evening they had their first substantial hot meal for days. However, this was just the prelude to the main event, which was their New Year's Day dinner with turkey and all the trimmings, followed by Christmas pudding and mince pies, all washed down with a pint of beer. Each man also received a packet of cigarettes. The local people had been generous, with one hotelier and a local brewery gifting the beer, and some gifts of cash through the local WRVS that helped fund the much-appreciated feast. The Battalion had made a good impression locally with their good behaviour and organization of local dances where, in the heart of England, Highland dancing to the music of the Battalion's Pipe Band became popular. The Battalion football team, taking on all comers, had an enviable record of only one defeat since their evacuation from Dunkirk. This success was not down to luck as the Battalion could call on some of their number who had been football stars in their civilian lives. These included former Chelsea player Graham Calder, Celtic player Tom Miekle, Hibernian inside forward James Mclean and Highland League players George Cormack, who played for Buckie F.C., and defenders John Hay and John Whitecross, who played for Keith F.C.

The 6th Gordons' training in the Midlands and East Anglia continued with advance notification given in June 1942 that they were to mobilize for service overseas; but, in reality, this was a little way off. Training in anti-tank procedures and tank hunting exercises were given special attention, with the men who had been in France well aware of the threat these posed to an infantry battalion. All the while, the battalion was being equipped with new Bren gun carriers and 2-pounder anti-tank guns to prepare them properly for this essential role. In October, some men were deployed to assist farmers in Norfolk with their potato harvest, which was not only profitable for them but also a bit of a welcome change from the hard training. For example, after a short leave at home in the Midlands, Private Leslie Tromans, who had enlisted in February 1942, sent a letter from King's Lynn describing the situation to his brother.

'Dear George,
Just a few lines to let you know I am okay, and got used to the army life once again. But we are having rather an easy time since I came back off leave. We have been on the farms, picking spuds, and they pay us a piece work rate of 4d a row, and you ought to see the length of the row: about a quarter of a mile long! I have averaged 3/6 a day. It's alright but a bit too much bending for me.'

Leslie's wages are expressed in the pre-decimal denominations of the time, i.e., four pence per row and three shillings and six pence per day. To put his earnings into a modern-day context, he was earning around £7 per day which compares well with his army pay of around £4 per day.

With so many men being conscripted into the armed services, there was a nationwide manpower shortage to harvest the crops. Harvest was very important because convoys bringing food into Britain were under a constant threat from German 'U' boats. The 1st Battalion London Scottish were also called upon to help farmers by harvesting hops while in Kent and sugar beets when stationed in Suffolk. The former had more of a holiday atmosphere, as traditionally whole families from London went down to Kent for the hop picking to earn extra money and it was a holiday in the countryside. In September 1940, this was a particularly enjoyable break as it was an escape from the horrors of the blitz which was ravaging London at the height of the Battle of Britain, where 'The Few' were engaged in heroic aerial combat in the skies above them in Kent. The end of the season was marked by a boozy celebration at a local pub where the soldiers and civilians partied together. There was the added bonus for the sex-starved young soldiers with the presence of young women who had accompanied their families. The beet harvest, however, took place during freezing conditions in the winter of 1941, with the crop not being harvested until it had been exposed to the frost to increase the sugar content. This was more of a chore and an alien task to those not engaged in agriculture in their civilian lives.

In November 1942, orders came for the 6th Battalion Gordon Highlanders to move back to Scotland and the battalion relocated to Darvel, Ayrshire. With embarkation for service overseas rumoured as being imminent, training was intensified. One man who would not embark with the battalion was Private Robert (Bob) Boyce, who fractured his knee during training and would have to wait for just over a year before rejoining his comrades. This was not, however, the worst case of accidental injury during the intense training and tragically, another accidental drowning occurred during an exercise. This was Private Robert Mclean, whose home was only 20 miles away in Wishaw; he was buried in the local graveyard at Cambuskenneth. Unfortunately, he is not the only 6th Battalion Gordon Highlander buried in this graveyard who was accidentally killed while on active service. William John Milne Belcher, also from Wishaw, was accidentally killed on 5 November 1943, shortly after being home on leave. He was given a funeral with full military honours. He was named after his uncle, William Johnstone Milne, who had emigrated to Canada and served with the Canadian Army during the First World War. He was awarded the Victoria Cross (VC) on 9 April 1917 near Thelus, France, during the Battle of Vimy Ridge. He saw an enemy machine-gun firing upon his comrades and crawled forward, killed the crew and captured the gun, then later repeated this action against a second enemy machine-gun crew. Unfortunately, he was killed shortly afterwards and his VC was awarded posthumously. Since he had no Canadian next of kin his VC was presented to his sister in Lanarkshire.

A highlight of the battalion's time in Ayrshire was the visit by King George VI on 18 February 1943, when he inspected the battalion at Morton Park, Darvel, and watched them execute various training exercises, including 'how to silently eliminate a sentry from behind,' expertly executed by Corporal David Tripney. When a photograph was taken to publicize the royal visit in the following day's newspapers, the King was pictured complimenting Sergeant William Graham while Lieutenant Colonel James Peddie looked on. The following day, Leslie Tromans wrote home to his family to report on his experience of the visit. He wrote, 'I had the surprise of my life yesterday, but I must say it was a great surprise. You see, we had orders to Blanco our equipment and clean everything up for someone important was coming on Thursday. Well, we were standing by our beds all toffed up, when the King walked in the billet. I thought I would drop through the floor, but he was just like his photo, except he was made up. He never spoke though, just inspected us, and shook hands with the officers and away he went. It was exciting though seeing him for the first time.'

Soon afterwards notice of embarkation was received, which allowed the men some leave prior to their forthcoming service overseas. At this point, where they were going to be deployed would remain a mystery.

# Chapter 5

# Embarkation for Overseas

In the spring of 1942, in preparation for future action overseas, the 6th Battalion Gordon Highlanders was being brought up to full war strength. They received large drafts of men from the King's Own Scottish Borderers, the Liverpool Scottish and London Scottish, furthering the relationship between the 6th Gordons and the London Scottish, both being elements of the 'Corps' of the Gordon Highlanders. Despite being readied for action overseas, the 6th Gordons, however, were not leaving Britain just yet.

At this time, the 1st Battalion London Scottish were also preparing to go overseas. After embarkation leave, they sailed from Gourock on 27 August 1942. On board was Private John McElroy, who was married in Chelsea just 12 days earlier while on leave. Unlike the 6th Gordons, only a small number of them – four officers and thirty-four other ranks – had seen action in April 1940 after volunteering for a force formed to counter the German invasion of Norway. This group had included James Peddie and J. Brian Clapham, who were both now serving with the 6th Gordons. The rest of the 1st Battalion London Scottish had remained in England after their mobilization and had not seen any action as they had been training in and around Kent and Suffolk, carrying out coastal defence duties.

Leaving the Clyde on board the troop ship His Majesty's Transport (HMT) *California*, the 1st Battalion London Scottish sailed in convoy into the Atlantic, then south to the west coast of Africa, calling in at Freetown, Sierra Leone. As was customary, the local vendors saw the convoy as a big 'pay day' so tried to approach the ships to sell the soldiers sweet treats and trinkets. They were, however, only in port for just sufficient time to replenish supplies and for the men's mail to be unloaded and sent home. The next port of call was Capetown, South Africa, where shore leave was allowed. Their voyage continued up through the Indian Ocean. The *California* finally docked in Bombay on 16 October 1942, where the men were able to disembark as their onward journey, still unknown, was to be aboard a different vessel. The men were grateful for a short shore leave after such a long journey and able to get their land legs back after having been at sea for over six weeks.

Their travels were far from over. Just over a week later they boarded HMT *Neuralia*; appropriately for the 1st London Scottish, their ship was built in the famous shipyards of the River Clyde in 1912. They sailed to the Persian Gulf, docking at Shat el Arab, and set up a transit camp at Zubayr some 15 miles west of Basrah. Their stay here was short and they boarded a train to take them to Kirkuk via Baghdad, where they had to change stations. This was a hot, dry and dusty journey of some 500 miles which took almost two days. In the previous 80 days, unlike Phileas Fogg, the principal character of Jules Verne's novel, *Around the World in Eighty Days,* they had not circumnavigated the world but had travelled some 16,000 miles. This had been an amazing adventure as very few of them had ever travelled outside the UK before. They had seen the colourful chaotic scenes in Sierra Leone, the sophisticated colonial style of South Africa, the exotic nature of the streets of Bombay and were now in the deserts of Iraq. Kirkuk was their home for the next four and a half months. The purpose of them being stationed in this remote location was the perceived threat of Nazi forces invading Iraq from the Caucasus in the north to secure the country's vast oil resources.

The principal reason for the degree of discomfort in this location was that they were housed under canvas during the winter months. The misery was compounded as it frequently rained heavily and conditions were very testing with mud and some flooding causing problems. Training had to continue with marches and exercises in heavy rain proving to be gruelling. One exercise involved crossing the Little Zab River, swollen by rains, which proved very demanding; unknown to them at the time, it was to be an invaluable experience for future operations. Another sorrowful incident occurred on 3 March 1943, when Private David Jenkins was accidentally shot during a training exercise. He had been in the army less than a year and had recently celebrated his twenty-first birthday. He was buried with full military honours locally in Kirkuk but now lies in the Military Cemetery in Mosul, Iraq.

To everyone's great relief, at the end of March 1943 orders came to move again. The unenviable train journey back to Baghdad was not a prospect relished by many. In Baghdad, they left the slow train for road transport, then crossed the Syrian Desert and travelled through Palestine and Gaza. On 7 April, the Battalion finally arrived on the east bank of the Suez Canal, opposite Ismailia, Egypt, about midway along the canal's course. They had been travelling for almost ten days with much of it through a fairly featureless and inhospitable terrain. The Battalion now learned that with their 168 Brigade comrades, they were to transfer to the 50th (Northumbrian) Infantry Division, which had suffered heavy casualties in Tunisia. Prior to this they were now to engage in intensive training in amphibious landing techniques on the Great Bitter Lake and on the Gulf of Aqaba. With the success of the final defeat of the Afrika Korps in Tunisia, many guessed they were in training to be part of an amphibious landing on southern Europe, but where? This was still a closely guarded secret.

When training commenced, it was a welcome change. The 1st Battalion London Scottish was camped in the desert near Kabret, and the amphibious training was at HMS *Saunders*, the combined operations centre. Kabret was on a small promontory jutting out into the Great Bitter Lake which formed part of the course of the Suez Canal. This promontory marked the division between Great Bitter Lake and Little Bitter Lake. The lake's name derived from the high salinity of the water, which gave it a bitter, salty taste. HMS *Saunders* was not a ship but a shore-based operation run by the Royal Navy to train Royal Navy personnel to operate landing craft alongside assault troops. The intense nature of the training was tempered by the opportunity for the men to relax by swimming in the lake, where the high salinity gave increased buoyancy and helped many men to learn to swim.

On 28 February 1943, six months after the 1st Battalion London Scottish left Britain from the Rivers Clyde and Mersey, the 1st Division, including the 6th Gordons, left Gourock, in the Firth of Clyde, and Liverpool, on the Mersey. The Gordons were on board the former Canadian Pacific liner the RMS *Duchess of Argyll*, which had been converted to a troop ship. The convoy rendezvoused before heading out into the Atlantic Ocean, going around the north of Ireland. As their convoy sailed for eleven days south through the Atlantic Ocean, there were, unfortunately, some ships sunk by enemy submarines. The evening before arriving at their destination, the officers of the 6th Battalion were the guests of the captain, who hosted a sumptuous dinner on board. There was a commemorative menu card which almost every officer signed; a copy survives in the collection of the Gordon Highlanders Museum in Aberdeen. The menu was far more extensive than anything available in strictly rationed Britain, offering tomato soup, fillet of lemon sole, braised ox tongue with spinach, roast stuffed turkey and cranberry sauce, cauliflower cream sauce, chateau potatoes, finishing with fruit salad and vanilla ice cream. The menu card also conveyed a good will message from the captain and the ship's company, expressing the hope they would be the first to welcome them on a victorious voyage back to Britain.

On arrival in port at Algiers on 9 March 1943, there was enemy aircraft activity in the form of Junkers Ju 87 Stuka dive bombers. These had a terrifying effect; as they dived on their target, the sirens fitted to their wings screamed. Understandably, the ship's captain was anxious not to be caught within the confines of the harbour, where it was impossible for him to manoeuvre. Like a lot of the senior naval officers, he loathed army personnel wearing their tacketty (hobnail) boots on board as he didn't want the paintwork on the decks damaged. He had insisted that while on board the soldiers only wear soft-soled shoes, which was a problem as he now tried to rush the Gordons off his ship so that he could get his ship back out to sea and comparative safety. Lieutenant Leslie Hatt complained bitterly as he, like the rest of his comrades, was ejected from the vessel still in his plimsolls. With no one keen to hang around the harbour area in the middle of an air raid, the orders were given to press on to escape the bombing. With darkness falling there was no option for him but to march in his plimsolls, while also loaded with his heavy pack. The Gordons were to camp at Baraki, a distance of some 15 miles to the south-eastern outskirts of the city; by the time the battalion arrived at its destination, after marching over rough roads during darkness, Leslie Hatt complained that his shoes were wrecked and his feet very sore. The next week was very busy, spent assessing the losses of equipment, obtaining replacements and planning their next move. After eleven days at sea, the men were pleased to be back on dry land getting some exercise and getting some acclimatization before moving forward to the front line in Tunisia.

Although the 6th Battalion arrived at Algiers safely, the ship which was carrying a lot of their stores and other equipment, including their transport, sports kit and the recently replaced drums, was sunk when about 400 miles off Gibraltar. The torpedo struck amidships, so fortunately there was no explosion. The crew, along with some attendant army personnel, managed to get into the lifeboats before she disappeared below the waves. Among those saved was Corporal Ronald Shand, a technical corporal of the 6th Battalion, whose job was to ensure the vehicles and equipment were stored correctly on board. He was fortunate to be picked up that evening by another ship in the convoy, which had broken down and was trying to catch up with the convoy when they were sighted. He also arrived at Algiers but was not allowed to land as he had become separated from his battalion, which had moved. He was returned to Britain in a returning troop ship and arrived back in Glasgow some two weeks later and was sent to Gordon Barracks in Aberdeen. On arrival there, he found that his identity and story was not readily believed and was only allowed some shore leave after a rigorous interrogation by an intelligence officer. He was then sent all the way back to Algiers but still not allowed to rejoin his battalion and was transferred to the Black Watch. He was frustrated by what he considered to be the Army's bureaucracy and it was a further seven months before he was able to rejoin his battalion.

# Chapter 6

# North Africa

On 16 March, the 6th Gordons set off on a three-day train journey eastwards along the coast to Annaba. The train had no corridor; it would stop in an apparent haphazard way, whereupon men would alight to relieve themselves. On one occasion, around forty men were left behind – although the communication cord was pulled, it was later found that it was not connected, so the train driver had no idea he was supposed to stop. These men were eventually reunited with the rest of the Battalion as they were picked up by the motor transport bringing up the stores and equipment. In Annaba, some time was allowed for rest and recuperation, and the men had the opportunity to swim in the Mediterranean. On 24 March, they moved to a troop concentration area at Teboursouk. During the hours of darkness the next night, they advanced into the front line, taking over a position south-east of Medez-el-Bab, relieving men of the 1st Battalion East Surrey Regiment. The British and the German frontline positions were on hills several miles apart. The area overlooked the Goubellat Plain, through which flowed the meandering Medjerda River. This facilitated farming of the area, with small farms scattered throughout, but the surrounding hills were rocky and barren.

The Germans had positioned artillery on the heights and there was sporadic shelling of the Battalion's position. Their observers had a clear view of any movement in the Gordons' positions, provoking an artillery or mortar bombardment which restricted any activity, including the bringing up of supplies, until the hours of darkness. Where possible, the men dug in on the reverse slopes. These artillery barrages were often very effective, causing casualties and were very demoralizing. On 23 April, heavy artillery and mortar fire caused casualties to men sheltering in their slit trenches. Private Erik Brammer, a stretcher bearer in A Company, ignored the danger of exposing himself to enemy fire and ran forward to provide medical assistance and treat their injuries, despite being wounded himself. The following day, he showed his courage again, going to the assistance of the casualties of an anti-tank crew operating in his company area. He was first on the scene; despite shells still landing in the area, he treated the men's injuries and supervised their evacuation to safety for further treatment.

One of those wounded on 23 April was Private John Henderson. He had already shown great courage and resourcefulness, but his luck finally ran out on this day. He had previously served with 5th Battalion Gordon Highlanders in France in 1940 and was captured at St Valery-en-Caux when the 51st (Highland) Division was forced to surrender there on 12 June 1940. He escaped from the column of PoWs being marched into captivity on 27 June 1940, at St Pol, France, with Private Tom Anderson, with whom he had done his basic training in Aberdeen. They slipped out of the column, hid in a wood and waited until the column passed. However, they were both recaptured at Boulogne looking for a boat. They were taken to Tournai, just over the Belgian border and less than 20 miles from Lille, where John Henderson escaped again, this time he went alone. He climbed a wall and was sheltered for about a month by some Belgian civilians who were working with the Resistance. From here, he went south and crossed the line of demarcation at Moulins by crossing openly at a bridge carrying hay on his back so that the German guard took him for a French peasant. He continued on to Agde and crossed into Spain, but he was arrested by Spanish police and sent back to Fort St Jean, Marseille, where Allied PoWs were being interned. He broke out on 11 April 1940, walked 25 miles to Arles and from there across the Spanish frontier. He was arrested again in Barcelona and ended in Miranda Prison, where he spent nine weeks. His plight became known to the British Consulate. After their intervention, he was released for repatriation and set sail from Gibraltar, arriving back in Glasgow in July 1941. After some leave, he was transferred to the 6th Battalion and so sailed to Tunisia with them. After being seriously wounded in Tunisia, John Henderson was evacuated back to Britain and was discharged from the army on 11 February 1944 on medical grounds. His co-escaper, Tom Anderson, unfortunately did not make a successful escape back to Britain, but spent the rest of the war as a PoW, ending up in Stalag 317 Markt Pongau, Austria. Another 5th Battalion man who was in France in 1940 was Jack Rainnie. He was wounded at the battle of Abbeville on 4 June 1940 and was evacuated back to Britain for treatment. After a period of recuperation, Jack Rainnie joined 1st Battalion Gordons and was, in 1941, an early recruit to the parachute regiment. He saw action at the battalion's first operation in November 1942, which was to capture and hold Beja, an important road junction in Tunisia. The mission was a success. In March 1943, while still in Tunisia, Jack 'acquired' a German MP38 Schmeisser sub-machine pistol which he kept through the Sicily campaign and is now on display at the Gordon Highlanders Museum.

Initially, the Germans controlled the plain through active patrolling and occupation of some of the farm buildings. It was realized this had to be dealt with before any substantial attack on their positions could be undertaken. Once some small patrols had established the disposition of the Germans more clearly, from 14 April the 6th Gordons engaged in more active fighting patrols to capture prisoners for intelligence and to make the Germans realize the area had become less secure for them. Patrols were always conducted at night and since the area had been strewn with mines this made the activity hazardous. With a whole 1st Division attack planned for 23 April, a priority was given to mapping and clearing these minefields. On the night of 20–21 April, the 6th Gordons were in a concentration area away from the front line when an attack was made on their position by a fighting patrol from the Hermann Goering division. This attack involved the 6th Gordons' B Company, but was successfully beaten off; there were casualties and vehicles destroyed. Private Jack Parker was killed when he was struck by a bullet through his throat. His civilian occupation was in the machine room of the *Yorkshire Evening Post* and it was sad for his former colleagues to see his death reported in their companion newspapers.

As planned, on 23 April the entire 1st Division formed up for what was to be the first full set piece attack the 6th Gordons were to be part of. Their objective was a group of hills known as 'Point 174' with the main objective being Gueriat el Atach. The Gordons' role was to secure the hills on the right flank of the main thrust. As the rain fell, Lieutenant Colonel Peddie led the way to the start line, a distance of some 20 miles. Everyone was fully laden with packs of rations and ammunition. The start line was over the Medjes to Tunis Road; as they marched, their route was jam-packed with tanks, trucks and guns. Zero hour was just after 02:00 hours on 23 April 1943; a huge barrage of artillery opened up. The plan was for the advance to follow closely behind this creeping barrage until they were at the enemy's positions. This moved forward fairly quickly, rather than creeping, so it was necessary to move at double time to keep up. The men were fairly exhausted after their 20-mile march before the attack began but adrenalin kicked in and everything went to plan.

When they reached the German position, they discovered the position appeared to have been abandoned but it was quickly realized the Germans had just fallen back to avoid the shelling and would almost immediately counter-attack in the hope of catching the attacking Gordons by surprise. The order was given to move forward and take up positions on the top of the downward slope; they quickly established a defensive position and awaited the German response. This came fairly soon, and they were subjected to mortar fire. The danger was not confined to shrapnel but also the detonation of these explosives on the bare rocky ground, which caused stones and rock splinters to fly up, ensuring the men kept their heads down. The mortar fire was followed up by German infantry, who were met by a terrific fusillade of bullets cutting many of them down. A larger and more widespread German counter-attack soon developed with their ensuing artillery bombardment. The threat to the Gordons' position on the hilltop was intensified when Tiger tanks started manoeuvring on the lower ground and strafed them. Soon British tanks and artillery responded. The Tiger which had been causing the Gordons so much grief was disabled by British artillery fire. It is believed this was the first relatively intact Tiger tank captured by the British; it provided useful intelligence on this fearsome weapon. Tiger tank 131 is now an exhibit at the Tank Museum in Dorset.

Lieutenant Robert (Bobby) Smith was also wounded on 23 April. He was struck on the head by a piece of shrapnel which tore a large hole in his steel helmet. The wound was considered so serious that it was thought that his helmet should not be removed until he reached the medical expertise at the field dressing station. On examination it was decided the helmet had done its job and his wound was less critical than first thought. Although a bit dazed, once he was bandaged up, he was able to return to duty and was given the helmet with the large hole as a souvenir of his lucky escape. Later he was seen by Lieutenant Leslie Hatt dashing through his position with a bandaged head and a pistol in hand which he thought looked reminiscent of a *Boy's Own* magazine action character. Much later, long after the war, Bobby Smith donated his 'lucky' helmet to the Gordon Highlanders Museum, where it is now on display.

This battle ensued for some time. In a separate phase on 24 April, the British 4th Division attacked a German position at a point known as 'Peter's Corner', a junction on the road to Tunis a few miles east of Medjez-el-Bab. The 4th Division forces passed through the Gordons' position, which was fairly close to their objective. This attack however, encountered strong resistance and did not succeed and it was disappointing for the Gordons to see the battered remnants withdrawing back through their position. On the night of the 25th, a message came to the Gordons that there were wounded men lying out in a minefield and it was decided that a rescue mission be undertaken. The Medical Officer, Captain George McIntosh, MC, another Keith doctor who had replaced Captain (Doctor) Lennel Taylor, was asked to assist. George McIntosh was no stranger to extreme danger when assisting wounded men. In 1940, while with the 3rd Division in Belgium, some wounded men were too exposed to be rescued from their positions on the Scheldt Canal. With complete disregard for his own safety, Captain McIntosh went forward to attend to their wounds. He was awarded his Military Cross for this action and a further action when he carried on treating men in the regimental aid post when he himself had been wounded.

Lieutenant Robin Bain and Captain McIntosh organized a party of stretcher bearers and they all set off into the minefield. Unfortunately, their movements triggered one of the S mines and four of the party were wounded, including Doctor McIntosh. This was calamitous as he was to have provided the main medical expertise. At this point Private Richard McPherson, one of the stretcher bearers, stepped forward to give the necessary first aid to those injured, but another mine exploded and Richard McPherson was also wounded. He continued to apply his first aid skills to all of the others and the rescue was completed. Unfortunately, McPherson's wounds proved fatal. For his courage and devotion to duty, he was posthumously mentioned in dispatches.

The mine fields strewn liberally over the area by the Germans as a defensive measure were a serious problem. Lieutenant Stanley Martin was injured on 26 April as a result of stepping on these hidden menaces and lost his foot. His war was effectively over. His rescue was carried out by stretcher bearers who risked their own lives to extract him from the minefield and deliver him to the care of the Medical Officer, Captain McIntosh, who was still suffering from his own wounds received in a minefield the previous day.

The Gordons were relieved from their position on 28 April and went into reserve positions. Their rest did not last long, however. On 30 April 1943, A and D companies were ordered to undertake a counter-attack on points 212 and 214. The objective was to relieve and rescue men of the Irish Guards who had suffered heavy casualties and were pinned down on the lower slopes of Djebel Bou Aoukaz, a steep hill some 250 metres high, which commanded the whole area and dominated the plain. This relief force moved forward in trucks led by Major Innes Flemming, with Captain John Crewdson following up with the ammunition and other equipment. As they moved across the plain, clouds of dust were churned up by the vehicles, which gave the German gunners an inviting target they couldn't ignore; this made the journey very hazardous. Some casualties resulted. Once in their starting position, the Gordons moved forward in their platoons toward their objective, which was almost half a mile away with little or no cover. While crossing the open ground, they came under fire from snipers and machine guns, resulting in a few more men being wounded before they reached the relative cover at the bottom of the hill. As the platoons scrambled up the slopes, a number were pinned down. One section of a following platoon led by Private John Lamb managed to bypass this bottleneck and they were joined by others. Together, they managed to reach the top of the ridge, but they were continually exposed to fire, with John Lamb being wounded in the leg. They directed the fire of the platoon's 2-inch mortars onto a machine-gun position which was holding them up. This forced the German machine gunners to break cover and, as they fled, the Gordons' Bren gunners repaid their murderous fire with interest. Sergeant John McConnachie, who was later awarded a Military Medal for his bravery, managed to reach his objective, but his platoon was severely depleted, having taken heavy casualties with almost the total loss of two of his sections. Fighting was intense and Captain Robert Rae managed to get his company up the slopes. He was progressing well when he was badly wounded, but he tried to continue to urge on his men, for which he was mentioned in dispatches. Captain Rae had to be relieved for medical attention and subsequently his arm was amputated as a result of his wounds. One of those killed was Lance Corporal Andrew Duke, who was originally from Kirriemuir, Angus. His wife, Betty, was living with her parents in Ascot, Berkshire, where she gave birth to a daughter, Norma, just four days after he was killed. The family story is quite sad, as Andrew's brother, George, was also killed in Sicily just three months later on 1 August 1943, while serving with the 1st Battalion Black Watch.

Under extreme pressure, with their position taking heavy machine-gun fire that created multiple casualties, A Company became severely depleted. Lieutenant Norman Lawrie came forward and led an attack over some 400 metres of exposed ground and the ferocity of this action resulted in their objective being taken successfully with the enemy resistance rapidly overcome. As the A Company commander, Captain Robert Rae, was seriously injured, Lieutenant Lawrie had to take over command of the entire company. He managed to withdraw his men to a less-exposed position, where Colour Sergeant Henry Garioch reorganized them to improve their capabilities in their collective defence.

The Gordons now held their position and, on 2 May, were reinforced by B Company, commanded by Captain Lindsay Bridgman. The Gordons braced themselves for a counter-attack, but mercifully it never came and the surviving Irish Guards, who were in a poor state, were evacuated successfully. Lieutenant R. W. (Bobby) Smith recalled that in recognition of their gallant rescue at point 212, the Irish Guards requested 6th Gordons send a representative party, including pipers, to the memorial service to commemorate their fallen comrades.

Later that month, for his proven leadership abilities, Henry Garioch was given a field commission, becoming 2nd Lieutenant Garioch. Unusually, he was allowed to remain with A Company. Henry was a very experienced soldier with fifteen years of experience rising through the ranks. He had served as a Regular soldier with the 2nd Battalion in Gibraltar and Singapore. He was also a very accomplished sportsman in many fields and was among the team who won the Malay Command Tug o' War 'Warren Shield' in 1937. He transferred to the Army Reserve in 1938 but, on the declaration of war, was called up as a Reservist.

There was a lull in the fighting for a few days, although the Gordons' position was subjected to artillery and mortar fire. This was a serious problem as the ground was so hard and stony that it was virtually impossible to dig in to improve their cover.

On 4 May, just before first light, the expected German counter-attack started with heavy mortar fire, followed by the appearance of tanks on the plain below. This was followed up by infantry surging up the hill towards their position. These were repelled by concentrated rifle fire and the exchange of grenades, but most telling was mortar fire directed by Sergeant Tom Bruce, who was mentioned in dispatches for his valuable action. The attack was well organized and groups of German infantry were able to close on the Gordons from their rear. Another major problem was the fire from tanks which had broken through the lines at a point known as Gab-Gab Gap, which was a flat area between the two hills, Djebel Bou Aoukaz and Dejebel Rhaouss. This menace was not something the companies of Gordons on the hill could tackle on their own; support was required from the battalion anti-tank guns, which they expected would be brought to bear as soon as was possible. Major Innes Fleming was fatally wounded, being shot through the head, and almost immediately Captain Lindsay Bridgman was also wounded. Lieutenant Norman Lawrie was again required to take over command, this time of all three of the rifle companies, which he achieved with coolness and courage while his position was under considerable pressure from fire of all kinds. He issued orders to reorganize their defences and repel the attack. As groups of determined Germans attacked from seemingly all sides, individual acts of courage helped stem the attack. Corporal Edmunds exposed himself to danger, jumping out and spraying the advancing enemy with his Tommy gun, stopping them dead in their tracks. Lieutenant Fordyce was wounded in the hand but refused to leave his post and subsequently lost a finger as a result of his wounds. He was among those to also be mentioned in dispatches for his actions in this battle. Amidst the fighting, the Gordons were taking a lot of casualties, keeping stretcher bearers Privates Sam Cochran, Tom (Tiny) Grimshaw and John Stevenson busy. Sam Cochran showed little regard for his own safety working under fire and as a result was wounded but continued to tend to the other casualties. He received a mention in dispatches for his courage, while Lieutenant Norman Lawrie was awarded a Military Cross. One of the saddest casualties was Corporal Ronald Hosler, who was killed on his twenty-fourth birthday.

On 6 May, after the threat to the Gordons' position on Djebel Bou Aoukaz had receded, stretcher bearer Private Erik Brammer observed men of the Duke of Wellington's regiment reach his location as they were advancing towards Djebel Bou Aoukaz as part of an attack to complete the elimination of that German strong point. The Duke's men received casualties from mortars and snipers and their advance was held up. Despite the danger, Eric Brammer ran across 40 metres of ridge exposed to enemy fire and took charge of the situation. He treated the wounded and, with the assistance of another stretcher bearer, evacuated a wounded man to cover. He displayed great courage and coolness on this occasion and earlier, on 23 and 24 of April at Medjez-el-Bab, and was awarded the Military Medal.

The Axis hold on Tunisia was coming to an end and a big offensive was launched on 6 May 1943. The following day, the Gordons were ordered to clear some pockets of enemy soldiers around Djedeida, a small town some 20 miles east of Tunis sitting on the Medjerda River. As they moved off in darkness, the weather broke and torrential rain made the unsurfaced roads impassable to wheeled vehicles. There was no alternative transport, so the men had to continue to their objective on foot. It was a thoroughly unpleasant march in the freezing cold wind and rain, dressed only in their lightweight khaki shirts and shorts. They were soaked to the skin and froze as they plodded on through the mud. Over the next two days the Germans they encountered all appeared to be happy to surrender. A German field hospital was discovered in a chapel in the village of Chaouat. This held a large number of German patients together with sixteen Allied wounded. No doubt the Germans who were taken prisoner were as relieved that their war was over as the British and American patients were delighted to be liberated. Soon afterwards, on 13 May 1943, German General Jurgen von Arnim formally surrendered, delivering all of North Africa into Allied hands and effectively ending the fighting in North Africa. The 6th Gordons heard this news while at Grombalia, some 25 miles south-east of Tunis, and their victory celebrations were greatly enhanced by the close proximity of a winery.

Next day, the Battalion moved the short distance to Hammam-Lif on the Mediterranean coast, where the men could relax, indulge in swimming in the sea and buy fresh fruit from the local vendors; a festival atmosphere prevailed for a few days. In keeping with the holiday spirit, during this short interlude between fighting and training, Private Arthur Mutch and a few friends from his company went into town to get 'Scotland for Ever' and a thistle design tattooed on their arms, which was intended as a good luck talisman. He knew how fickle the fortunes of war could be as his older brother, John, was serving with the 2nd Battalion Gordon Highlanders in Singapore and taken prisoner by the Japanese in February 1942. The local tattoo artist had no idea what a thistle looked like, so Arthur sketched out the design and wording of the slogan for him and this design was immediately tattooed onto Arthur's forearm. The next man in the queue was happy enough with the artist's handiwork, based on Arthur's design, so he got the same tattoo. Soon there was a queue of Gordon Highlanders right up the street awaiting their turn. The tattoo artist was a very happy man having made a nice profit that day.

The battalion moved again to Sousse and a small detachment of officers and men went to Tunis to participate in the victory parade on 20 May, marching within the ranks of contingents from the whole 1st Division. The salute was taken by Supreme Allied Commander, American General Dwight D. Eisenhower. The parade was led by the drums and pipes and they played the Gordons' regimental march 'Cock o' the North' as the Gordons passed the saluting base.

The business of war and the complete defeat of the Nazis was far from complete. Everyone knew the holiday period would soon end, and so it did, signalled when a large draft of men from the Black Watch transferred to the Battalion to replace the heavy losses of the Tunisian campaign. Intensive training then began with landing craft and practising boarding and disembarking ships by scrambling nets. This could only mean that their next mission would involve an amphibious landing on some enemy shore. The location of this was finally revealed to the 6th Gordons as the small Italian volcanic island of Pantelleria, a strategic base for planes and submarines which had been active in the enemy siege of Malta but also threatened future Allied operations in Sicily and southern Italy. This was codenamed Operation Corkscrew. The island was considered by the Italian fascist leader, Benito Mussolini, as an impregnable fortress.

At daybreak on 11 June, three rifle companies of the battalion sailed from Sfax on the *Queen Emma* and *Princess Beatrice,* while HQ Company and the remaining rifle company sailed out of Sousse on the *Royal Ulsterman.* The short crossing over a calm Mediterranean Sea took only a few hours, but was long enough for the men who were to assault the island's shore to contemplate with some trepidation as to what the day would bring. This was also the first full-scale attack on enemy home territory and the first amphibious attack the Gordons had experienced. The orders were for the 6th Gordons to land in the second wave and assault the mountain in the centre of the island. The landings had been preceded by four days of bombing; a short time after the first wave landed, the island's garrison flew the white flag and surrendered, just as the 6th Gordons were assembling to transfer to landing craft. The announcement of the surrender roused a loud cheer from the men who were convinced they were just about to attack the heavily defended shore with the high probability of numerous casualties. Consequently, they were able to land on the island without a shot being fired. As part of the spoils of war, an Italian officer surrendered his Beretta pistol to, now Captain, Bobby Smith and this is now part of the collection of the Gordon Highlanders Museum. The battalion also found that the island's garrison had two large military bands, one Italian and the other German. As they were made prisoner they were relieved of their instruments and Lieutenant William (Willie) McHardy, recorded that on leaving the island these instruments were mostly in the possession of the Gordons. Willie McHardy had only recently rejoined the battalion after being commissioned from the ranks and spending some time as an instructor at the regimental HQ in Aberdeen. Pantelleria was to be his first action and he was disappointed to have returned to the Battalion after all of the fighting in Tunisia was over. The Battalion left the island on 16 June.

The victory in North Africa and the recent operation in Pantelleria had delivered thousands of German and Italian PoWs into Allied hands. On returning to Tunisia the 6th Gordons were detailed to take over guarding around 10,000 PoWs. The location was at Ghardimaou, Tunisia, which was about 50 miles inland and on the border with Algeria. The weather in the height of the summer was very hot and dry and facilities for showering and proper sanitation were virtually non-existent. The poor hygiene was inevitably an issue; this attracted swarms of flies and many men fell ill as a result. The PoWs were held in several enclosures made of 'concertina' barbed wire, which were situated in an olive grove, each holding around 1,000 PoWs. The 6th Gordons' task was ensuring security by patrolling the perimeter, which was a couple of miles long, but the unsatisfactory fence was easily surmounted and the olive trees gave ample cover for any prisoner who wished to attempt an escape. The duties also included the administration of the camp, which included a hospital for wounded Germans. Not only was there the requirement to provide food and water but maintaining a record of their prisoners was also necessary. The latter proved difficult as, with the insecure nature of the fences, PoWs could also move from one caged enclosure to a different one, so record-keeping was a bit of a farce. All of this was bad for the morale of the Gordon Highlanders and Willie McHardy thought this was not really a job for frontline soldiers like the 6th Gordons. The Battalion did manage to improve matters by bringing in temporary showers and controlling the fly population, but the saving grace was the formation of a small camp on the coast where each Gordon was given a few days leave. To everyone's relief, both the PoWs and Gordons, the PoWs were transferred and this temporary camp closed after three weeks, but the battalion remained in place for a further month.

A return to normal soldiering was welcome, even though this meant a period of strenuous training in mountain warfare. There was some relief and a sense of occasion when the battalion took part in a parade of the whole 1st Division in Tunis on 4 September 1943, where General Eisenhower again took the salute. It was clear that the 6th Gordons' time in North Africa was drawing to a close. The war was progressing into Italy and it was likely this would be their next theatre of operation; this was still a few months away. Mountain training resumed, which further posed the question: Where would they be deployed next? As the 1st London Scottish were preparing for their first action, the 6th Gordons had already seen quite a lot of action in Tunisia. It was the final defeat of the Afrika Korps in Tunisia which ended their two-year dominance of the whole North African theatre. The regiment of the Gordon Highlanders could take pride in their part in this defeat beginning with the famous pivotal victory at El Alamein in October 1942. Montgomery's forces had included the 1st and 5th/7th battalions, while the 6th Battalion were involved in the final victory when German General Jurgen von Arnim surrendered on 13 May 1943.

# Chapter 7

# Sicily

The 168 Brigade, which included the 1st Battalion London Sottish, had been operating as an independent brigade group since being detached from the 56th Division in April 1943. This was all set to change. After their amphibious training was complete, they enjoyed a short period of rest at Gaza. They joined the 50th Northumbrian Division, with which they would be part of the invasion of Sicily. The convoy set sail from Alexandria, Egypt with the 1st London Scottish aboard the former Polish ship *Kosciuseko*, which was also Clyde-built. The 1st Battalion London Scottish knew that they would see their first action of the war very soon and they too were about to invade an Italian island.

The Allied landings on Sicily, codenamed Operation Husky, took place on the night of 9–10 July. British and American forces attacked the south-eastern corner of the island with the British Eighth Army pushing directly north up the east coast while the American Seventh Army forged north and west. The 1st London Scottish were not involved in the initial landings and landed at Syracuse on 13 July, which had already been captured. They were not, however, the first men of the London Scottish to have been in action in Sicily.

A full two years earlier, on 29 August 1941, two of their number, Lance Sergeant Robert Brown and Lance Corporal John Ferguson, who had volunteered to join the Commandos, took part in a daring raid in Sicily. The objective of the raid was to disrupt enemy communications by destroying the bridge on the coastal railway between Palermo and Messina. The target chosen was where the railway crossed the river Torrente Furiano near Acquedolci on Sicily's northern coast, some 5 miles east of Palermo, the island's administrative centre. At this point, the bridge crossed the wide river valley and had several spans. John Ferguson had some experience of operating behind enemy lines and had taken part on previous raids in July when he had blown up trains on the Sicilian and the southern Italian coast.

On 19 August 1941, the Commando raiding party boarded the Royal Navy submarine HMS *Triumph* of the 10th Submarine Flotilla, which was operating out of their base on Manoel Island in the natural harbour between Valetta and Sliema, Malta. They were welcomed aboard by the boat's captain, Commander Wilfrid Woods. Once the men were aboard, HMS *Triumph* slipped her moorings and sailed out into the Mediterranean. After three days, HMS *Triumph* approached the north coast of Sicily, off the mouth of the Torrente Furiano. She remained submerged and a survey was made of the target area by periscope. Since all looked quiet it was intended to land a reconnaissance party after midnight, but the sea was quite rough and it was decided to await calmer conditions, which occurred by that evening.

The reconnaissance party was due to go ashore that night but before the Commandos could be released a signal was received with orders for the submarine to attack a fleet of Italian warships which was passing through the Straits of Messina that separate the island of Sicily from the Italian mainland. Commander Wilfrid Woods put the reconnaissance party ashore shortly after midnight, on 24 August 1941, in folboats (collapsible canoes) and they returned to the submarine after an hour, reporting that the bridge was unguarded and they had not encountered any opposition.

Commander Woods knew the bridge wasn't going anywhere so his priority had to be to engage the enemy fleet while it was transiting the confines of the Messina Straits. He postponed the Commando operation and set sail for the straits. In the early hours of the morning on 26 August, he sighted the Italian ships and fired two torpedoes. He observed, with some satisfaction, that the Italian heavy cruiser *Balzano* had stopped and smoke was rising from her. She did not sink but was out of action. Despite taking immediate evasive action, Commander Woods then found himself being hunted and under an accurate and intensive depth charge counter-attack, which was extremely harrowing for the Commandos and the submarine's crew. The commander eventually managed to evade his attackers and return to his original mission.

HMS *Triumph* was back on station off the mouth of the Torrente Furiano the next afternoon and preparations were made for the Commando party to go ashore. Around midnight, just as the canoes were about to be launched, there was another change of plan forced on the operation. A fishing boat, which had not been spotted in the mist, strayed into the area. Although it was sunk, their mission had been temporarily compromised, so Commander Woods took his boat back out to sea. He returned in two days and made another survey of the target by periscope. Under the cover of darkness in the early hours of the next morning, 31 August 1941, the twelve-man Commando team set out in their canoes after being dropped off just under a mile offshore.

Initially, the operation went well, and two spans of the twin-track railway bridge traversing about 120 metres were demolished, cutting a major link between Sicily's capital, Palermo, and the Italian mainland, through the ferry port of Messina. The damage was substantial and it took months to repair. At about 03:00, the explosions were heard by the crew of HMS *Triumph* as they waited for the return of the raiding party. Meanwhile ashore, disaster struck as the raiders were compromised and most failed to turn up at the rendezvous point. Only five men were picked up and seven were missing. As it became light, HMS *Triumph* had to leave the area, returning the following night to await stragglers, but none arrived. Reluctantly, Commander Woods set sail for Malta. It was later discovered that the missing men had been captured and these included John Ferguson and Robert Brown. Both men, in common with the other members of their raiding party, were awarded gallantry awards, with Robert Brown and John Ferguson both receiving Military Medals. In their medal award citations both were commended for their great courage, determination and resourcefulness, with John Ferguson being singled out for particular praise as after three separate successful missions being described as 'an able, zealous and fearless soldier who has assisted in dangerous work with important results'.

Malcolm Munthe was another Gordon Highlander set to create havoc on the island of Sicily. He was a member of a prominent Swedish family with royal connections, but in 1939, he enlisted into the Gordon Highlanders as a private soldier. His potential was quickly realized; he was commissioned in December 1939 and very soon afterwards recruited into the Special Operations Executive (SOE), where he carried out special operations in Scandinavia. He was forced to leave Norway in July 1941 because of his involvement in a plot to assassinate Heinrich Himmler, head of the Nazi SS, while he was in Oslo. In Sicily, Malcolm Munthe commanded a small SOE unit whose task was to make contact with Italian anti-fascist elements and encourage them to revolt and to form guerrilla bands. On one occasion his band posed as refugees and he dressed himself as an old woman and rode a donkey carrying bombs hidden inside melons which were padded with pine needles.

Once ashore, the 1st Battalion London Scottish established itself in an olive grove outside the city. After four days the battalion started their march forward towards the front line. They had waited in vain for trucks to assist in the movement of their equipment and stores, so each man was carrying a heavy pack. After a few days' rest and in the cool of the morning this was fine, but as the sun climbed into the cloudless Sicilian sky and the temperature soared, men began to suffer from exhaustion, dehydration and heatstroke. Local transport had to be commandeered until the army's promised transport arrived, which only became available the next day. The battalion's first action took place on the night of 15–16 July, when one company was required to assist an attack to hold Primosole Bridge, constructed of steel girders with a span of some 125 metres crossing the River Simeto, south of Catania, on the main road from Syracuse to Catania. This was an important strategic position as Catania Airfield was less than 10 miles to the north. The bridge was being contested heavily after a force of British paratroopers had captured the bridge intact. One of these paratroopers was Jack Rainnie, the former Gordon Highlander wounded in France in 1940, who still had the German Schmeisser sub-machine pistol he had acquired in Tunisia. Half his platoon was dropped in the wrong location but the remnants still managed to help secure the bridge intact, despite fierce enemy resistance. After a German counter-attack they were effectively surrounded and the 'Paras', who had expended almost all of their ammunition, were forced into a small perimeter to the south. The Germans were able to re-establish a defensive line on the northern side of the bridge. Next day, the bridge was retaken and a small bridgehead re-established by the Durham Light Infantry. The 1st London Scottish was ordered to move into position to perform a counter-attack role should the enemy try to retake the bridge while the Durhams were attacking to enlarge the bridgehead. It became apparent that strong enemy machine-gun posts had been left in scrub and vineyards behind the attacking Durhams and A Company of the 1st London Scottish was ordered to deal with the threat. A platoon led by Lieutenant John Gillan moved out to tackle the Germans' machine-gun positions, but they were well concealed and it was essential to establish their exact positions so that they could be eliminated. Lieutenant Gillan, armed with a Bren gun, and Private Arthur Proctor fearlessly exposed themselves while firing on the German positions to draw their fire, while the rest of the platoon was sent on a flanking manoeuvre. Captain Hugh Attwooll, who commanded A Company, was situated in the rear and as a result of Gillan and Proctor's actions was able to pinpoint the German machine-gun position. The threat was eliminated by the 2-inch mortars of Lieutenant Gillan's platoon and the assistance of a Sherman tank sent forward by Hugh Attwooll. As a result of their courageous actions, John Gillan was awarded a Military Cross, while Arthur Proctor was awarded a Military Medal.

This was a small action but next day the whole battalion saw action. Zero hour for the attack was 10:00 pm on a fine bright moonlit night on 17 July. The battalion's 'start line' was located just on the northern side of Primosole Bridge. The terrain was flat and bare between the battalion's start line and their objective, which was a deep artificial irrigation canal, named the Fosse Botaceto, almost 2 miles away. The advance was carried out in virtual silence, with no opposition being encountered until they were within 300 metres of their objective, where they expected there would be a supporting artillery barrage just before they made their final assault. Unknown to the attackers, the artillery barrage had been cancelled; so, fatally, the attack went in without that support.

The attack was met with a fierce storm of machine-gun fire along the whole front, with some close-quarter fighting having to be undertaken to capture a farm which had been fortified by the enemy. With no cover, the whole battalion was caught out in the open and when the artillery support finally came, it fell beyond the objective so had little effect on the enemy. The attack was thrown into complete confusion as the men sought cover in the shallow ditches on the field edges, but their situation was dangerous as their movements were silhouetted in the moonlight and visible to the German defenders. This was the first experience of battle for these young soldiers and the noise of gunfire, grenades and mortar explosions all numbed the senses as the air was peppered with screams, moans and expletives. In the darkness, disorientation was also a factor, along with real horror at seeing some of their comrades cut down by the intensity of the enemy fire.

It was clear that the attack had failed and, just before dawn, a withdrawal was ordered as it would be impossible to hold the forward positions in daylight. During this battle Private Jim Rennie, who was a D Company signaller, braved continuous shelling, mortaring and machine-gun fire and worked tirelessly to repair broken telephone lines to maintain the communications between the company and the battalion HQ. The confusion of the battle led to reports of losses much higher than had actually occurred, but as the battalion regrouped, it was found that there were numerous casualties, with twelve men killed, many more wounded and some captured. This was therefore a very black day to mark the first full battalion action of the war. One of those wounded and evacuated to a hospital in Tripoli, Libya, was Lance Corporal Alexander Whitehead, who died of his wounds four weeks later and never saw his son, who was born shortly after he left Britain for service overseas.

The battalion remained in position for almost two weeks, when patrols were sent out to establish the enemy strength and disposition. Private Arthur Proctor demonstrated his fearless nature and devotion to duty yet again when, just two days after his action with Lieutenant Gillan, he penetrated some 300 metres behind enemy lines and noted their strength and positions, returning safely to report his findings.

After some heavy fighting on the whole division's front, Catania was taken and further advances were possible with only sporadic resistance. The Germans were retreating while the Italians were surrendering in droves. The campaign to capture Sicily continued and the 1st London Scottish were next in action on 10 August 1943 on the southern slopes of Mount Etna at Viagrande. In what was to be a feature of the whole Italian campaign, the enemy cleverly used the natural topography to assist their defences and hard fighting resulted. The resupply of water, rations and ammunition was very difficult due to the rough steep terrain, which was resolved to a degree by the use of mules. The terrain was not the only obstacle to getting around as Lieutenant Neil Will found to his cost. As the Battalion's Signals Officer, he was travelling by motorcycle to deliver an important message to the commanding officer when a shell burst in front of him, wounding him and knocking him off his machine. Courageously, he picked himself up and delivered his message before seeking medical assistance. That same day, a German Spandau machine-gun position was holding up Captain Hugh Attwooll's A Company. Captain Attwooll, armed to the teeth with grenades and a Thompson submachine gun ('Tommy Gun'), went out alone and hunted down the German position, holding his fire until he was within range. When he opened fire, he took the Germans totally by surprise and those that survived his attack fled and the advance was able to continue. Two days later at St Verina, in another close action, he moved between his platoons while exposed to small arms fire, encouraging them and directing their fire to good effect. Even after being blown off his feet by an exploding shell, he continued to perform his duties and next day led a patrol to see if the enemy were still holding their positions. For his courageous actions over the preceding days, he was awarded a Military Cross. During this action, despite the area being swept by machine-gun fire, stretcher bearer Private George Martin showed great devotion to duty when he went out to rescue a seriously wounded man, only to find he was already dead when he reached him.

With the advance covering another 12 miles, elements of the 1st Battalion London Scottish reached the town of Macchia on 12 August, where they found that the strategic river crossing was being held by a strong enemy force. At this time in the year, the river was practically dry, but the river's channel still created a significant obstacle requiring the use of the bridge to make further progress. Private William Cinderby was with the leading section when they came to the river and found the bridge blown. Without warning, a machine gun on the north bank opened up, wounding Corporal J. Strachan and Lance Corporal John Davers. Bill Cinderby dived into a nearby doorway, surveyed the scene and eventually located the machine-gun post hidden in thick undergrowth across the river, some 200 metres away. Its hidden position gave no warning of the danger before the Nazis opened fire. He assessed the situation and saw the enemy had a clear, open field of fire to where his two comrades were unable to move, lying in the road injured. There was absolutely no cover available to him but despite the obvious danger, Bill went forward and dragged Corporal Strachan to safety and applied first aid. Daringly, he went forward again to rescue John Davers. In a callous act, there was a second burst from the machine gun which killed John Davers. Despite there being little hope, Bill still checked to confirm that his comrade was in fact dead before returning to cover and safety. Bill Cinderby was a brave, compassionate soldier and in recognition of this he was awarded a Military Medal. Later in the war, he was wounded twice. In Macchia, the enemy put up stiff resistance and casualties mounted. Bill Cinderby was not alone in showing great compassion and courage towards his injured comrades. On 14 August, George Martin, assisted by some other stretcher bearers, endeavoured to help every wounded man, although this meant they were frequently being exposed to enemy fire. All of the wounded were rescued and successfully taken to shelter. For this and his earlier acts of selfless courage two days earlier at Sevenerino, George Martin was also awarded a Military Medal. The capture of Macchia proved to be the end of the Sicilian campaign for 1st London Scottish as they went into reserve until the next phase of the Italian campaign.

There followed a period of rest and recuperation, with the Battalion camped in olive groves on the lower slopes of Mount Etna, the largest and most active volcano in Europe, which was fortunately quiet during this period. The welcome news that Operation Husky was at an end came on 17 August with the complete occupation of the island of Sicily. The 1st London Scottish had been in Sicily for thirty-five days and in almost continual action for twenty-eight of them. The men enjoyed this period where they could go swimming in the sea and regroup before training began again. The Germans had successfully fled over the Straits of Messina to mainland Italy and the Italians signed an unconditional surrender on 3 September, but this was not publicized until five days later, which was to allow the Allied invasion of Italy to get underway and surprise the Germans. This was a short period to enjoy the pause in the fighting. There was even time, on 26 August, to meet up with the 1st and 5th/7th battalions of the Gordon Highlanders, who were with 51st (Highland) Division. The massed pipe bands played at Castiglioni where, afterwards, a party was held in the officers' mess, where the three Pipe Majors provided music for the Highland dancing.

The Gordons with the 51st (Highland) Division were set to leave Sicily for Britain but that was all they knew. Their next operation was to take part in the Normandy landings, which were almost a year away and still a closely guarded secret. The 1st London Scottish, however, were to follow a different path. While still in Sicily, they heard of the three-pronged attack on the Italian mainland by combined British and American forces while they awaited orders for their next move, but that was unknown until October.

# Chapter 8

# The Battle for Monte Cassino

The 1st London Scottish was now to rejoin the 56th Division, their old Division prior to their detachment, with the rest of 168 Brigade for training and involvement in the invasion of Sicily. In preparation for this they moved north to Messina on 11 October 1943. The Division, without 168 Brigade and the 1st London Scottish, landed at Salerno in south-west Italy on 9 September 1943. This was part of Operation Avalanche, a joint American and British operation, which commenced with amphibious landings which were met with unexpectedly fierce resistance. The 56th Division came ashore just west of Battipaglia, roughly in the centre of Salerno Bay, and in the middle of the invading force. Heavy resistance was encountered, but they managed to get ashore and by the end of the first day had pushed about 6 miles inland.

It was five weeks later, on 14 October 1943, after the bridgehead was secure, that the 1st London Scottish, as part of 168 Brigade, landed at Salerno from Landing Craft Infantry (LCI) vessels. Their vehicles had crossed the Straits of Messina from Sicily and had driven up to Salerno after the whole area south of Salerno had been successfully captured by British forces. The British had landed at Reggio di Calabria, in the 'toe' of Italy, and Taranto, in the 'heel' of Italy, around the same time as the Salerno landings. The 1st London Scottish was camped outside Salerno and while the reforming operation was taking place, some lucky men were able to get permission to visit the Roman ruins at Pompeii. The brigade then received orders to join the rest of the 56th Division in the Caserta area just north-east of Naples.

Major Malcom Munthe was again in action after the Allied landings at Salerno. While in southern Italy he was working with an Italian officer, Captain Antonio Ricci, who was captured by the Germans but managed to escape. Captain Ricci then began to organize resistance in Italy north of Salerno, crossing the front line a number of times to liaise with Malcolm Munthe. Over the nights of 21–23 September 1943, Munthe and his SOE team rescued Benedetto Croce and his family as German troops surrounded their house. Signore Croce was Italy's leading anti-fascist senator and a respected liberal philosopher. Captain Ricci was injured whilst assisting Munthe on this mission. For his work with the Italian (anti-fascist) Resistance, Malcom

Munthe was presented with a seventeenth-century Andria Ferara mortuary-hilted broad sword with an engraved inscription. The sword had been in Captain Ricci's family for centuries and had hung in his ancestral home since the seventeenth century. The sword was engraved: 'Presented by Italian Resistance. With the true thanks of the Italians who fight against Fascism and who always loved British freedom and courage, to the British officers and men who saved them at Sorrento, September 22, 1943, led by Major Malcolm Munthe of the Gordon Highlanders.' This sword is now part of the collection of the Gordon Highlanders Museum.

After the capitulation of the Italian Government to the Allies, Naples was the scene of a citizens' revolt. This was a vicious struggle with the occupying Germans executing Italians protesting about the occupation of their city. Resistance fighters were able to better arm themselves with weapons stolen from an Italian Army store and began an armed uprising alongside mass riots. With the situation becoming increasing difficult for the Germans to control and the imminent threat of the Allies approaching from the south, the Germans negotiated safe passage from the city but not before destroying the port facilities and much of the city's infrastructure. This was a bitter blow to the Allied cause as one of the main aims of the Salerno landings was to capture the large port of Naples intact to enable resupply. Allied soldiers entered the city on 1 October 1943 and work began rapidly to restore the port to an operational state.

On 20 October, the 1st London Scottish moved forward, crossing the Volturno River, which had been used by the Germans to enhance their position in the 'Volturno line', their first line of defence as they doggedly defended the Italian peninsula. With the river crossing in full view of their line in the hills beyond, the Allies suffered heavy casualties in the attempted crossings. Once the crossing had been achieved, the Germans merely fell back to their next prepared defensive line, known as the 'Barbara line'. This was the position when the 1st Battalion London Scottish entered the fray, moving into the line in the hills where artillery attacks were common and frequently caused casualties. Unfortunately, the first casualty of the battalion on the Italian mainland, in this new phase of the Italian campaign, was Medical Officer Captain Bryan Rowlands. He was wounded by shrapnel on 23 October and had to be evacuated. His post was filled with Lieutenant James Pugh, also of the Royal Army Medical Corps.

It was necessary to send out patrols to establish the disposition of the enemy. It was on two of these patrols that Private Jim Rennie again showed his courage under fire and played a critical role for the patrols he supported. On 27 October, near the village of Visciano, a patrol led by Lieutenant Gillan,

MC, came under heavy machine-gun fire and contact with the company HQ was severed for a time. Private Rennie dutifully worked to restore communication even though he was exposed to a hail of fire and restored communications so that artillery and mortar fire could be laid down to assist the patrol. His courage and expertise on patrol was called for again just two days later when out again supporting a patrol led by Major Penman. In an exposed position, he maintained wireless communication while his position was subject to continuous heavy mortaring. For these actions and his earlier vital contribution during the attack beyond Primosole Bridge in Sicily, in July, he was awarded the Military Medal.

After the active patrolling had gained sufficient intelligence on the disposition of the enemy, a dawn attack was made on the strong, well-prepared enemy positions protecting the town of Teano, the capture of which was the objective of the attack. This was achieved on 31 October after the enemy withdrew from the town, fearing encirclement and capture. The battalion suffered heavy casualties, with five men killed and twenty-five wounded, two of whom died of their wounds. This was a baptism of fire for the new medical officer. It was déjà vu for Private David Dalrymple as he was wounded for a second time; the first time was in Sicily, in the first whole battalion attack and then, just three months later, he was wounded in the first battalion attack in the Italian mainland. Around this time, the Commanding Officer of the Battalion, Lieutenant Colonel Henry (Harry) J. Wilson, had to be evacuated as he had contracted malaria and was too ill to carry on. Major A. T. (Torance) Law assumed command.

Although now considered to be a disease of underdeveloped countries in the tropics, malaria was a significant problem for the Allies in Italy during the war. The disease was endemic in pre-war Italy and it is an astonishing statistic that during the operations on Sicily in 1943, the number of soldiers hospitalized through malaria exceeded the number wounded in battle. The Italian Government had been trying to combat the disease through measures like better land drainage and medical interventions. Malaria is a disabling disease which is caused by a parasite harboured by mosquitos and spread to humans by insect bites which infects the victim through the bloodstream. The disease is characterized by a variety of symptoms, ranging from fevers, chills and nausea to lethargy. It is spread by the malaria mosquito, which breeds in stagnant water. The war exacerbated the problem significantly; in addition to the naturally poorly drained areas such as swamps, stagnant pools formed in shell holes, bomb craters and areas deliberately flooded as a defensive barrier by blocking drainage canals and ditches. The Nazis understood the threat from the disease and, in an attempt to recruit this tiny insect to their cause, deliberately flooded the Tiber Delta south of Rome and even breached some tidal defences to allow the inundation by sea water, as brackish water was more conducive to the survival of the mosquito larvae. This was a callous act as it placed the civilian population at risk as well as the Allied soldiers. The soldiers were, however, particularly vulnerable to attack by the disease-carrying mosquitos as they invariably had no natural immunity to the disease; they slept in the open air or sheltered in buildings with no windows or doors and without mosquito nets, etc. Sergeant John McElroy was allowed five weeks leave in January 1945, and came back to Britain to see his wife, who he married just days before he embarked with the 1st Battalion London Scottish for their overseas posting three years earlier. He had been wounded in the fighting on the River Garigliano in November 1943 and unfortunately, fell ill with an attack of malaria when he arrived home on leave. His family had difficulty in obtaining quinine to treat his illness and his father complained to the authorities that it was very unsatisfactory that soldiers who were fighting on the front line were unable to receive proper medical treatment for this ailment which was affecting many of the men.

Moving into November, the weather broke and turned colder and very wet; it was no longer 'sunny Italy'. As the Germans fell back, they had previously constructed a series of strong defensive lines using the geographical features, such as the rivers and mountain ridges, to good advantage. Since these features generally ran across the width of Italy from the Tyrrhenian Sea in the south-west to the Adriatic Sea in the north-east, they hindered the advance of the Allies, making their progress slow and very costly in lives. At the beginning of November, the 1st London Scottish moved forward to the Calabritto area at the base of Monte Camino, a towering mountain which was defended in depth by the Germans as part of their 'Bernhardt defence line'. During the month of November 1943, there were more displays of conspicuous gallantry which were very different in character. Some were over a period of time, demonstrating cool-headed bravery for a sustained period, whereas there was also quick, bold action exhibiting raw, impulsive courage.

The forward company's position at Calabritto was fairly close to the enemy's front line; from their elevated location, the Germans were able to observe any movement by the 1st London Scottish during the hours of daylight. Consequently, when they were being relieved on 10 November 1943, this had to be undertaken at night. Just as the hand-over was taking place, their position came under a heavy barrage from artillery and mortars; when his platoon commanders reported to him that they had successfully handed over to their relieving unit, Major Ian Will ordered his men out of the village, as planned. The German artillery attack was followed up by an infantry attack which had a degree of success. Major Will, then realising the danger, ordered his men back into the village to assist the relieving company of the 10th Royal Berkshire Regiment and a ferocious battle ensued with some hand-to-hand fighting before the attack was successfully beaten off. During this action, Ian Will distinguished himself by disregarding his own safety and despite heavy enemy machine-gun fire, he moved among his men encouraging them and reorganizing their defences until the position was restored. However, all of the exits out of the village were now held by the Germans, so they were surrounded, cut off and unable to make any contact with their supporting British units. Sergeant Alexander Watt was ordered to take two men from his section and outflank an enemy position which was endangering one area of the village. Leaving the rest of his men in the safety of cover, he led two of his comrades into positions where they could support him with their Tommy guns. Alex then crawled forward, under intense machine-gun fire, and got to within throwing distance of the Germans. He assaulted their position with grenades, which had the desired effect and drove them off. Major Will kept his men in the village for the next two days to assist in the defence until the whole front had been stabilized by a counter-attack by other companies of the 10th Berkshires, also part of 168 Brigade. For his courage; cool, calm leadership; and as an example to his men, Major Ian Will was awarded the Military Cross. In recognition of his courage in assaulting a German position alone, Sergeant Alex Watt was awarded the Military Medal.

Lieutenant Alex Buchanan, a London Scottish officer, was acting as the Brigade Liaison Officer and was tasked with communicating messages between the Brigade HQ and the battalions. On four occasions he went forward to the Berkshires' position where the road was continually subjected to enemy artillery fire. On one of his trips, as he approached the Berkshires' Battalion HQ area, it came under a particularly heavy barrage. With complete disregard for his own safety, he went forward and delivered the message from Brigade and then he waited until he could understand the full situation so that he could report back to Brigade. For this action and many other occasions when he displayed coolness and courage, he was awarded the Military Cross. Communications were particularly vital during the time when the battalion was being relieved and contact with forward companies had to be maintained. During the five hours of continuous bombardment, the lines were frequently broken. Lance Corporal John Johnston, one of the battalion's signallers, was tasked with ensuring communication was maintained so, without regard to his own safety, he braved the firestorm and located and effected repairs as necessary. For his courage, he was awarded with the Military Medal.

The Battalion was constantly conducting patrols and reconnoitring the enemy positions, but casualties occurred regularly, such as Private Tom Robinson, who hailed from Orkney and was killed on 19 November 1944, just over a month before his twenty-first birthday. He was called up to join the Gordons on his eighteenth birthday but before this had been keen to do 'his bit' and had volunteered to join the Home Guard. Orkney was a highly strategic location, with Scapa Flow being the base of the Royal Navy's Home Fleet. The Battalion mounted regular fighting patrols to counter the enemy patrols, who were engaged in the same activity. These patrols were also attempting to capture enemy prisoners to gain vital information. On 23 November 1943, near Vandria, Corporal Albert Gee spotted a German patrol coming his way, but they suddenly disappeared from view in this rugged landscape. He was ordered to take his men and try to find the Germans and deal with them, with the hope that they might also capture some of them. The Germans were located in a deep wooded gully and Albert directed his Bren gunner to give covering fire and set up a sniper to deal with any offensive move by any German who dared show himself. Alone, Albert crawled forward and shouted in English, 'Come out Gerry, I have got you covered.' The response from the Germans was almost immediate and surprisingly, also in English. Their reply was, 'Come and get me Tommy,' to which Albert instantly responded, 'OK, I'm coming,' almost as if he was playing the child's game of hide and seek. As he advanced quickly over the open ground, the German patrol panicked and started to run, but the German Feldwebel (NCO) was wounded and captured, later providing much-needed intelligence. For his daring and somewhat audacious approach, showing great individual courage, Corporal Albert Gee was awarded a well-deserved Military Medal. Unfortunately, Albert was himself wounded just twelve days later.

The next big battle for the Allied cause was to take control of the mountain. While the 1st London Scottish played a supporting role, they were not directly involved in the battle for the mountain but were given the task of occupying the summit of Mount Camino. The battalion continued to conduct numerous patrols and made a surprise attack to capture the village of Rocca d'Evandro on the western side of the mountain and on the approach to the Allies' next formidable obstacle, the River Garigliano. The capture of this village was not only a surprise to the Germans but also to the 201st Guards Brigade, who had been allocated the task of taking the village. This was the last significant action of the year, and with the battalion going into reserve, some leave to Naples was granted to a lucky few. As the end of the year approached, thoughts turned to Christmas and Hogmanay, when the celebrations were traditional and there were welcome parcels from home. The men could reflect with pride on the past year. They had been tested in action for almost the whole of the previous six months, and although their casualties had been significant, they knew they had distinguished themselves. On their experience in the previous two months, they anticipated the new year would be even more testing, a notion that would prove to be correct, but nobody could foretell what the future held in store.

The 1st London Scottish were back in action on 11 January 1944. The advance had reached the River Garigliano, but it was necessary to remove the remaining German defensive position on the southern side of the river before a full-scale attack could be made across the river. This was the first objective of the Battalion.

The Germans had fortified two farms; an attack by a patrol was unsuccessful, as it lacked the necessary numbers and firepower to overwhelm the defenders and a number of casualties were incurred. The importance of eliminating this enemy strongpoint meant that the attack had to be renewed, and this was made by the whole of D Company under the command of the intrepid Captain Hugh Attwooll MC, supported by artillery and mortars. Operation Haybag was successful, but again there were heavy casualties. It was being held with only a small force when it was lost in an enemy counter-attack; among the missing was Private Leslie Ireland, recently transferred from the Highland Light Infantry. Such was the confusion with casualty replacement that the movements of men between units was often well ahead of the transfer paperwork. Leslie Ireland was first listed on a War Office casualty list as missing and serving with the Highland Light Infantry. This was corrected to him serving with the Royal Scots Fusiliers before another correction to the Gordon Highlanders (1st Battalion London Scottish). Fourteen others were initially listed as missing Seaforth Highlanders but later their regiment was corrected to the Gordon Highlanders (1st Battalion London Scottish). This group's fortunes were mixed, with six eventually being confirmed as killed in action. The other eight were reported as prisoners of war, of whom three died of their wounds while in German hands. A number of other wounded men who were reported as Seaforths were also later confirmed as Gordon Highlanders.

Another attack was mounted on the farm on the night of 12 June 1944 and a fierce firefight ensued, with Lieutenant Edward Blamey taking a leading role while rallying his men to keep together in the darkness and smoke of the battle scene. He personally led the assault on the farm building with grenades and his platoon were gaining the upper hand when reinforcements arrived in the form of another platoon under the command of Sergeant George McKay, whose orders were to mop up the last remaining resistance on the objective. Despite his platoon suffering significant casualties from enemy shell and mortar fire, he led his men to the destruction of two enemy posts at a critical stage in the battle. The last remaining enemy position south of the river was therefore eliminated. The eradication of this last stronghold of the Germans south of the river was at a high cost in casualties, with thirty-two men killed or died of wounds, twenty-three wounded and seven taken prisoner. Lieutenant John Gillan, MC, who was posted missing after the first attack, was found to have died at the scene of the battle. He was a very brave officer, having exposed himself to enemy fire in an attack in Sicily on 16 July 1943, for which he was awarded his Military Cross. He was then wounded later that month and now killed in this dangerous action. Lieutenant Rory Adamson, who was left to command the platoon which was to hold the position overnight, was killed during the German counter-attack. Sergeant George McKay's work was, however, not yet done that day, as he volunteered to lead a party of stretcher bearers back to the ruined farm where the battle had taken place to recover their numerous casualties. This was not without risk; although the enemy had been eradicated from south of the river, they were not far away on the opposite bank and had the farm under observation, effectively targeting it with artillery and mortar fire. George McKay successfully led the stretcher bearers back to recover the casualties, but he was also wounded in the process. After the sadness of losing so many close comrades, there was positive news for Lieutenant Blamey and Sergeant McKay. Both were recommended for and received gallantry decorations. Edward Blamey received a Military Cross and George McKay the Military Medal.

At the Casablanca Conference held in Morocco in January 1943, the 'Big Three' (Winston Churchill, Franklin D. Roosevelt and Joseph Stalin) agreed that after victory in North Africa was complete, the next campaign should be to attack Italy, which Churchill referred to as the 'soft underbelly of Europe'. This was not without debate, but it was agreed that the objectives were knocking Italy out of the war and tying down German forces away from the Russian front and France, where the next main Allied thrust would take place. It was expected that once the Allies invaded, the Germans would withdraw to a defensive line in northern Italy along the River Po. After Salerno, the Allied advance was slowed by the weather. During this period, it had been raining relentlessly for weeks. The rivers and streams were now raging torrents and the roads were a sea of mud; it was very cold, with winter having set in with a vengeance. This did nothing for the morale of those fighting in this mountainous region, as the Allies pushed forward, trying to give the Germans as little time as possible to prepare a defensive line closing the road to Rome and beyond. One soldier serving with the 56th Division artillery support was later to become famous as an actor and comedian. This was Terrance Milligan, famously known as 'Spike'. He wrote that while he was enduring physical illness, terrible weather, lack of success in their efforts and terrible losses among his comrades, this meant that he became severely depressed to a point where he had to be hospitalized. Doubtless, he was not alone in this general feeling of despondency and Signalman Keith Spooner, along with others in the 1st Battalion London Scottish, also felt their nerves affecting their morale. Nevertheless, somehow men generally got through each day with dogged determination, but they could certainly have told Winston Churchill that they had yet to find any 'soft underbelly', and with the incessant rain and cold, nor had they found 'sunny Italy'.

The Garigliano River proved to be a significant obstacle to the progress of the Allies through a combination of the weather, making the river deep and very fast flowing, and through being under observation by the enemy, which possessed the high ground on the northern side, lying in wait in well-camouflaged dugouts armed with machine guns and mortars. The banks of the river were devoid of cover, crisscrossed by ditches and streams and heavily mined so even getting to the river and constructing a crossing point was impossible in daylight hours. A night crossing by boat was the only option. The plan was to cross the river in strength with a three-pronged attack by the British 5th, 56th and 46th Divisions. The attack was scheduled for the night of 17–18 January 1944. The 5th Division was to attack across the river closer to the coast towards the town of Minturno where the terrain was flatter, and the other two divisions were on their right further up the valley, with the 56th Division in the centre. Private Andrew O'Brien, who was serving with the 6th Battalion Seaforth Highlanders, part of 17th Brigade of the 5th Division, was part of the initial assault across the river by boat and was among the first to get across, but he was wounded in the face. He got the rest of the men off the boat and, despite suffering with considerable pain, he made a further three crossings during which there was intense artillery fire. He managed to land the rest of his platoon and only then did he himself land where he accounted for a number of Germans in the subsequent action. His heroism was rewarded by a Military Medal. After recovering from his wounds, he transferred to the 1st Battalion London Scottish.

The London Scottish was not part of the assault by the 56th Division, which was initially successful, catching the enemy unawares, but the Germans were able to reorganize quickly and mounted a series of ferocious counter-attacks. The 1st London Scottish was called forward on the night of 20 January to occupy a position on Mount Damiano, near the town of Castelforte, and was immediately involved in heavy fighting. The next day Major Algernon Borthwick attacked a strong position held by the Germans. Leading from the front, he successfully drove the enemy from their position. For this and a subsequent action three nights later, he was awarded the Military Cross for the gallantry and leadership he demonstrated.

On the night of 23–24 January 1944, Major Borthwick was ordered to carry out an attack to restore the situation on the main Damiano ridge. He led his company up the mountainside and personally knocked out a machine-gun post, killing the German machine gunner with his pistol. Almost as soon as the attack had begun, Major Borthwick was wounded, but refused the assistance of the stretcher bearers; he considered that they were already fully committed to helping the other men more seriously wounded than he was, so he made his own way back to the aid post for treatment. The heavy fire was taking its toll when the only other officer with the company was wounded soon afterwards. Lance Sergeant Rowland Hancock, the platoon commander, ordered a section of his platoon to carry out a right flanking movement against some enemy machine guns which were holding up the advance; almost as soon as he had issued the order, he was killed. There was no platoon sergeant, so the section consisted only of a lance corporal and four men, who were joined by Private George Mitchell, the 2-inch mortar man from the platoon's HQ.

Despite the odds against success, they advanced up the steep rocky slope in the darkness. The enemy waited and opened fire at point-blank range with a heavy machine gun. Without hesitation, George Mitchell dropped the mortar he was carrying, seized a rifle and bayonet and charged up the hill, alone, through intense Spandau fire. Miraculously he reached the enemy machine-gun position unscathed, jumped into the weapon pit, shot one German and bayonetted the other, silencing the gun. This allowed the rest of the platoon to continue their advance, but almost immediately, the leading section was again held up by the fire of a group of strongly entrenched Germans who were pouring sustained rifle fire down onto them. George Mitchell, again realizing that prompt action was essential, valiantly rushed forward into the assault, firing his rifle from the hip, apparently completely oblivious of the hail of bullets which was sweeping the area. The remainder of his section followed him and arrived in time to complete the capture of the position in which six Germans were killed and twelve more made prisoner. The situation was still far from secure and just as the section was reorganizing, another enemy machine gun opened up on them at close range. Once more George rushed forward alone and, with his rifle and bayonet, killed the crew.

This small band of gallant soldiers now found themselves immediately below the crest of the hill, and they came under heavy small arms fire and grenades dropping on them from above. It was obvious that to remain where they were was suicidal so the choice was to withdraw and lose the ground they had taken so far or give one final drive. George Mitchell's ammunition was exhausted, but in spite of this, he urged the men for one further effort and again led the assault up the steep and rocky hillside. Dashing to the front, he was again the first man to reach the enemy position and was mainly instrumental in forcing the remainder of the enemy to surrender. Tragically, a short time later, a German who had surrendered and therefore had his life spared, picked up a rifle and treacherously shot George Mitchell through the head. He died instantly.

Throughout this operation, which was carried out on a very dark night up a steep hillside covered in rocks and scrub, George Mitchell displayed courage and devotion to duty of the very highest order, fearlessly exposing himself to fire and showing a determination not to accept failure. This greatly inspired his comrades so that, together, they succeeded in overcoming and defeating the more numerous enemy force which had the significant advantage of the high ground and prepared defensive positions. As a result of his outstanding acts of daring that night, he was awarded the Victoria Cross, the highest and most prestigious decoration available to any member of the British Armed Forces. Unfortunately for George Mitchell, this was a posthumous award. This was the only Victoria Cross (VC) awarded to any soldier of the regiment of the Gordon Highlanders during the whole of the Second World War. (The award of this decoration is very rare, with only 181 awards being made during the whole of the Second World War; just twenty-two of these were awarded for the whole of the Italian campaign.)

George Mitchell's Victoria Cross was presented to his family by King George VI at an investiture in Buckingham Place on 17 July 1945. George's father, Edward Mitchell, had served for twenty-five years with the Royal Scots Fusiliers, including during the whole of the First World War, joining in August 1914. Whilst this was a very proud moment for the family, the Second World War must have been a traumatic time for George's parents as George's elder brother, David, was killed in action just two months before George. He had also been serving in Italy as were his other two brothers, Charles and Edward. While the battalion were in Iraq, David was in the same platoon as his brother George, but he transferred to the Argyll & Sutherland Highlanders, with whom he was serving when he was killed on 30 November 1943.

In 1959, his brother gifted George's medals to Farmer Road School, Leyton, North London, which George had attended. The school was renamed George Mitchell School in his honour. By a remarkable coincidence, another pupil of this school was also awarded the Victoria Cross. This was to John (Jack) Cornwall in 1916 during the First World War for an action at the Battle of Jutland. His award was also posthumous. He was just sixteen years old when he died and was the youngest naval recipient. This makes the George Mitchell

School the only comprehensive in England to have had two Victoria Cross recipients as pupils. Some years later, the London Scottish Museum bought George Mitchell's medals, which is where they remain in their safekeeping as part of the museum's collection. The money received for the medals was used to fund improvements to the school.

The position on Mount Damiano was held. The 1st London Scottish were relieved on 26 January and crossed back over the Garigliano River for some rest. There was however, a very sad postscript to the actions during this period. It was discovered that one of a new draft of men joining the Battalion, Private David Allan from Aberdeen, was in fact only sixteen years old; so he should not even have been in the army, and certainly not in the front line. It was decided that he couldn't be a combatant but that he could be a stretcher bearer. Unfortunately, the group he was with triggered a trip wire attached to a Teller anti-tank mine, killing two men and seriously wounding David. He later died of his wounds and was the youngest Gordon Highlander to die during the whole of the Second World War.

On 27 January 1944, it was announced that the Commanding Officer, Lieutenant Colonel Wilson, was leaving the Battalion to take up a post with the Army Welfare Service. Major Torrance Law was promoted to Lieutenant Colonel and resumed command. This was not the only change for the Battalion, as just two days later they were ordered to Naples with the rest of 168 Brigade, arriving at Giuliano, on the northern outskirts of Naples, at the end of the month. Naturally rumours abounded as to the reason behind this move, particularly when there was still no sign of a breakthrough of the German defences towards Monte Cassino. The men didn't have to wait long for an answer; the reason was to be made clear within days.

# Chapter 9

# Operation Shingle: Anzio

The 6th Battalion Gordon Highlanders took their leave of Tunisia on 5 December 1943 when they boarded the SS *Cuba* at Bizerta, just north of Tunis, leaving the small harbour in lighters and joining the ship which was lying just offshore. The choppy sea didn't make for a very comfortable crossing, but it was mercifully short. Nevertheless, the ship's pitching and rolling made the task of climbing up the scrambling nets a bit tricky. This troop ship, although built on the Tyne in 1923, was previously owned and operated by a French cruise ship company. After the capitulation of France in June 1940, it was considered to be an enemy vessel being operated by Vichy France. She was captured in the Atlantic in October 1940, taken by the Royal Navy as a 'war prize' and converted to a troop ship. Once the Battalion was all safely aboard, she set sail for Italy, arriving at Taranto in the 'heel' of Italy. After disembarkation, the Battalion travelled up the coast by rail through Bari and Barletta to Canossa, then by road to Spinazzola, a small town in the hills of Puglia. Here they set up camp and were billeted in a school, but some were under canvas, which was not ideal as it was cold with snow on the ground. It was here that the news was received that the Battalion were being transferred from the 2nd Division to the 1st Division. They remained here for the rest of the month; as 1943 ended, the 6th Battalion Gordon Highlanders were enjoying the Hogmanay festivities despite the cold icy conditions. A move was in the cards, and 1944 began with their relocation to Santa Lucia, about 30 miles south of Salerno. While here, some leave to visit Naples was permitted. Sergeant Douglas Tait was one of those who chose to experience the pleasures of the city and recorded in his diary, 'Naples looks lovely from a distance. At close quarters it stinks!' His visit wasn't all a disappointment, however, as he went on to write, 'Saw Vesuvius for the first time. A lovely sight.' Douglas had been married back home in the Rosehearty Manse near Fraserburgh, Aberdeenshire, in February 1942, and had hardly seen his wife, Ena, since. Walter Lindley, fresh from completing his basic training, arrived into the port of Naples with a draft of reinforcements which had come directly from Britain on the troop ship the RMS *Samaria*. His first impressions were that there had been a lot of damage to the harbour through bombing and the efforts of departing Germans destroying as much of the port facilities as they could. With Walter was Bob Boyce, he was returning to the Battalion after his injury during training in Ayrshire, just before departure for Tunisia. Inevitably, this meant he had to endure quite a bit of ribbing from his former comrades who had spent the previous months fighting in North Africa while, as they saw it, he had been languishing safely back in Britain.

Santa Lucia was their base for their intensive training for landing on the beach from landing craft. This training lasted for two weeks with a final 'dress rehearsal' landing in darkness on the beach at Salerno the night of 18–19 January 1944. It had been clear to all that they were about to embark on an amphibious landing north of the Gustav line, but where? The local vendors of fruit and other treats, working from small boats from Naples, were confidently announcing to the soldiers already embarked on the landing ships (LSTs) of the assault convoy that they were bound for Anzio, which was supposed to be a closely guarded secret. Everyone knew that the port of Naples was a nest of German spies and since landing at Anzio appeared to be common knowledge, the 6th Gordons expected the worst and that their landing would be strongly opposed.

The reasoning behind the Allied invasion of Sicily and the Italian mainland was to knock Mussolini's Italy out of the war. It was optimistically expected that the German forces in Italy would fall back to northern Italy and defend a line north of the River Po in Lombardy. When the Germans decided to defend Italy in depth from the Gustav line, anchored on Monte Cassino, the Allied advance up the Italian peninsula became bogged down. This caused tensions in the alliance as the constant demand for men and resources was seen by the Americans as a distraction from the planned, but still top secret, invasion of Normandy. In their view, this gave a more direct and shorter route to the Nazi capital, Berlin. One clear strategy to break the stalemate at Cassino was to make a flanking manoeuvre around the Gustav line. A seaborne invasion north of the line made perfect sense, as the Allies enjoyed almost complete air superiority and also controlled the whole Mediterranean Sea, while the German lines of communication and supply to Cassino were long and also vulnerable to air attack. The idea had been considered initially but not progressed until the end of 1943, when it was resurrected by Winston Churchill, who was the most enthusiastic proponent of the whole Italian campaign. Again, the planning for the invasion of north-west Europe took precedence, and all the available landing craft were redirected to the south of England. Churchill did, however, manage to argue successfully that a small number of these vital specialist craft be held back for a short period to allow an amphibious landing to be made north of the German line at Monte Cassino. The planning went ahead, but with the time-limited availability of landing craft, it meant this was rushed.

This joint British and American action named Operation Shingle was under the overall command of British General Sir Harold Alexander and American General Mark Clark. The target was decided as Anzio, a small resort 30 miles south of the Italian capital, Rome. Anzio was ideal on paper as it had a harbour and a sandy shoreline suitable for the landings. Until the landings took place, Anzio was known only as a holiday resort for modern-day Romans, although it had attracted tourists from ancient times, known then as Antium, where the Emperor Nero, perhaps Rome's most notorious emperor, was born in 37 AD.

The British contingent for the operation was the 1st Infantry Division, commanded by Major General Sir W. Ronald Penney. This Division comprised the 2nd Infantry Brigade (6th Battalion, Gordon Highlanders, the 1st Battalion Loyal Regiment, the 2nd Battalion, North Staffordshire Regiment); the 3rd Infantry Brigade (2nd Battalion, Sherwood Foresters, the 1st Battalion, Duke of Wellington Regiment and the 1st Battalion, King's Shropshire Light Infantry); and the 24th Guards Brigade (1st Battalion Irish Guards, the 1st Battalion Scots Guards, and the 5th Battalion Grenadier Guards), supported by the 46th Royal Tank Regiment. The American forces, commanded by Major General John P. Lucas, were more numerous, including the 3rd (US) Division and the 1st (US) Armored Division which, together with other British and American support units, amounted to some four divisions.

The embarkation point was the Bay of Naples, where the Allies had made the port fully operational again. The loading of the equipment and vehicles, which all had to be waterproofed, and the embarkation of the men took all day. This resulted in a long boring wait for the men before the ships set sail. The convoy of over 250 ships put out to sea on the evening of 20 January, initially heading south around the Island of Capri and out into the Tyrrhenian Sea in an attempt to confound the enemy spies in Naples and keep them guessing as to where the blow might fall. The sea was calm and the convoy assembled at a rendezvous point just east of enemy-held Corsica, which it was hoped the enemy spies would have concluded was the intended final destination and target for the assault. The voyage proved uneventful arriving at their true destination in the final hours of 21 January with 'H-Hour' preset for 02:00 hours on the 22nd. ('H-Hour' is a code word used in planning the operation which is a device to keep the actual hour for the start of the operation secret. Subsequent actions are then described as H+1, etc. This permits the entire operational timetable for the attack to be scheduled in detail with the various stages planned long before a definite day and time for the attack is decided by the high command. The same principle explains the use of the code letter 'D', meaning the undisclosed day when an operation begins.)

Admiral Lowry's armada anchored off Anzio just after midnight. It was still almost two hours to H-Hour, just enough time to make the final preparations and check of weapons. As the time ticked down, the men of the assaulting units were brought up from the dark holds, organized on the deck of the LSTs and loaded into the small assault boats. When everything was ready, these were lowered into the sea and cut loose to allow them to manoeuvre into their assaulting formation. Men were naturally anxious at the prospect of hitting the beach well behind enemy lines and possibly met by withering machine-gun fire from the well-guarded shore, where the defenders had all the advantages of position, preparedness and cover. The 6th Battalion's last amphibious attack had been the invasion of the island of Pantelleria just over six months earlier. Many of the men could recall their feelings then, when just as they were being organized on deck prior to storming the shore, the Italian island garrison gave up without a fight, an outcome which gave them cause to cheer. However, they knew their current foe from their experiences of fighting the Germans in France and Tunisia and knew they would not give up without a fight, so they were braced for a tough landing. The British were to attack a stretch of sandy shoreline a few miles up the coast just north-west of Anzio designated as 'Peter Beach'. The Americans were to capture the small ports of Anzio and Nettuno and the shoreline to the east, designated as 'X-Ray Beach'. To create an element of surprise there was to be virtually no preliminary bombardment of the shore, except for a massive rocket salvo just a few minutes before the attack was launched. It was expected that the beach would be heavily defended, possibly mined, and strewn with barbed wire obstacles; it was hoped these rockets would destroy the majority of these defences.

The 6th Battalion Gordon Highlanders were among the first troops of the 1st Division to get ashore. The landings were completely unopposed and to everyone's great relief, it appeared that the operation had achieved complete surprise. The Germans had either decided to ignore the rumours going around Naples that Anzio was the intended target or thought it was a sort of bluff spread by the Allies to deflect attention from Civitavecchia, which their intelligence considered would be the most likely target for an invasion. Civitavecchia is about 75 miles north of Anzio and also north of Rome. To boost the deception, Allied bombing raids targeted the port of Civitavecchia in the days before the Anzio landings and, simultaneously with the Anzio landings, Royal Navy ships bombarded the shore as a mock invasion was staged.

Just ten minutes before H-Hour came the first surprise for the men circling in their landing craft; the enormous salvo of rockets was launched with a deafening noise and a spectacular impact on the shoreline, momentarily lighting up the dark night. The men could only marvel at the tremendous power that had just been unleashed. This was a tremendous boost to their morale as it looked impossible that any shoreline defence force could survive such a colossal impact. A second surprise awaited them a short time later, when their landing craft came to rest on a shallow sand bar a short distance from the beach. When the ramp was lowered and the men stormed out, they got a shock as they jumped into the cold sea water which was waist deep. They were cold and wet, but the adrenalin kicked in and they forged ahead and onto dry land. Fortunately, the beach at Anzio held few defensive obstacles apart from a few mines which were successfully detected and disarmed. The first objective was to get a few miles inland but dense scrub just behind the beach made a direct exit impossible and they initially had to go along the length of the beach until a gap was found. Many were still wondering if this was an elaborate trap, but they began to advance inland through the scrub and into the Padiglione Woods. They were still on their guard for a sudden counter-attack, but happily accepted their prize.

The 6th Gordons pushed on to the northern side of the woods but remained in the fringe, which gave them cover from the air and observation of the country beyond; it was almost flat for the first 10 miles then, at first gradually, then very steeply, sloping up towards the Alban Hills, just 20 miles due north at a height of around 900 metres. These hills were later to dominate the battlefield with their commanding views over the whole beachhead area. The entire bridgehead area was cut by deep drainage channels, both natural and artificial, which were swollen with water due to the wet winter weather. Their first objective, which was Campo di Carne on the Anzio Albano Road, was achieved by mid-morning. The entire bridgehead was flanked by two features which aided its defence. On the west was the Moletta River and on the east the Mussolini Canal, a large drainage channel constructed by the orders of the Italian Fascist leader to drain the once-mosquito-ridden Pontine Marshes, which had successfully turned the land into a fertile area. This was now dotted with two-storey stone-built farm buildings, known locally as *podere*, which were all built to a standard plan. For the Allies, the canal provided an excellent barrier against enemy tanks attacking their right flank as it had high levees and a considerable width and water flow. For the enemy each farm (*podere*) could become a stronghold which a few men could defend against a much larger attacking force, often requiring artillery or tank support to overcome the defenders.

At Campo di Carne, the 6th Battalion then awaited further orders, still wet from their unexpected early morning dip in the sea and cold in the near-zero air temperature. It wasn't until the following day that orders were received to move forward and everyone was wondering why the delay when there appeared to be no opposition. To the soldier on the ground, it seemed that the momentum of the operation and the element of surprise was being frittered away. More small advances were ordered but by the evening of 24 January, the 6th Gordons were still less than 10 miles north of the Anzio Harbour. At this time the battalion was on the western edge of the Anzio Bridgehead at a position overlooking the Moletta River Ridge and astride the minor road running from the village of San Lorenzo, on the west, to the flyover, on the east, which crossed the main road from Anzio to Albano, eventually leading to Rome.

There was general frustration with the lack of action and seventy-two hours after landing, the 6th Gordons had hardly seen any Germans. Word had got around that there were a small number of Germans found in the town who were engineers planning to destroy the harbour facilities, but they had been caught totally unawares. Most were captured while still in bed and the harbour was made fully functional for Allied shipping by the afternoon of the first landings, although men and equipment were still being landed on the beaches. One of the beach masters on Peter Beach was a Royal Engineers Major named Denis Healey, a veteran of the North Africa and Sicily campaigns. He went into politics after the war and continued to serve his country as an eminent politician, being Secretary of State for Defence in 1970 and Chancellor of the Exchequer in 1974. The logistics operation was going so well that Peter Beach was closed three days after the landings and the harbour at Anzio and a section of X-Ray Beach used for all later landings of men and supplies.

Major General John P. Lucas, the American general in operational command of the Anzio operation, was a cautious man and concentrated on consolidating the beachhead area and getting as many men and as much equipment ashore as quickly as possible before going on the offensive. He had seen the near failure of the earlier landings at Salerno, when the Germans had almost succeeded in pushing the assault forces back into the sea, and was determined to be in a strong enough position to defend the beachhead before advancing inland. Back in London, Winston Churchill, who had been buoyed up by the initial news that the landings had achieved complete surprise, unrealistically expected the Allies to be in Rome within days. Dismayed by the lack of progress, he is famously quoted as complaining, 'I had hoped we were hurling a wildcat onto the shore, but all we got was a stranded whale.'

Meanwhile, the Germans were not idle. Although they were initially totally surprised by the landings at Anzio, they already had a contingency plan for such an eventuality, even though they had no idea when or where it might be required. This was known by the code name 'Case Richard'. The German supreme commandant in Italy, Generalfeldmarschall Albert Kesselring, recovered from his surprise very quickly and activated his contingency plan. He was able to draw on his reserves from north of Rome, and other units from the south of France and as far away as Yugoslavia were ordered to relocate to Anzio. Kesselring appointed General Eberhard von Mackensen as his operational commander, who quickly organized the defences around the Anzio Bridgehead. The result was that the Allied divisions ashore were soon opposed by a numerically much larger and stronger force which had many more tanks and heavy artillery. The short window of opportunity to capture the high ground of the Alban Hills and cut the German supply routes south to the Monte Cassino front was lost. This was not the only disappointment for the Allies. It had been expected the landings would force the Germans to draw units from the Monte Cassino front, weakening it and increasing the likelihood of a breakthrough which would then link up with the forces at Anzio and cut off the retreating Germans. Kesselring did not, however, oblige; he did not weaken the Monte Cassino front, instead using reserve forces from elsewhere.

The 6th Gordons remained in position west of the flyover and overlooking the Moletta River for the next few days until 30 January. By this time, several of their patrols had encountered Germans and inflicted casualties, but they also had come under heavy shelling. Despite Allied air superiority, there was also a random air raid on 27 January, when a bomb hit the Battalion HQ and resulted in casualties. One of these was Erik Brammer, MM, the stretcher bearer who had disregarded his own safety to go to the assistance of wounded men in Tunisia. It was while carrying out his duties as a stretcher bearer that he was killed. Private James Clark died on the same day and they were the first fatalities of the 6th Battalion in Italy.

Elsewhere in the Bridgehead, a reconnaissance operation of the Carroceto area on 24 January by a small British force in Bren gun carriers found it to be held by the Germans; they also took artillery fire from the Aprilia (known as 'the factory') area. At dawn on the next morning, in dreadful weather with freezing rain and sleet, the Guards Brigade was ordered by General Penney to advance to take these positions so that a further advance by the full Division could follow. The Guards succeeded in their attack, but this was at the cost of heavy casualties which were increased significantly when the inevitable German counter-attack took place; but the position was held. The Divisional advance to capture Campoleone Railway Station began on the afternoon of 30 January. The action was in tandem with an American advance on the eastern side of the Bridgehead targeting Cisterna Station and the major road transport links south from Rome to Monte Cassino.

The British 3rd Brigade, supported by tanks from the 46th Royal Tank Regiment, was then tasked with taking Campoleone Railway Station and cutting the strategic rail link south. Their advance successfully punched their way a distance of almost 5 miles into enemy-held territory, creating a long, narrow bulge into the German defensive line. However, Campoleone Station, the main objective of the assault, was not reached and the attack faltered just short of the objective. This long, narrow salient was very precarious as the long flanks on either side required defence from the enemy forces pressing from all sides. The Guards and 3 Brigade had taken heavy casualties during the attack, so the defence of this long, narrow salient required additional resources. The narrow nature of this salient was not the intended outcome of the attack on 30 January, but came about due to the failure of the British to reach Campoleone Station and the Americans to reach Cisterna and then for both forces to link up, which would have broadened the Allies' front and been more easily defended. It had been intended that the British attack would secure a position beyond the railway line, but the failure to reach this meant the Germans could use the high railway embankment to cover their assembly and give them a secure line of defence.

On 30 January, the 6th Gordon Highlanders were finally on the move inland, but only as far as Carroceto. They took over a position which was a group of flat-roofed buildings known as 'the factory' after their appearance, rather than their purpose. In reality, this was a small village concerned with the agriculture of the area, but the buildings were all of a similar style with flat roofs and built as part of the Italian Fascist's development of the marsh area. The following day they moved into a position about 2 miles north of Aprilia to defend a section on the eastern flank of the salient.

The Battalion was deployed very thinly, as the length of the line they had to cover extended for just over 1 mile, resulting in gaps in their collective line and between them and the units to their right and left, all facing the enemy positions to the east. A and C Companies were deployed furthest forward but C Company was in a hollow about 20 metres lower and had no line of sight with A or D Companies. To compound their isolation further, D Company was some 500 metres behind them while B Company was located further back still with the Battalion HQ in the rear. This was made a strong point with the battalion's Bren gun carriers assigned to assist in its defence. The battalion's disposition was far from ideal. There were bush-covered gullies and ditches running from north to south, feeding into the Fosso di Spaccasassi, which bounded the eastern edge of the British salient. The lie of the land had given way from the flat coastal plain to a more undulating landscape as the land began to rise to the summit of the extinct volcano which was the Alban Hills. This meant that all the Companies were largely out of sight of each other which made it virtually impossible to provide mutual support. The network of ditches and ravines were, however, helpful to the enemy as they provided a protected, concealed location where they could infiltrate behind the British lines and assemble. These gullies were over 10 metres deep, so were also an obstacle to Allied tanks. To compound the 6th Gordons' precarious situation, the ground sloped fairly steeply upwards away from their position, so the Germans could observe their lines and react to any movement, generally by shelling that position. This had the result that movement was mainly restricted to the hours of darkness. In addition, having oversight of the British strength and defensive positions also gave the enemy the ability to plan how best to make their attack. With all of these worrying features their location proved to be an inauspicious setting for the 6th Gordons as the inevitable German counter-attack was likely to test them and the rest of the 1st Division to the limit.

In the larger context, the role of 6th Gordons, together with the 1st Battalion Loyal Regiment, was to plug the gap between the British 3rd Brigade at the apex of the Campoleone salient, and the Reconnaissance (Recce) Regiment positioned to the south-east at the base of the salient. These three regiments were responsible for over 4.5 miles of front so all were spread very thinly. On the opposite side of the salient facing west was the 24th Guards Brigade, comprising the 1st Battalion Irish Guards, the 1st Battalion Scots Guards and the 5th Battalion Grenadier Guards, spread just as thinly. A strong counter-attack was anticipated as the Germans had established a strong force on the three sides of the salient projecting into their lines; it was clear that, strategically, they could not allow this to continue. A flanking attack could cut off the 1st Division's 3rd Brigade, which was located at the apex of the bulge into the German lines.

The next few days were relatively peaceful, but A Company's position, the furthest forward, was heavily shelled. The full German attack was launched at 23:00 hours on 3 February and began with a heavy artillery barrage which particularly impacted on the 6th Gordons area. The Battalion HQ was shelled continually for a full twenty minutes and sporadically afterwards. This artillery barrage was, as expected, followed up by an infantry assault. This initially fell on the western flank held by the Irish Guards; when one of their companies was overrun, this allowed the Germans to cross the Carroceto to Campoleone road (the Via Anziate) and infiltrate between B and D Companies of the 6th Gordons. The mortar position of D Company was over-run, but quickly retaken by a platoon led by Lieutenant William Fordyce, which removed the threat for a short time. Shortly after midnight, Lieutenant Henry Garioch reported hearing Germans digging in to the east of A Company's position in an area of 'dead' ground, which threatened his and D Company's position.

A proposed counter-attack by A Company to clear this threat was set for 04:00, but this was changed to a plan to attack with B, C and D Companies with covering fire being provided from A Company. After the Germans had overrun the Irish Guards' position and gained control of the eastern side of the Via Anziate road, A Company was under the additional threat from the Germans on their west flank and D Company had a similar threat. This was compounded when it was found, that at around 04:00, a strong force of Germans, estimated at around two companies in six separate pockets, had dug in behind them and C Company. The result was that the forward Gordons' positions were being gradually surrounded on all sides. A local counter-attack by a single platoon of C Company, led by Sergeant Duncan McCallum, was launched against the Germans behind C Company's position; this was driven back when they sustained heavy casualties, including Sergeant McCallum, who was killed. After the moon had set, there was virtually no visibility – a situation compounded by the foul weather. When there was a penetration of Germans between B Company's position and the forward companies, the danger was clear. Corporal James Moir was with Number 10 Platoon and he held their position, constantly firing on and harassing the enemy which had dug in about 100 metres in front of them. The Battalion counter-attack was postponed when it was learned that a squadron of tanks from the 46th Royal Tank Regiment was being made available to assist them. The 6th Gordons were not entirely without support and 266 Field Battery of the 67th Field Regiment, Royal Artillery provided continual and much needed heavy firepower throughout the battle on 3–5 February.

The individual companies were not within sight of each other; it was also dark and raining, with all the fixed telephone lines being cut by the artillery barrages. The job of a signalman was to go out and crawl along the path of the telephone line to find the break and repair it. On this occasion this task fell to Sergeant Joe McIntosh. He bravely disregarded the ground being swept by machine-gun and artillery fire, searched for the severed connections and made repairs as quickly as he could. However, it soon became obvious that the constant shelling made the task unsustainable because as soon as he had repaired one break another occurred. In the absence of fixed telephone line communication, maintaining the wireless contact between them became vital. The Battalion Signals Officer, Lieutenant James Leckie, realized this imperative and took personal charge of the Battalion HQ wireless set no. 18 and ensured that messages were relayed as appropriate. This was not without risk as the poor quality of the signal meant that he mostly had to operate in the open while exposed to enemy fire. He was not alone in having to brave the enemy fire on his position to maintain communications. Lance Corporal

Alex Paterson, the wireless operator for B Company, could only get reception when he operated his no. 18 set while he was half out of his trench; he bravely stuck to his task, constantly exposed to enemy fire, and continually did his important duty for almost twenty-four hours. Meanwhile, the poor quality of the reception on the radio set was not the only issue. Early in the action the no. 18 wireless set at B Company had been damaged and was out of action, so the only means of communication between the platoons was by a runner. Private Alex Mennim filled that role and despite the company coming under constant machine gun, mortar and shell fire he never hesitated to leave the shelter of his trench to carry messages to and from the Company's platoon commanders. This was a vital duty carried out during a very dangerous situation.

Although the Battalion HQ was well to the rear of the other companies, the threat to the Battalion came from both flanks, so it was also under threat. Sergeant Major John Underwood efficiently organized the defence of the HQ and despite artillery pounding their position and small-arms fire constantly sniping, he moved around the position, urging his men to remain vigilant, and returning fire. Captain Robin Bain commanded the Battalion Bren Gun Carrier Platoon; they were constantly in action and inflicted heavy losses when driving off enemy attacks. When a message came in that B Company were running short of ammunition, he loaded one of the Bren gun carriers and drove it up to their position, which was extremely hazardous as his route was being constantly subjected to enemy fire.

Corporal Ian (Jock) Cobban was in charge of the Signal Platoon Dispatch Riders and he was ordered to bring up a small arms ammunitions truck from the rear echelon. The night was pitch black and as he travelled up to the Battalion's position, the sleet drove into his face, partly blinding him as he rode. He then crashed headlong into a shell crater and was thrown off his motor bike. Apart from being a bit shaken, he was relatively unhurt, so found another machine and set off again. As he continued, he was then blinded by dense smoke from a burning farm building and, unable to see his way, he collided with a lorry. Although he was now considerably shaken up by his ordeal and accidents, his condition was exacerbated by the effects of the heavy shelling going on in that area. Bravely, he picked himself up and completed his objective, bringing up the ammunition to the front line in good time. Jock Cobban was a pre-war 6th Battalion man who served with the Battalion in France and Belgium in 1940, being evacuated from Dunkirk and going on to serve in North Africa. Unfortunately, the following month, he was killed when there was a direct hit on his dugout, leaving a widow with his young son back home in Huntly, Aberdeenshire.

While the decision on launching the counter-attack on the infiltrated enemy position was delayed several times, Lance Corporal Jim Agnew found that when dawn broke he was faced with a large enemy force dug in and also under the direct observation of an enemy Tiger tank. With great courage and without considering his own safety he crawled out of his trench and threw grenades at the Nazi soldiers, killing many and keeping their heads down until the company was made ready to mount its attack. Jim Agnew was not alone in displaying a huge degree of personal courage as B Company was coming under imminent threat. Sergeant John Thain took over a captured enemy machine gun which he used to beat off an enemy attack from his own position even though fully exposed to the enemy. He reportedly gave burst for burst of machine-gun fire as the enemy advanced until unfortunately, he was killed by a shot to his heart by an enemy sniper. The orders given to B Company were to hold their fire until the enemy was right on them. This was to avoid giving away their positions. After a preliminary bombardment with artillery and mortars the company knew this would likely be immediately followed up by an infantry attack. This strategy worked almost perfectly. Lieutenant Edward Grace admired the discipline of his men who, although nervously waiting for the enemy to attack and try to kill them, waited until he gave the order to fire. This proved to be highly effective in surprising the Germans who were unaware of the Gordons' position until it was too late for them to avoid the hail of rifle fire which decimated their number and checked their attack. Later, in a counter-attack, Corporals Moir and Tripney, leading their sections with great skill and dash, followed Lieutenant Grace into the enemy positions, driving out those they couldn't kill or capture.

When the Sherman tanks from the 46th Royal Tank Regiment arrived at the Battalion HQ they were immediately ordered forward, but before they advanced, Captain Thomas Tregellas identified a German self-propelled gun and an anti-tank gun which posed a serious threat to the tanks. He commanded the 6th Battalion's Anti-Tank Platoon but had previously served for eight years with the London Scottish. He acted quickly and, with the anti-tank guns under his command, he directed fire at the enemy with great effect, knocking out the threat to the tanks which could now proceed. The British tanks arrived at B Company's position just before daylight at 06:15. Major Lindsay Bridgman had readied his company for the assault on the enemy positions and the attack went in without delay. The Germans in front of his position, which were behind D and C companies' position, were also readying themselves to attack, unaware of the British intentions and the new situation of tank support. B Company's attack caught the Germans as they were emerging from their slit trenches and with the assistance of the British Sherman tanks succeeded in inflicting heavy casualties and while clearing the enemy from the front of their position took around 100 prisoners. This counter-attack was unable to get as far forward as D Company's position as it became impossible to cross the ridge between the two Company's positions; heavy opposing anti-tank and machine-gun fire was being directed at them, with the enemy guns outranging that of the Sherman's. This meant that the Germans were able to hold their position on the ridge threating A Company's flank.

At this point in the battle, shortly after 07:00, Sergeant George Cormack and Corporal George Wilson were manning the only anti-tank gun in A Company's position. George Wilson spotted eight Tiger tanks, emerging from a farm, some 1100 metres away, coming down the minor road from the direction of Campoleone and heading for their position. This was reported to the Company Commander, Major David Hutcheon, who was awaiting the promised tank support. Major Hutcheon ordered the company to withdraw to a deep ditch between his and C Company's positions, which he believed would afford more protection from the impending tank and likely infantry attack, until his own tank support became available. The order to withdraw was not immediately followed by George Wilson and George Cormack. They believed it was their duty to have a crack at the enemy tanks so kept them under observation. They saw their opportunity when the enemy tanks emerged from the dead ground some 400 metres in front of them. The two Georges worked together and carefully edged out of their trench. George Cormack loaded the anti-tank weapon while George Wilson lay on the ground and prepared to fire. Their opportunity to 'kill' one of these tanks came when one of the Tigers turned to the side while the others continued to approach head on. George selected the tank broadside on, took aim and fired, scoring a direct hit with his first shot, which struck just above the tank's tracks. He fired twice more to make sure and there was a great deal of satisfaction when the tank went up in flames. The two Georges then came under intense machine-gun fire when, inevitably, after they had fired, their position was identified. With no more vulnerable targets available, they knew they could do no more and withdrew. Sadly, George Cormack was killed that day.

As the battle progressed, A Company lost communication with the others, so Lieutenant Henry Garioch was ordered to make his way back to the Battalion HQ, which was located in the farm buildings some distance to the rear, and report their situation. Unfortunately, as he made his way back, using the course of a natural ditch to give him some cover and concealment, he was surprised when challenged and captured by some Germans who had infiltrated behind the Gordons' lines. While the battle raged all around them and the noise was intense Henry's luck was about to change. When an artillery barrage fell around their position the Germans dived for cover and he was able take his chance to get away. He realized further progress towards the Battalion HQ was impossible so he returned to report this to his Company Commander, Major David Hutcheon.

With the lack of communication, the Commanding Officer in the Battalion HQ needed information on the situation on the ground with his forward Companies. At around 08:30 the Adjutant, Captain James Williamson, volunteered to go forward on foot to ascertain the situation but, due to the intense machine-gun and rifle fire from the Germans holding the ridge to the west of the Battalion's position, he was unable to get much further than 300 metres beyond B Company's position. This was about a kilometre from the most forward Company. As he observed the former positions of the forward companies, he heard voices which were unmistakably German then, without warning eight German soldiers emerged from the bushes and were surprised to be confronted by Captain Williamson who promptly took them prisoner. Despite failing to reach his objective, his efforts were not totally in vain as he was able to report back to the Battalion HQ that the Germans were holding the ridge so were dominating the positions of the forward companies. This was vital information for the Commanding Officer and enabled him to make a plan to recover the situation.

Major Hutcheon was very concerned that the lines had been so completely compromised and he was out of touch with the rest of the Battalion. He decided he would attempt to get back to the Battalion HQ himself but, before his attempt had even started, the squadron of Tiger tanks got within range of his position. The tanks raked A Company's position with machine guns and high explosive shells. This was a prelude to an attack by German infantry from their position behind the Company's position so they were surrounded on all sides. A Company's position was then overrun by the enemy, with almost all of the company being killed, wounded or captured, including the Company Commander, Major David Hutcheon, who was fatally wounded by a burst of machine-gun fire. The Tigers then moved along the ridge and gave the same treatment to D Company and again their only option was to surrender to the accompanying German infantry. With the German Tiger tanks now occupying the former positions of A and D companies, C Company's position was exceedingly precarious with the worst possible likely outcome. The loss of both the companies on their right meant that, not only were they being bombarded from above, by the tanks on the ridge to their east, they also came under fire from the enemy who had infiltrated the position behind them. They also had no choice but to surrender.

Some twenty men from A Company and two men from D Company got away but none from C Company came back to the Battalion HQ or B Company which was in their rear, although it was still not very clear about the full circumstances of the forward actions, it was certain that there had been a catastrophic loss. Meanwhile B Company, supported by the Sherman tanks, held fast despite heavy concentrations of fire against them from their flanks and the positions formerly occupied by A and C companies. The Germans were now close to succeeding in their objective to recapture all the ground taken a few days earlier following the attacks of the 23rd Infantry of the 24th Guard's Brigades, which had created the long, narrow salient projecting into the enemy's lines almost as far as Campoleone Station. If they achieved this by the actions on the flanks, as were taking place against the positions held by the Guards and the 6th Gordon Highlanders, 23 Brigade would have been completely cut off. With the loss of the forward companies the artillery support became increasingly important. Despite the dangers of machine-gun fire, mortars and heavy shelling, Major David Shepherd, the Commander of 266 Field Battery of the 67th Field Regiment, Royal Artillery, together with his second in command, Captain Graham Jupp, had established a forward observation post which was in an exposed position. These two officers had acted coolly and skilfully and directed the fire of the Divisional Artillery onto enemy positions, with great effect, blunting the enemy's attack.

Sergeant Douglas Tait recorded in his diary for 3 February that 'at 23:00 all hell let loose. Jerry put down terrific barrage, followed by all-in attack. I fired my gun until red hot. Jerry couldn't make it on our flank.' For his entry for the following day, 4 February, he wrote, 'I thought we had them well in hand. Did a bit of sniping. Spandau fire came at us from all angles. A runner managed to reach us with word we were the only flank left & almost cut off.'

General Ronald Penney, the commanding officer of the British 1st Division, knew he had to commit his reserves to stabilize the situation and prevent the Germans breaking through. 168 Brigade of the British 56th Division had been moved from the Monte Cassino front and landed at Anzio the previous day, 3 February. This included the 1st Battalion London Scottish and no sooner had they arrived than they were thrown into the line. It was fortuitous that they joined their fellow Gordons and a council of war was quickly arranged between the commanding officers of both battalions, Lieutenant Colonels James Peddie and Torrance Law. Both men knew each other from their former association when they were both serving with the London Scottish. After being made aware of the dire situation Lieutenant Colonel Law decided to counter-attack the Germans as soon as his battalion could be brought forward. B Company of the 6th Gordons was still holding resolutely and the counter-attack was to be launched from that firm base. This attack went in at 16:00 and was supported by the tanks of the 46th Royal Tank Regiment, which had been supporting the 6th Gordons, together with the continued artillery support of the Royal Artillery, which was being directed by Major Shepherd and Captain Jupp.

In the driving rain and sleet, the 1st London Scottish was transported to the front line as a matter of urgency. Even before they managed to get in position they suffered casualties from enemy artillery. Once assembled their attack involving three companies with fixed bayonets began at 3:30 in the afternoon of 4 February. They immediately suffered more casualties as they emerged from the cover of the 6th Gordons' positions and crossed some open ground but after heavy fighting and heavy casualties, the lead assaulting company (A Company), led by Captain James Findlay, got to within 200 metres of their final objective but were being held up by murderous machine-gun fire from both flanks. The rescue of the 3 Brigade, trapped at the tip of the Campoleone salient, depended on the objective being taken and Captain Findlay urged his remaining men on, leading from the front to clear the houses on either side of the road. They took their final objective after two hours of fierce fighting. This was not the end, however; the London Scottish was continually counter-attacked but miraculously, they withstood the enemy onslaught and held the position and so kept the Via Anziate open long enough to allow the survivors of 3 Brigade to withdraw. Once this was accomplished, the few survivors of A Company, which were only Captain Findlay and five other ranks, were ordered to withdraw. The battalion's success had come at a huge cost with the loss of 120 men killed, wounded or captured, little consolation for the many casualties they had inflicted on the enemy, including the capture of some thirty Germans. Colour Sergeant Robert Samuel, an Aberdonian serving with the London Scottish, noted that many of the Germans surrendered at the sight of the cold steel of the Gordons' bayonets. Once the position had been secured, B and D Companies of the London Scottish held their positions for a few more hours then withdrew through the remnants of the 6th Gordons. Both battalions then relocated back about a mile, where a new defensive line had been established, but the Germans had largely succeeded in eliminating the bulge into their line and now prepared to go on the offensive.

That day, 4 February 1944, was a momentous one for the Regiment of the Gordon Highlanders, with two of its battalions having been involved in fierce fighting and suffered hugely in terms of the casualties. In addition to the losses of almost the whole of the London Scottish A and D Companies, the 6th Gordons had lost almost the whole of their A, C and D Companies. Among these casualties there were many tragic family stories, with some of those killed leaving young families without a father. Back home in Keith, Banffshire,

Mrs Isabella Milton received the news of the death of her husband, Francis, which was further grief following the loss of her brother, William Mackie, killed two years earlier, in a mine-laying accident while he was serving with the 2nd Battalion Gordon Highlanders in Singapore. Her husband's death was also mourned in Queensland, Australia, where he was born and his parents still lived. They also had the worry of Francis's brother who was with the Australian Army. He had been captured in Singapore and they had received little news about him, so couldn't be sure if he was still alive. The loss of any family member was a huge blow and difficult to come to terms with. Leslie Tromans was one of those seriously wounded in the counter-attack made by B Company of the 6th Battalion and his family were first informed that he had been wounded, and then of his death, after he died of his wounds just four days later. Leslie's father wrote to his commanding officer, Major Lindsay Bridgman, asking for information; he replied, telling how proud he should be of his son, as he had 'fought like a lion'. In the attack launched by the 1st Battalion London Scottish, there was perhaps one of the saddest losses. Twins Thomas and John Cairncross from Newburgh, Fife, had been called up on their nineteenth birthday. After their basic training with the Black Watch, they had been posted to Italy and transferred into the 1st Battalion London Scottish shortly before Anzio. Both twins were killed on 4 February, so were not only born on the same day but died on the same day. Their time in the army had been very short and fate had not allowed them to have any battle experience before being thrown into the intensive fighting in the defence of the Campoleone salient. On receiving a letter from the War Office that their son Leslie was missing, the family of the Gray twins from Aberlour, Banffshire, had already been through the anguish of the fear that a son may have been killed after receiving similar such news in 1940. Leslie's twin brother, Thomas, had also been serving with the 6th Gordons with the BEF when he was posted missing. They had feared the worst then, but a few months later there was great relief when they heard that he had been captured at Hem, France, and was a prisoner of war. The best they could hope for now was that Leslie was captured and not killed at Anzio. There were also numerous men wounded that day. Captain William Dallas was leading a patrol that was ambushed when all of his men were killed and he received shrapnel wounds to his back and leg. He lay injured all night until picked up by a German tank in the morning and taken to a German field hospital. He was operated on by a German doctor but without any anaesthetic as the Germans had also had a huge number of casualties that day and had run out. After his emergency treatment, Captain Dallas became a prisoner of war.

The officers and men of both battalions of Gordon Highlanders had shown great courage and had played an important part in preventing the Germans from breaking through. As a mark of the ferocity of the fighting and the high degree of courage displayed, numerous gallantry decorations were awarded. Captain James Findlay from Aberdeen became the first officer of the 1st Battalion London Scottish to receive the Distinguished Service Order in the Second World War. There were also numerous awards for the 6th Battalion Gordon Highlanders. Major Lindsay Bridgman was awarded a Military Cross for his leadership of B Company on 4 February and a subsequent action three days later. Lieutenant Edward Grace, who commanded a platoon of B Company, was also awarded the Military Cross, as was the Adjutant, Captain James Williamson. Corporals George Wilson and James Moir together with Private Alex Mennim were awarded the Military Medal, while Lieutenant James Leckie, Regimental Sergeant Major James Underwood, Sergeant John Thain, Corporals Jock Cobban and David Tripney and Lance Corporals Alex Paterson and James Agnew all received mentions in dispatches, in addition to which James Agnew also received the American Silver Star. Royal Artillery Observers Major David Shepherd and Captain Graham Jupp, who were directly supporting both Gordons battalions throughout 4 February, were both awarded Military Crosses for their courageous actions that day. Battalion support came in many forms and Quartermaster Captain Charles G. Munro, MM, was awarded the order of the MBE for his efficiency in maintaining a supply of rations to the front-line soldiers, confirming the importance of the B Echelon to the success on the front line. Charles Munro had been the 6th Battalion's Quartermaster from before the war and served in France and Tunisia. He had been awarded his Military Medal in the First World War when serving with the 7th Battalion Gordon Highlanders.

The action which was included in the citation for Major Bridgman's Military Cross occurred when, under his command, B Company of the 6th Gordons was placed under the command of C Squadron of the 1st Recce Regiment. They moved into a position near Padiglione at around 11.00 pm on 7 February but it was a bright moonlit night and the enemy immediately had them under observation. The predictable result was that they were heavily shelled as they dug in. They withstood continued enemy attacks throughout the night, but at daybreak elements of the Recce Regiment, together with a platoon of B Company, were overwhelmed by a fierce attack made in strength under the cover of a smokescreen. Major Bridgman realized his position was the only impediment preventing the enemy from breaking through a gap in the open ground. His company was now isolated from other British forces but they held on all through the day, while all the time reporting on enemy movements in front of them, which was invaluable intelligence. When darkness fell, it was possible to reinforce the line and stabilize the position on either side of them. Major Bridgman had again demonstrated his coolness and courageous leadership under circumstances of extreme jeopardy. It was not only Lindsay Bridgman who was delighted to receive this recognition but he took the news of the award modestly. His Batman, Pat Murray, took it upon himself to write personally to Mrs Bridgman and was the first to give her the news of the award and some details of the actions which led to her husband's award for gallantry. In his letter he mentioned that the company were at one point surrounded and had to deal with tanks and flamethrowers, but Major Bridgman was determined to hold out to the last man to thwart the attack, which lasted for some three days.

By noon on 5 February, all of the British units had fallen back to straighten the defensive line to just about 1 mile north of Carroceto and Aprilla ('The Factory'). It was now time to take stock of the situation as both battalions had been seriously depleted, but the 6th Gordons were especially weakened. Not only had three forward companies been virtually wiped out, B and HQ Companies had also suffered considerably. In order to strengthen the 6th Gordons, a Company from the Durham Light Infantry was placed under the battalion's command, but this company was inexperienced and had not seen any action previously. Other reinforcements arrived in due course for both battalions, but these were all without combat experience, most just recently having completed their training in the UK. However, the lack of reinforcements meant it was impossible to return to full strength for some months.

The main objective now was to prevent the Germans breaking through and pushing the Allies back into the sea. Continual actions were necessary to close gaps in the line. In one such action on 8 February, elements the 1st London Scottish were sent to support the 10th Royal Berkshires, but in the early hours of the following morning, the situation deteriorated after heavy shelling of the position. During this bombardment, an artillery round scored a direct hit and knocked out one section of the mortar platoon of 168 Brigade's support company. This killed their officer, Lieutenant Ronald Gordon, and wounded six others. Sergeant Vernon Fraser took charge of the situation and was fully aware that the forward infantry required his mortars to harass the enemy and impede their advance. Despite the danger to his own life, he bravely moved from mortar to mortar, all of which were under sustained and accurate fire, encouraging and inspiring his men to endure and persist in this vital task. For his courageous efforts, he was awarded the Military Medal. Despite all efforts, the forward positions were overrun, which also involved the loss of the most forward platoon of C Company of the London Scottish, with Lieutenant Douglas Elgood and all of his men captured. D Company of the battalion suffered a similar fate; all of the thirty men surviving from the action to relieve the 6th Gordons in the Campoleone salient on 4 February, went missing. Captured with them was their company commander, Captain Hugh Attwooll, MC, whose heroic war had come to an end. The enemy were eventually stalled in their attack when Allied bombers made a concentrated attack on the 168 Brigade's front. The battalion moved into reserve and counted the cost of the previous seven days, i.e., since arriving in the beachhead at Anzio. The rifle companies had been the most heavily impacted, but the battalion's total loss was about one third of its entire strength.

Aerial reconnaissance showed the Germans amassing armour and artillery for an attack. One of the most worrying features was the appearance of huge calibre railway guns located at Campoleone with a further piece located at the mouth of a tunnel at Albano. The troops dubbed this gun Anzio Archie. With the Germans holding the high ground of the Alban hills, their artillery observers had an uninterrupted view over the whole beachhead area. These big guns were able to target any area within the entire beachhead area but were out of range of the smaller calibre artillery available on the beachhead. It was necessary therefore to rely on the Air Force and the naval ships lying in the bay as the only way of attacking these monsters, which were in turn, also able to retaliate and target the ships.

Since the beachhead area was restricted, enemy bombing and artillery fire from the hills did not need to be very accurate to wreak havoc. The constricted area meant that even fairly random shells exploded ammunition dumps and threatened other facilities and the men in the rear areas. A dreaded hazard were the German high velocity 88-millimetre artillery shells, which travelled at such a high speed there was absolutely no warning of their approach and no time to take cover. On 17 February, when the 6th Gordons were in a rest area well behind the front line, the area was hit by a barrage of these shells, killing the Signals Officer, Lieutenant James Leckie. The same shell seriously wounded the Intelligence Officer, Lieutenant James Methven, who was taken to hospital. In effect, nowhere was safe and this included the hospital area, located near the coast in the American sector of the beachhead. The risk of shellfire or stray bombs was a very real threat, not only to medical staff but also to the already wounded patients. This earned the hospital area the name of 'Hell's Half Acre'. Seriously wounded soldiers would be evacuated back to a hospital in Naples. One of those was Leslie Sudderick of the 1st London Scottish, who wrote home to his parents in Lancashire, reporting that he had been wounded twice on the Anzio beachhead. The first injury kept him in hospital for five days, but the second necessitated his evacuation to Naples, where he recounted that he had to be evacuated from the first hospital as Mount Vesuvius had erupted. This stay in Naples was perhaps a providential experience for Leslie as, soon after the war ended, he returned to marry his Italian sweetheart, Clelia, in Naples.

Major Malcolm Munthe was also active at Anzio, where he was often seen wearing the kilt of Gordon tartan and accompanied by his friend and comrade, Captain John Gubbins, who also wore a kilt of Cameron tartan. Both were courageous men and would appear very resolute and unmoved by exploding artillery shells around them. Unfortunately, tragedy struck on 6 February when they were with the 6th Battalion Gordon Highlanders. During a German counter-attack on the beachhead, Munthe was badly wounded, receiving shrapnel wounds to the head and chest. Afterwards he said, 'I heard a terrible thud as though someone had hurled a dining table against my heart. I was certain I was dead.' His comrade, John Gubbins, the son of Major General Sir Colin Gubbins, who was the head of the SOE, was killed instantly in the same incident.

The Germans had taken the initiative and were pressing the Allied lines, resulting in artillery attacks and infantry attacks having to be repulsed; this required reinforcement of the units under attack with other resources from within the division. On 9 February, following orders from the 168 Brigade commander, Sergeant Robert Mitchell led a section of the 1st London Scottish Bren gun carriers forward to assist the Royal Berkshires. The position was overrun and they were not heard from. As the Berkshires were still under pressure, the battalion's rifle companies had also to move forward to give support. Twenty-three men were subsequently posted missing, with Sergeant Mitchell and three others taken prisoner.

On the same day, at Padigleone, a number of 6th Gordons C Company were wounded after heavy shelling and mortaring of their position. Private Alex Hadden, a stretcher bearer, led them with a carrying party to the regimental aid post (RAP) to ensure they received appropriate medical treatment for their wounds. The only route to the RAP was down the bed of a watercourse, which was in flood, so they had to wade through water which was waist deep. With the steep sides, it was not easy to climb out, especially during wet weather when the banks were slippery. This was not the only hazard with which they had to contend, as the enemy might be lurking around any corner. During the evacuation, the enemy bombardment continued with shells also falling in the ravine they were navigating, but they managed to succeed in their mission and delivered the injured men to the RAP Alex Hadden was not able to relax over the following period. Just a few days later, on 14 February, the company were again subjected to heavy mortar fire and inevitably there were casualties. Without hesitating, he ran across 100 metres of open ground, which was still under fire, to attend to the wounded and escort them back to safety. The following day he was almost a casualty himself. After a shell exploded near the Company HQ, he was blown clean off his feet by the blast. He was badly shaken but otherwise unhurt, but could barely stand. Almost immediately there was a direct hit on a farm a little way in front of the Company HQ and a call went out for stretcher bearers to assist the injured men. Captain Leslie Hatt didn't think Alex was fit enough to continue and advised him that he shouldn't go but he protested that it was his duty to go to the injured men's assistance, so he collected his medical kit and again ran across open ground exposed to enemy fire. When he got to the farmhouse he found a scene of carnage. There were many injured British and American soldiers. He set about dressing their wounds while the whole time their position was continually under fire. While he worked, he heard an ambulance pass; he attracted its attention, guided it to his location and helped get some of the injured into the vehicle. After its departure, he waited until its return to ensure the others were also evacuated, all of the time working alone due to the loss of the other Company stretcher bearers, who were all being exposed to danger. On hearing about Alex Hadden's selfless courage over a number of days, his commanding officer, Lieutenant Colonel James Peddie, recommended him for an award of the Distinguished Conduct Medal. For an enlisted man, this decoration is second only to the Victoria Cross as an award for gallantry. His recommendation was countersigned by the commanding officer of 2nd Infantry Brigade but on reaching the Divisional Command it was downgraded to the Military Medal, which is also only awarded for acts of exceptional bravery. A mention in dispatches was also made for the actions of Private Patrick Gordon, who was also busy as a stretcher bearer on the battlefield at Anzio.

The courage of the stretcher bearers in both battalions was incredible and another example of their daring and dedication took place on 24 February 1944. The incident began when four seriously wounded men arrived at the London Scottish A Company headquarters, which was located in a river bed around 800 metres north of the Anzio Lateral Road. An ambulance was summoned but not sent; it was explained that it was too dangerous for any vehicle to proceed to their location in daylight. The evacuation would have to wait until darkness fell. Hearing this, the stretcher bearers, Privates Patrick Duffy and William Doran, volunteered to carry the casualties back for treatment, but the company commander said it was too dangerous as the route was subject to almost continuous artillery and machine-gun fire. Privates Duffy and Doran asserted that they were confident they could achieve the evacuation and insisted on trying so were permitted to attempt the dangerous task. Over the next two hours they successfully carried three of the cases the 800 metres to safety where they could receive treatment for their injuries. On the fourth trip, the stretcher and the patient were blown out of their hands, killing their charge and wounding the two of them. This was a painful blow, but they had achieved an extraordinary task at great risk to their own safety. Both men were awarded the Military Medal for their courage and devotion to duty.

The hazards of the beachhead area were ably described by Sergeant Douglas Tait who wrote in his diary for 10 February, 'Was sleeping alongside carrier with Larry when small butterfly bombs landed at our feet. Luckily the shrapnel rose over our bodies, blew Larry's jacket to pieces and riddled the carrier's cover. I was struck with the covering of bomb, thought my end had come. Only a small puncture in my back.' With typical ironic nonchalance the next day his diary entry was, 'Learnt a lesson last night. Dug a slit trench! It's worth the sweat.' What Douglas Tait was referring to was the anti-personnel bombs dropped by, generally, a single German aircraft flying over the beachhead at night. The American soldiers nicknamed this regular visitor as 'Popcorn Pete'. These aircraft dropped 1,000-pound bombs which would explode in mid-air and disperse numerous smaller bomblets which fluttered down to explode near the ground, sending shrapnel in all directions. The noise of the numerous bomblets exploding in rapid succession gave rise to the association with popcorn popping.

The Allies were now on the defensive, so measures were put in place to protect the forward positions. John Rose, a corporal in the 6th Gordons Pioneer Platoon, was laying mines when one exploded prematurely; sadly, he was killed. Mines, laid by both sides, were rightly feared by the soldiers as they not only killed but if the result was not fatal, the injured man was often terribly maimed. The situation in the Anzio bridgehead was developing into somewhat of a stalemate. This type of warfare needed the men to show a dogged determination as amply demonstrated by Sergeant Peter Shand. After the loss of 6th Gordons C Company, on 4 February, at the age of just twenty-three years, he took over command of a platoon of the reformed C Company. This was comprised of young soldiers with little or no active service, let alone battle experience. On 12 February, the company moved forward and took up a position almost 2 kilometres north of the flyover crossing the main road from Anzio to Rome. The platoon's position was on an exposed forward slope in an area devoid of any natural cover, so staying below ground and out of sight was essential during daylight hours. The enemy still held Carroceto, which was on higher ground, so the Germans had complete observation over their position. The consequence of this was that snipers and mortaring were a constant threat. One night, a strong enemy patrol attacked their position. Sergeant Shand showed exceptional leadership by ignoring the hail of bullets flying through the air and thudding into the ground all around him; courageously, he darted between each section of his platoon. He encouraged his men and directed their fire with such effectiveness that the patrol was driven off. This was not an isolated example of coolness and courage; his leadership inspired his men, which kept them alive and turned them into highly efficient battle-hardened soldiers which brought successful results. Notwithstanding him being relatively young himself, his dogged sustained courage and leadership was rewarded with the Military Medal.

Over the next prolonged period, the 6th Battalion occupied a position on the east side of the flyover with alternate periods of three weeks in the line or the reserve. The vicinity around the flyover was very uncomfortable as it was a frequent aiming point for enemy artillery. The area was constantly under their observation, which restricted any movement to the hours of darkness. With this troglodyte existence below ground for most of the day, the battle of Anzio was becoming very like the trench warfare of the First World War. One consolation was that some of the German shells failed to explode and turned out to be duds; nevertheless, the live rounds continued to cause many casualties.

Despite their exposed position, the men had to be constantly resupplied with food, water and ammunition. This was the job of the quartermasters and C Company were fortunate to have the brave and quick-witted CQMS George Melville serving them. On 19 February, he was informed that part of the route up to his company had been taken by the enemy. He knew his comrades needed resupply, so despite this news, he was determined to do his duty. George Melville was a very experienced soldier who had served as a 'Regular' with the 1st Battalion for twelve years before he was wounded in France in 1940. He was posted to the 6th Battalion in 1943 after recovering from his injuries. George prepared himself and his carrying party to fight their way through, but luckily the information he had been given proved incorrect and the rations were delivered without too much of a problem. This was not so straightforward just three nights later. When he and a party of men were again delivering rations to the area, they were heavily shelled, leading to a number of casualties with some of his own carrying party among those injured. Coolly he took charge of the situation and arranged to have all the wounded evacuated and ensured other men took the place of the injured so that he could complete his mission. He stayed in the area until he was content that rations had been delivered to every platoon and then started to make his way back. The shelling had left the whole area cratered by the explosions; in the darkness, he drove his carrier into one of these holes and became immobile. The units nearby were unable to provide him with assistance to tow his vehicle out of the shell hole, so he had no option but to walk back to the B Echelon base, a distance of 4 miles, to get another carrier and return to get his own vehicle. It was a remarkable feat that he achieved success and managed to recover his carrier and return to safety before dawn, after which his movements would only have attracted lethal attention from the enemy artillery. Unfortunately, just a month later, George was killed when there was a direct hit on his dugout.

The Germans continued to press all along the front probing for weakness and exploiting the lie of the land to infiltrate into the British positions. Another dire situation arose on the morning of 23 February. The continued bad weather had the defending soldiers shivering miserably in their partially flooded dugouts while more-determined attacks were made against the 1st London Scottish, which were beaten off but not without casualties being sustained. It was little consolation that the German casualties were much greater, but the line was held firm. These attacks continued over the next few days and the now much-weakened A Company position was overrun. When the reserve D Company counter-attacked to restore the position, Lieutenant Douglas Kenilworth was wounded. A valiant effort was made by Sergeant Watt, MM, together with Signaller Frank House to rescue him, but he died while he was being transported back to the aid post. In the ebb and flow of these continually changing actions, Frank House was captured two days later. There were a very high number of casualties resulting from shrapnel from artillery and mortars. On 28 February, Private Arthur Baxter was wounded by shrapnel to his leg. This was potentially a personal disaster for Arthur who in civilian life was a professional footballer. He was a player for Dundee FC and Barnsley FC. One of his most memorable experiences was in the Scottish Cup final in front of a crowd of 75,000 fans at Hampden Park, Glasgow, on 4 May 1940. He joined the army in 1941 and while undergoing his basic training at Bridge of Don Barracks, Aberdeen, played for Aberdeen FC. (The Dons). After his training he was posted to the 1st Battalion London Scottish and was the captain of the battalion football team. Fortunately, he recovered from his wounds and was able to return to duty.

The German attacks continued, but the 1st Battalion London Scottish were a spent force, having taken part in some of the fiercest fighting in the Anzio Beachhead and having unsustainable casualties of over 60 per cent of all ranks killed, wounded and captured. Their record was a proud one, preventing a German breakthrough on many occasions and the officers and men had been awarded many decorations for their courage. They were relieved and left the beachhead. Before the 1st Battalion London Scottish left Anzio, Sergeant John Thom was given special leave to go and meet up with his older brother George, who was serving with the United States Army in 77th Ordnance Depot Company. George had left his hometown of Huntly, Aberdeenshire, fourteen years before when he emigrated to the USA. He lived in New Jersey. The brothers hadn't seen each other for many years so this was a special occasion and there was a lot to talk about. The joy of this reunion was, however, short-lived. On 24 February, just two days after their meeting, George Thom was killed at Anzio and is buried in the American Military Cemetery at Nettuno.

The two Gordons battalions were again to pursue different paths, but their war was to continue in Italy. While the 6th Battalion Gordon Highlanders remained at Anzio, the 1st Battalion London Scottish sailed from Anzio to the Bay of Naples on 11 March 1944. They sailed away, leaving many of their comrades behind, killed, wounded or captured. Due to the large number of casualties earlier, a number of B Echelon troops, who had little or no combat experience, were used to make up a combined company of the 1st London Scottish. This was commanded by Captain Angus McFadyean, who had taken charge of the unit only two weeks earlier when, on 25 February, they were in a desperate defensive action against a large determined attacking enemy force. Despite being together for only a short time, they had been moulded into a coherent unit, successfully beating off two large enemy attacks. Angus McFadyean was very active himself, leading counter-attacks with grenades and automatic weapons, while encouraging all of his platoons and making sure their position was secure. By the time the Germans withdrew, their dead amounted to over fifty, eleven others were captured and a large number of their weapons were bagged, including fifteen Spandaus. Captain McFadyean was recommended for the Distinguished Service Order but this was downgraded to the Military Cross. Unfortunately, this was awarded posthumously, as he was subsequently killed on 9 March, just two days before the battalion left the bridgehead.

After leaving Anzio, the London Scottish set up camp at Sarno, some 15 miles down the coast from Naples at the foot of the volcano Mount Vesuvius, which was grumbling ominously. The battalion stayed in the town for only a few days and on 17 March, Vesuvius started to erupt in earnest with lava bombs being ejected from the crater. Fortunately, these were crashing down the northern side of the mountain, away from their location. Before the situation became worse, the battalion moved to the outskirts of Taranto and sailed from the port to Egypt on 29 March.

The stalemate on the beachhead had an effect on the men's outlook, but morale remained high. When the Germans dropped propaganda leaflets from the air on 15 March, the reaction was that they were useful when the army issue 'form 00' was unavailable. Douglas Tait completed his daily diary with, 'I wish I had something fresh to write, but no! The days drag by, shells going this way, shells going that way, then some bombs at night to break the monotony.'

He did however have something different to write when he was given a few days leave at the beginning of April. He was sent to Salerno, although he would have preferred Naples; but he visited Pompeii and was disappointed to have missed the spectacle of the volcano erupting. He did however notice that there was still a lot of volcanic dust in the streets of Salerno. He reported, 'The nights feel strange. It's so quiet I keep waking up wondering what is wrong. Maybe it is sleeping between white sheets that kept me awake.' The break lifted his spirits as he was able to meet a friend in Naples and attended Irving Berlin's show, *This Is the Army*. He was even able to be a little flippant about his return to Anzio, 'Back on Beach-head & had the usual welcome. They couldn't even wait until I landed. The ship was shelled in the bay.'

As the spring weather started to dry out the ground after months of incessant rain, the Allied tanks were more able to manoeuvre and 6th Gordons patrols were sent forward to probe the German defences. However, sniping and artillery fire was a constant treat for the forward companies. On 3 May, a small group of reinforcements were moving up to join the recently reformed C Company, but before they had even reached the Company's position, Private Matthew Barrett was killed and five other men with him were wounded. The enemy artillery often targeted the Allied guns and mortars and on 8 May German mortars counter-batteried a 6th Gordons' mortar position where Sergeant George Hardie was in command. A direct hit caused the ammunition to explode and he was wounded in the face but refused to be evacuated for treatment until he was satisfied that the ammunition was replaced and the unit kept functioning. Earlier he had braved a heavy concentration of artillery fire in the area manned by his platoon to rescue two of his comrades who were in shattered dugouts. With shells exploding all around him, he extricated the two men and dressed their wounds before seeing them to safety. He was awarded a Military Medal for his courage and subsequent tireless work. It was not only the enemy artillery which caused casualties. On 30 May 1944, there was a tragic incident of friendly fire when an artillery barrage fell short: thirty-eight men of the 6th Gordons were wounded and Corporal Frank Handy was killed. This was the start of the breakout and the British divisions pushed north-west over the Moletta River with great success. C Company were attacking German positions on a hill north of Fosso Dell Vajarella when, around mid-day, the enemy resistance stiffened and the company started to suffer a number of casualties. Seeing the situation, Private William Pickard displayed exceptional courage by leading a party of stretcher bearers over open ground despite concentrated enemy fire to assist the evacuation of the wounded over a distance of more than a kilometre. As the action continued and other units passed through C Company's position, many further casualties occurred through that afternoon. William Pickard continued to work in evacuating the numerous wounded over an extended period of nine hours while continually under fire, saving an estimated forty or fifty men. His devotion to duty earned him the award of the Military Medal.

The breakout was successful on the whole front with the Americans making huge advances in the north-east. The better weather allowed the Allied air superiority to pound the retreating Germans to great effect. The warmer, drier conditions allowed the Allied armour to advance and along with them the infantry, ready to mop up as the advance proceeded. Finally, the Americans entered Rome on 4 June and General Mark Clark had his day of glory, but his decision to make the liberation of Rome his priority, rather than cutting off the retreating German forces from the Monte Cassino front, was controversial. One consolation was that the speed of the Allied advance after the breakout surprised the Germans and prevented them from putting their demolition plans for the city's bridges and some monuments into effect. The British halted about 10 miles south of Rome on a hillside overlooking the Italian capital. There was a feeling of relief, combined with satisfaction that their mission had been achieved, but the human cost had been enormous. Many could look back and remember comrades who, for one reason or another, failed to see the 'Eternal City'. So many had been killed and many more wounded, some with life-changing injuries, such as Arthur Mutch, whose leg had to be amputated after a mortar shell blast, or Alfred Price, who lost an arm due to shrapnel injuries from an artillery shell and Alex Brandie was partially blinded, losing his right eye. There were also hundreds missing and although it was believed that most had been taken prisoner, their fate remained uncertain.

The Anzio campaign was described in poetic fashion by Sergeant J. Miller of C Company, 6th Battalion Gordon Highlanders, who penned some verses in Doric, a Scots dialect spoken almost exclusively in north-east Scotland. While still on the beachhead on 20 April 1944, he wrote:

'It was twa o'clock in the morning and a blast of Januar' win'
Was ruffling up the wavelets as the ship came sneaking in.
Ghostly ships in the half light, crammed with grim-faced men
Peering into darkness at a coast they didna ken.
As the ships came on the beaches and ground on the golden sand
Out poured those veteran warriors with their battle cry, 'Bydand'.
The Gordon lads had landed and history's page will glow
With the glory of that landing on the beach at Anzio.

'Then it was on, on, on for the battle must be won
And they knew within their hearts did every mother's son
That among the trailing vines
Through wire and through mines
They must breach the Jerry lines
And the Gordon line must hold.

'As they fought their way across the plain, they raised their tired eyes
To the distant line of hills, their foremost major prize.
They knew that once upon those heights and astride the Appian Way
No matter what the Boche might do they were there to stay.
But plans have miscarried or may have gone "agley",
No man can tell the reason, if they did go astray.
For the Gordons got their orders and instead of pushing on,
They toiled and dug their trenches to make the line more strong.

'So it was hold, hold, hold, though you're soaking wet and cold
For Highland hearts are brave and Highland hearts are bold,
And hold the line you must
Till you're trampled into the dust
For our cause is right and just
And the bridgehead <u>must</u> be held.

'So they dug their trenches deep and made ready to stand fast
For they knew the Hainies and the stalemate couldn't last.
Yet for days they stood their guard in the sticky mud and slime
And grumbled at inaction and the waste of precious time.
Then the fury of war unrolled and the hun unleashed his might
And half our noble company was lost that bloody night.
Still they fought from out their trenches and in turn they cursed and prayed
But through the night of horror they held the line they made.

'For it was fight, fight, fight, with all our strength and might
And when the dawn came sneaking in and chased away the night
There on the Pontine Plain
Lay the bodies of the slain
But they had not died in vain
For the Gordon line still held.

'When the days of tears are o'er and the blast of war is blown
And Liberty and Peace are seated once more upon their throne,
When the chroniclers and historians set out old history's page
'Bout noble deeds and daring battle that did wage,
Foremost of all heroes and first of all the fights
Will be the Gordons' famous stand through those long dreadful nights.
And when the aged greybeards bring battles back to min'(d)
'Twill be the glory of the bridgehead where the Gordons held the line.

'Then 'twill be cheer, cheer, cheer, for the lads who paid so dear,
Who stood and fought against the foe with hearts that felt no fear.
Their glory, worth and fame
Will always be the same
Revered will be the name
Of Gordon lads who held the line in the Anzio Bridgehead.'

The glory days were short-lived, however; the eyes of the world turned to Normandy where the Allied landings of D-Day took place on the early morning of 6 June. The use of the word 'D-Day' for these landings, as if the incidence was a unique event, was somewhat of an irritation to the soldiers in Italy who had already taken part in several amphibious landings, including Sicily, Salerno and Anzio.

The British forces in Italy were not to be denied their moment of celebration for the enormous task they had played such a massive part in achieving. On 8 June, the Drums and Pipes of the 6th Battalion Gordon Highlanders led the Black Watch, the Royal Scots Fusiliers and Seaforths to march through Rome. The parade passed the Colosseum and the Victor Emmanuel Monument (the Altare della Patria or 'Wedding Cake' building) and finished by playing at the Vatican, all while receiving a rapturous welcome from the Romans with the skirl of the pipes and the sway of the kilts having their 'usual' effect. The mixed pipe band of pipers with just a few drummers that played in Rome was brought together by Captain Hamish Henderson, a Scottish musician and poet who grew up in Glenshee, Aberdeenshire. He was serving with the Intelligence Corps. He also marched alongside the pipers as they paraded through the city. On 12 June they played again and in an interview with a British war correspondent in Trajan's Forum, Hamish Henderson described the pertinence of some of the tunes being played, which included *The Crossing of the Garigliano*, *The Shores of Anzio* and *The Roads That Lead to Rome*. The music for the tune *The Shores of Anzio* was composed by Piper Frank

Stewart, who played that day and was a member of the 6th Battalion Gordon Highlanders Pipe Band.

Back home in Scotland, Sergeant (Piper) Tom Keith's wife was pleasantly surprised when she was watching the newsreel at the cinema in Buckie, Banffshire and recognized her husband. She was filled with pride seeing her Tom marching through the streets of Rome lined with cheering crowds as he played his pipes at the head of the parade. The newsreel played nationwide but just 12 miles away in Keith, the battalion's headquarters town, Corporal (Piper) Tom Smith's wife was equally delighted to see her husband. Both women hadn't seen their menfolk since they were on embarkation leave in February 1943. After the parade, the pipers and drummers were given time to view the historical sights Rome had to offer. High on everyone's list was the Colosseum. Pipe Major William Boyd of the 6th Gordons was admiring the building while chatting to Pipe Major William MacConnachie, 2nd Royal Scots Fusiliers. Both were distracted when a curious incident took place. An Italian woman sneaked up behind them and started to feel the cloth of Willie MacConnachie's kilt before he politely shooed her away. (It is believed she was an Italian dress designer and was interested in the fabric of this male garment, with which she was unfamiliar, but had noticed the favourable reaction of the crowds to the men wearing it.)

Many other men of the 6th Gordons were given leave to sightsee in Rome, something most had dreamed of from the day they landed at Anzio, but never expected this would be over four months later. Sergeant Douglas Tait visited St. Peter's Basilica and was introduced to the British Secretary for the Vatican. There was now time to pause, reflect and relax for a short period before training resumed. The novelty of being able to walk around in the open, even in daylight, felt unnatural and took a little time to get used to. The 6th Gordons had set up camp about 10 miles south of Rome; in addition to visiting the city's sights, the men of the Battalion enjoyed the opportunity to swim in the sea at the Ostia Lido, where, in pre-war days, the Romans had flocked in their thousands to spend a weekend at the seaside, escaping the stifling heat and claustrophobia of the city. With the higher ambient June temperature, the Gordons found this dip in the sea was much more to their liking than their obligatory dunk in January at Anzio during the amphibious landings.

After the Normandy landings on D-Day, 6 June 1944, the main focus of the war shifted to north-west Europe. This was also the focus of media attention back in Britain. It was reported that Lady Nancy Astor, the member of Parliament for Plymouth Sutton, who was well-known for her outspoken views and lack of understanding of current affairs, used the phrase 'D-Day Dodgers' to describe the men fighting in Italy, although she later denied saying this. This incensed the men who had suffered bitter fighting in that country and the response from the ordinary soldier was the composition which became known as *The Ballad of the D-Day Dodgers*, which was sung to the popular war-time song *Lili Marlene*. The words differed depending on where in Italy it was being sung and who was doing the singing. In essence, it was a cynically satirical song pointing out, in a humorous way, but with ironic bitterness, the trials they had endured and the sacrifices they had made given that they had already undertaken several of their own 'D-Day' landings in Sicily, Salerno and Anzio. The various versions were collected by Hamish Henderson and one version is shown below.

'We are the D-Day Dodgers,
Out in Italy,
Always on the vino,
Always on the spree.
Eighth Army skivers and their tanks,
We live in Rome, among the yanks.
We are the D-Day Dodgers,
We're out in Italy.

'We landed at Salerno,
A holiday with pay.
The Jerry brought his bands out
To cheer us on our way,
Showed us the sights and gave us tea,
We all sang songs, the beer was free.
To welcome the D-Day Dodgers,
To sunny Italy.

'Anzio and Cassino
Were taken in our stride,
We did not go to fight there,
We just went for the ride.
Sicily and Sangro are just names,
We only went to look for dames,
For we are the artful D-Day Dodgers,
In sunny Italy.

'On our way to Florence,
We had a lovely time,

We drove a bus from Rimini,
Right through the Gothic Line,
Then to Bologna we did go,
And went bathing in the River Po,
For we are the D-Day Dodgers,
Way out in Italy.

'Dear Lady Astor,
You think you know a lot,
Standing on your platform
And talking tommy rot.
You England's sweetheart and her pride,
We think your mouth is too bloody wide
From the D-Day Dodgers,
Out in sunny Italy.

'Look around the mountains,
Through the mist and rain,
See the scattered crosses,
Some that bear no name.
Heartbreak and toil and suffering gone,
The lads beneath, they slumber on.
They are the D-Day Dodgers,
Who'll stay in Italy.'

Cap badge of the Gordon Highlanders.
(*Gordon Highlanders Museum*)

Cap badge of the London Scottish.
(*Gordon Highlanders Museum*)

Gordon Barracks, Aberdeen Above 1935 and below recent

No. 9 Infantry Training Centre. (*Gordon Highlanders Museum*)

The 1st London Scottish cleaning their weapons, Barjissia near Basra, Iraq 1943. (*London Scottish Regiment's Trustees*)

Group of 1st Battalion London Scottish at 'comfort stop' on train from Basra to Kirkuk, Iraq 1943. (*London Scottish Regiment's Trustees*)

The 1st London Scottish, Iraqi Desert, 1943. Private Joseph McGarrity in front row, third from left. (*Courtesy of Jim McGarrity*)

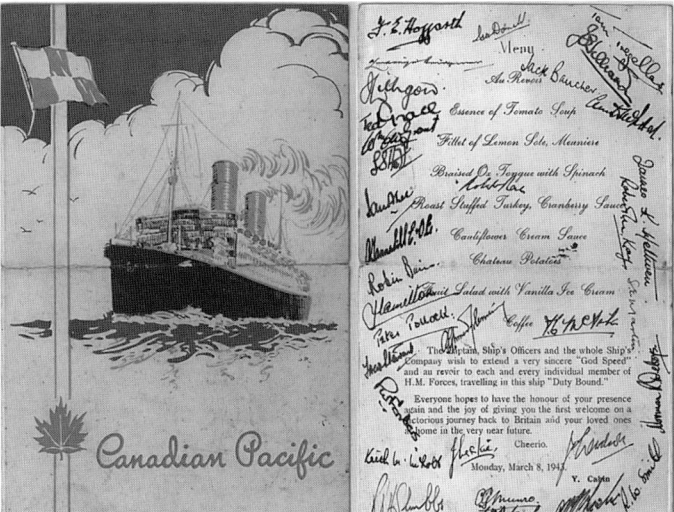

Signed menu card from officers' dinner before landing in Algiers, March 1943. (*Gordon Highlanders Museum*)

Corporal John Miller (1st London Scottish) inspecting abandoned German equipment in a Sicilian square, 1943. (*Gordon Highlanders Museum*)

Lieutenant Leckie (first left, back row) with his men, Tunisia, January 1944. (*Gordon Highlanders Museum*)

R.W. (Bobby) Smith after the Second World War. (*Courtesy of Michael Drummond Smith*)

Steel helmet punctured by shrapnel, which saved R.W. Smith's life in Tunisia. (*Gordon Highlanders Museum*)

Italian officer's Beretta pistol surrendered to R.W. Smith in Pantelleria. (*Gordon Highlanders Museum*)

Monte Cassino. (*Author's collection*)

Private George Mitchell, VC, 1st London Scottish.
(*Gordon Highlanders Museum*)

The Victoria Cross. (*Gordon Highlanders Museum*)

Painting by Joan Wanklyn depicting the action on Damiano Ridge on the night of 23–24 January 1944, for which Private George Mitchell was awarded the Victoria Cross. This painting currently hangs in the Drill Hall of the London Scottish in London. The original painting is in colour. (*London Scottish Regiment's Trustees*)

The Anzio Lateral Road, Anzio Bridgehead. (*London Scottish Regiment's Trustees*)

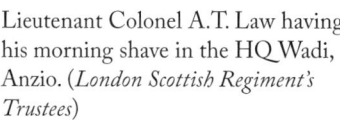

Lieutenant Colonel A.T. Law having his morning shave in the HQ Wadi, Anzio. (*London Scottish Regiment's Trustees*)

Signaller's dugout in Wadi in the Anzio Bridgehead. (*London Scottish Regiment's Trustees*)

Gordon Highlanders Pipe Band at the Anzio Bridgehead hospital area, 1944. (*Gordon Highlanders Museum*)

The 6th Gordon Highlanders marching through open country, Italy 1944. (*Gordon Highlanders Museum*)

The 6th Gordon Highlanders' pipers, Rome 1944. Corporal Tom Smith in foreground. (*Gordon Highlanders Museum*)

Gordon Highlanders commanding officers' meeting near Rome, August 1944. Left to right: lieutenant colonels A.T. Law DSO, J.B. Clapham and James Peddie DSO. (*Gordon Highlanders Museum*)

The 6th Gordon Highlanders 'S' Coy Bren-gun carrier crew, Florence 1944. Left to right: Sergeant Tait, Private McLeod, Private McKay, Private Stewart and Lance Corporal Thomson. (*Gordon Highlanders Museum*)

Sergeant James Lobban, 6th Gordon Highlanders, Florence 1944. (*Courtesy of Michael Lobban*)

The 6th Gordon Highlanders (far left) marching into Biforco, Arrow Route, September 1944. (*Gordon Highlanders Museum*)

Lieutenant Colonel Brian Clapham (left), 6th Gordon Highlanders, Gothic Line, 1944. Note the men's mud-stained clothing. (*Gordon Highlanders Museum*)

The 6th Gordon Highlanders working with 67th Field Regiment Royal Artillery, 1944. Major David Shepherd MC RA is the forward observer on the right. Note the pack mules. (*Gordon Highlanders Museum*)

The 6th Gordon Highlanders Christmas 1944 air graph. The Cock o' the North is the regimental march. (*Gordon Highlanders Museum*)

Private Douglas Ledicott (6th Gordon Highlanders) with Bren-gun carrier. (*Courtesy of David Howie*)

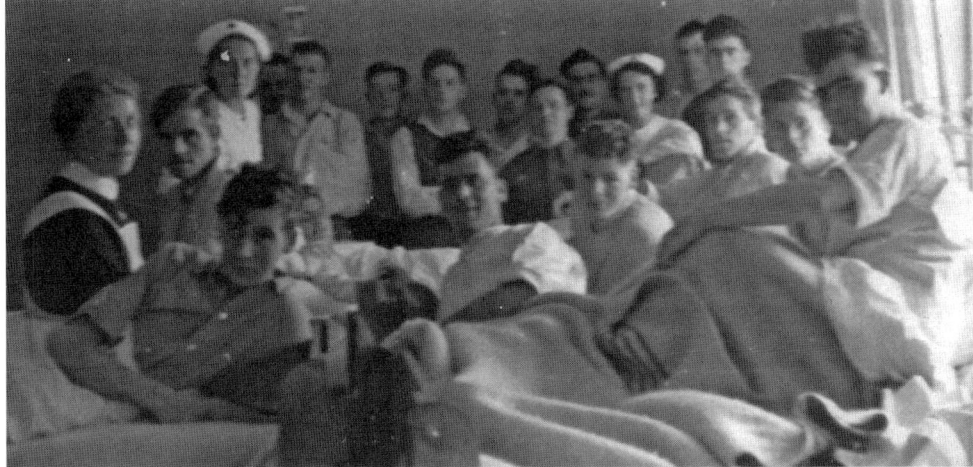

C Company of the 1st London Scottish marching from Morciano, north Italy. (*London Scottish Regiment's Trustees*)

Private Robert Frame (extreme right) with nurses and other patients, Calvariberg Hospital, Holland 1940. (*Courtesy of Anne Hunter*)

The military funeral for Robert Frame organized by the Germans, 7 June 1940. Thousands of Dutch civilians lined the streets to pay their respects. (*Courtesy of Anne Hunter*)

Lieutenant James Sinclair taking an exercise class at Obermassfeld Lazarette, Stalag IXC. Note the German guard patrolling the fence. (*Courtesy of Hellen Mutch*)

Chess pieces carved by Corporal Andrew Haldane (1st Battalion London Scottish) in Stalag 7A (Moosburg). (*Courtesy of Dennis Jones*)

Tin trunk made by Lance Sergeant W. Graham in Stalag 7A (Moosburg) from Canadian Red Cross Maple Leaf butter cans. (*Courtesy of George Graham and Gordon Highlanders Museum*)

Lieutenant William D. Dallas (far left, with spectacles and beer glass) celebrating his liberation from Oflag 79 (Braunschweig, Germany) in April 1945. (*Courtesy of Donald Dallas*)

The 6th Gordon Highlanders Anzio Memorial, showing both sides. (*Gordon Highlanders Museum*)

British Anzio Beachhead Cemetery, 1944. (*London Scottish Regiment's Trustees*)

Cassino War Cemetery. (*Gordon Highlanders Museum*)

Captains C. Douglas, E. Hall, A. Donald and W. McHardy at the pyramids, Cairo 1945. (*Gordon Highlanders Museum*)

Corporal David Hoy, 1st Battalion London Scottish, being presented with his Military Medal by Brigadier J. Scott Elliott DSO at Pola, Croatia (formerly Yugoslavia) on 25 June 1945. (*London Scottish Regiment's Trustees*)

The 1st London Scottish Pipe Band performing in St Mark's Square, Venice 1945. (*London Scottish Regiment's Trustees*)

The 1st London Scottish on VE Day, 8 May 1945, at Pola, Yugoslavia, cheering at the end of the speech by Prime Minister Winston Churchill. (*London Scottish Regiment's Trustees*)

The 6th Gordon Highlanders Pipe Band, Damascus 1945. (*Gordon Highlanders Museum*)

# Chapter 10

# The Arrow Route

After the liberation of Rome, there was a short interlude, where officers and men of the 6th Battalion Gordon Highlanders could relax and were given opportunities to visit Rome. The commanding officer, Lieutenant Colonel James Peddie, left the battalion at the end of June, after almost exactly three years in command. He was awarded the Distinguished Service Order for his leadership and although his role in Tunisia and Pantelleria was recognized it was his steely determination and organization at Anzio which was the primary reason for him being given this prestigious decoration. During the defence of the Campoleone salient he ensured that his Battalion HQ was secure, even though contact with some of his forward companies had been lost and his position was subject to continual small arms fire and shelling. This meant that he ensured a secure HQ was available for planning the counter-attack by the other Gordon Highlanders present, the 1st Battalion London Scottish, which launched its counter-offensive from the firm base secured by the 6th Battalion's B Company, ultimately preventing an enemy breakthrough.

At the beginning of July, the 6th Gordons returned to training, setting up their base in the Alban Hills, which they had looked up to for months with mixed feelings of dread and a desire to occupy that lofty position overlooking the whole bridgehead of Anzio, which the German artillery observers used to such effect. They engaged in mountain training and river crossings on the River Tiber. In one exercise, a novel innovation known as 'artificial moonlight' was trialled. This involved powerful searchlights being shone at a low angle towards the enemy positions which was designed to illuminate enemy positions while the glare dazzled enemy observers so the Allied patrols could venture forward. This new technique also created opportunities for Allied units to move into forward position more easily than in the pitch black of a moonless night. On 10 August 1944, the time had come to rejoin the battle and the battalion moved north and occupied a position overlooking the River Arno east of the 'Renaissance City' of Florence.

After a short period where patrols crossed the river, the Germans started to move out of the city and into the mountains to the north. The 6th Gordons were then ordered to enter the city on 17 August, but this was not without hazard. The Germans had demolished all of the bridges, with the exception of the ancient arcade-lined Ponte Vechia, which was an architectural and historic treasure. The Germans hoped that leaving it standing demonstrated they were being respectful of the city's history; they also concluded it posed no threat, as it was totally unsuitable for heavy military traffic. Many of the narrow streets were booby-trapped, which had to be cleared by the engineers. The occupation and defence of the city was a difficult balance as care had to be taken that no engagement provoked an enemy response which could endanger the numerous historic architectural sites. Although the Germans had ostensibly withdrawn from the city, they were often encountered by patrols and firefights would occur. Local partisans assisted the Gordons, but they were something of a law unto themselves. They took revenge against fascist sympathizers, including women, killing them without mercy. Sergeant Douglas Tait recorded in his diary that while out on patrol, 'If you meet anyone after dark, shoot first then ask questions. The Partisans, the Fascists & our old friend Todesch (Jerry) prowl the streets & shoot up each other.' In addition to this were the lurking German snipers which the 6th Gordons were tasked with mopping up. This required a great deal of courage against an unseen enemy but there were advantages to having the majority of the locals, who were pleased to have been liberated, on their side. On one occasion, the Germans were occupying the buildings on one side of the street while, unknown to the Germans, the Gordons had taken up occupation of the other. The water was cut off on the Gordons' side and it wasn't possible to leave their position without giving away their position to the enemy. However, in the intense heat of Florence, the men required water in order to maintain their position to keep the Germans under observation. The situation was resolved by recruiting the help of some local people. Armed with buckets, they brazenly went to the Germans and asked for water, which was furnished and surreptitiously delivered to the thirsty Gordon Highlanders. The locals were however, not always a help. When Sergeant Duncan Rankin was defusing a mine, he was fatally wounded when an Italian civilian inadvertently touched a trip wire and caused it to explode before he was able to disarm the device. He was later posthumously awarded a mention in dispatches for his work in Italy where, as an experienced member of the Pioneer Platoon, he had been involved in many mine-laying and defusing operations.

It was not just the enemy who presented a danger. Corporal Arthur Cruickshank was wounded in an accident and had to be evacuated back to Britain for treatment. This was just a month after his brother had been killed in France. His family lived in Aberdeen and there were four other brothers serving with the armed forces, making it a sad and stressful time for their mother. Among the many mothers with worries about their offspring was the mother of Alex Downs who was wounded in the legs in Florence and hospitalized. Her other son was a prisoner of the Japanese. Shortly after Alex Downs returned to duty he was wounded again; such was the attritional nature of the fighting.

There were also lighter moments in Florence. On 23 August 1944, the 6th Battalion Pipe Band played to an enthusiastic crowd in the historic Piazza della Signoria, with its stunning Renaissance architecture, and where Michelangelo's iconic statue of David stands. This musical performance by the Drums and Pipes of a Scottish Highland regiment was a novel experience for the Italian crowd, where the children were especially fascinated by their unique sound; the thousands of Florentines present demanded several encores. The Pipe Major was Sergeant Willie Boyd, who had served with the battalion for eleven years. Originally a native of Keith, Banffshire, he worked in one of the local wool mills. Just prior to the outbreak of the war he moved to Galashiels, the centre for the wool industry in the Scottish Borders. Shortly after this, some good news was received from France where the reformed 51st (Highland) Division was in the vicinity of Dunkirk in September 1944. Two of the 6th Battalion's drums, which had been jettisoned in 1940, were recovered.

Once Florence had been secured, it was time to pursue the enemy ever northwards. The 1st London Scottish, with the 56th Division, were already working their way up the eastern side of Italy while the 6th Gordons, with the 1st Division, were taking a more central route. On 3 September 1944, the 6th Battalion left the city and drove to the north on the main road from Florence to Bologna. They encountered trouble on their first day; ten men were wounded when the 3-ton troop transporter truck they were travelling in struck a mine. The battalion moved into the mountains, where the fine summer weather deserted them and rain and mist impaired visibility. Patrols probed the mountainous terrain of Monte Montello, almost 1,000 metres above the plain, to identify enemy positions. These operations were intrinsically dangerous as the enemy was often concealed. During one of these patrols, a platoon of A Company spotted the enemy. While they worked out a plan to eliminate the threat, one section stayed forward and kept them under observation, unaware that they too had been spotted by an enemy sniper. Suddenly, without warning, shots rang out, killing the section leader, Lance Corporal William Beaman, and Private Thomas James. The platoon returned fire with interest and drove off the Germans. The casualties' bodies were recovered and brought down the mountain by mule, which was the only means of transport in this rugged terrain. In common with dealing with all casualties, an officer was given the assignment of writing to the dead man's family. On this occasion the task fell to the Company Commanding Officer, Major Lewis Smith, who had the harrowing task of writing to their relatives to offer condolences and brief details of the circumstances of their loved one's fate, which was hoped would provide some comfort. Like so many of his fallen comrades, William Beaman was still a young man who was barely twenty-one years old with all his life before him until he was cut down prematurely. It was, however, especially sad writing to the widow of Thomas James, whose husband had only recently transferred to the Gordon Highlanders from the Royal Artillery. His wife had just recently given birth to their daughter, and Major Lewis Smith was aware how thrilled he had been to receive the news of her birth and that his wife and baby daughter were safe and well. A photo of his baby daughter was found in his personal belongings but he was never to meet his little girl as she was born shortly after he left Britain when he was posted to Italy.

The 6th Battalion returned to Florence for a short period in reserve. After returning to the city, a contingent of the battalion spent some time near the small town of Fiesole, just outside and to the north-east of the city. One of these men was Private (Signalman) Bob Boyce, who recalled that they spent two nights in a palatial villa owned by a former associate of the famous Italian opera singer Enrico Caruso. The owner had five daughters who were all opera singers in their own right. This small group of Gordon Highlanders were royally entertained by the old man regaling them with tales of his travels around the world on tour with 'The Great Caruso'. The highlight of their stay was when they were treated to an impromptu concert by the daughters singing arias from some of the great operas with their father accompanying them on the piano. It was realized that despite their grand surroundings, the family were short of food, and the Gordons happily provided them with some of their rations, including hard tack biscuits, corn beef and Maconochie's beef and vegetable stew, which was produced by Maconochie Brothers, an Aberdeenshire company based in Fraserburgh. The soldiers universally thought this was pretty awful cuisine, but it was enthusiastically received by their hosts.

The call of duty was never ending, and after only a few days it was back to the mountains and the war. What lay ahead was the formidable Gothic Line, a defensive line constructed by the Germans, maximizing the advantages of the mountainous terrain with steep ridges. The only means of advance was by rough tracks where mule transport was invariably the only way to keep the battalion supplied with ammunition and rations. The Gordons who had worked with livestock in their civilian lives had the unenviable task of cajoling these animals into contradicting their reputation for stubbornness, but not always with success. This was the Arrow Route which necessitated traversing a succession of ridges and valleys, from where the enemy had to be dislodged. This inevitably resulted in many casualties. Their first objective was Mount Gamberaldi, which was the highest peak in that vicinity at a height of almost 900 metres, with a sharp ridge heavily defended by the Germans. The weather was atrocious with driving rain and visibility reduced by thick mists. The conditions underfoot made progress difficult, with the men slipping and sliding backwards, sapping their energy and slowing their progress. Just prior to the attack going ahead there was an artillery barrage to soften up the enemy positions; as A Company of the 6th Gordons assaulted the heights, they were met by accurate Spandau fire and grenades and failed to take the position. There were a number of casualties, which included Lieutenant James Waddell being killed. This brought more sad news to his family back in Bishopbriggs as, only three months earlier, they had received the news that his younger brother, John, who was just twenty years old, had been killed while serving with the RAF.

This was not the only consequence of the attack. The Germans also replied with a barrage of mortar fire which went over the heads of the forward troops and landed on the Company HQ causing further casualties, including Signaller Bob Boyce, who was seriously wounded by shrapnel to his back. At this point, the Royal Artillery officer, Lieutenant Hoodless McIntyre, who was attached to the 6th Gordons, took over the operation of the wireless despite already being wounded himself. Unfortunately, he was hit a second time, this time fatally, and the 18 wireless set was completely destroyed. Bob Boyce was more fortunate and was evacuated, but this was to be the end of his war. Without a radio to send messages between the forward Company and the Battalion HQ, the task fell to runners, which was the only alternative. This was a difficult task for them, taking into account the enemy's fire and the distance and gradient between them. However, the dreadful weather turned out to be their friend on this occasion as, after three days, it was found that the weather had forced the Germans to withdraw for the summit of Mount Gamberaldi, so the 6th Gordons were able to occupy their objective. Bob Boyce had lost consciousness when he was taken to the Regimental Aid Post where he was treated by the Battalion Medical Officer, only coming to just as dawn broke. Because of the steep gradient, the only way he could be evacuated to hospital was to be carried on a stretcher where, due to the wound in his back, he had to lie on his front. His stretcher was being carried by four men who found the going tough so after a time they had to lay his stretcher down on the steep, rough mountain path and take a rest. While he was lying there, Bob noticed an elderly Italian woman coming towards them, looking as if she was carrying all her worldly goods in her sack. She stopped, knelt down and placed her hand on Bob's forehead, closed her eyes and muttered something which Bob didn't understand. He wondered if she was just saying a prayer for him but worried that she was giving him the last rites. Then she rummaged in her sack and took out a beautifully coloured religious card illustrating Christ on the cross and placed it on the stretcher in front of Bob's face. Bob was able to say *grazie mille* to thank her before she left. He felt eternally grateful to her, a total stranger, who showed him such consideration and kindness when she appeared to have her own troubles.

On 29 September, a second objective of Il Casone was given to D Company. The attack was led by Lieutenant Willie McHardy's platoon, who were ordered to approach the objective from the west, where their silent approach was concealed from the Germans. It was already nightfall and the visibility was made worse by the foul weather. On their ascent, the path split, going on either side of a rocky spur. Willie split his platoon and sent one half up the right-hand path while he took the rest of his men up the other side of the spur, which led to the crest of the ridge that the Germans were holding. Unfortunately, just before the final assault could be made, the element of surprise was lost when a member of the right-hand section accidentally dropped a Bren gun; the Germans were alerted and opened fire on that section. In the darkness, Willie and his Batman, who was by his side, did not know exactly where the German positions were, so fired at the muzzle flashes; the ensuing screams told them they had successfully hit their target. With the Spandaus silenced, they went on with the rest of the platoon and managed to achieve their objective. The weather conditions on the top of the ridge were so bad that it was impossible keep standing, as the wind would blow men off their feet. It was therefore unsustainable to remain there very long, so they withdrew partly down the mountain. The relentless work of taking the various peaks continued with their next objective being Mount Romano, but the exhausting actions in atrocious weather conditions meant the men were deadbeat. Thankfully, on 1 October, they were able to withdraw for some rest and reorganization to Borgo San Lorenzo. The succeeding period was spent with short periods patrolling and some small actions and periods back in Borgo San Lorenzo. The manpower requirements in north-west Europe took priority over Italy, which meant there was a lack of reinforcements. To compensate for this, C Company had to be broken up to bring the other three rifle companies up to strength. This situation remained largely unchanged until the end of the year.

On 17 October 1944, the 6th Gordons went into the line at Monte Ceco, taking over the position from another British unit. It was an unsettling scene with dead bodies lying around, many lying in slit trenches full of water. The weather and the terrain made for difficulties, although the persistent rain didn't appear to hamper the German artillery. Walter Lindley thought it was one of the hardest places they had to fight; this was where his friend, Albert Swain, with whom he had transferred into the Gordons from the Royal Artillery in November 1943, was killed. Walter was with the forward platoon on the top of the hill and was relieved that the artillery shells were going over their heads, but Albert was in D Company, who were further back down the reverse slope, which caught the full force of the bombardment. Other casualties included Harry Barnes, who was also killed. The stretcher bearer Bill Pickard, who had been awarded the Military Medal during the advance on Rome, was wounded, as was William Gordon, also a stretcher bearer, who had also been in action at Anzio.

The advance of the Allies had virtually stalled with the trials of the weather and the mountainous terrain which always favoured the defender. The next major operation which included the 6th Gordons was the relief of the Americans on Monte Grande by the British 1st Division, which took place on 5 November 1944. From the summit of this mountain, at some 600 metres high, the city of Bologna could be seen just 12 miles north as the crow flies. Willie McHardy viewed the city one morning as the mists cleared and the white buildings were unveiled, but this was as close as he got to the city. The short distance was, however, barred by a series of mountains with steep sides and deep valleys. The mule trains again proved invaluable in supplying rations and ammunition to the forward troops, but the conditions were so taxing with the incessant rain and mud, it was even difficult for these hardy animals, which could just manage one trip per day. The main mule track was very steep where it passed the position occupied by Sergeant George Hardie and the mortar platoon. He took it upon himself to go out every night, ignoring the rain or enemy fire, to assist the mule drivers to traverse the steep section past his area. The positions on Monte Grande were exposed to enemy observers and any movement during daylight hours was usually met with shellfire. The situation worsened for the forward troops after it snowed, as the fresh earth thrown up by the men digging and maintaining their slit trenches pinpointed exactly where they were and made them an easy target for the enemy's fire. The result was that it was impossible to leave their trenches during the day and the Gordons had to sit tight shivering with the wet and cold, unable to move about to get their circulation going or generate some warmth. The rocky ground made it difficult to dig the slit trenches to any depth so it wasn't even possible to stand up without the risking a sniper's bullet or a burst of lethal Spandau fire. The Germans were, however, not the only ones who were watching and reporting on the opposite side's movements. The 67th Field Regiment (Royal Artillery) was one of the 1st Division artillery support units; in November 1944, they were supporting the 6th Battalion Gordon Highlanders. Captain Harold

Parker, an artillery observation officer from the 67th, set up his observation post in a church tower and from his vantage point he was able to spot enemy gun flashes and report these so that defensive and counter measures could be taken. Unfortunately, it was not long before the Germans worked out that his eyrie in the church tower was being used for observation of their activities and targeted it with their own artillery. The church and its tower received several direct hits but he held on, even when falling masonry and the church bells came crashing down, leaving him badly shaken and bruised. He stubbornly refused to give up his viewpoint as it was the best available and he knew anywhere else would be less satisfactory. His equipment was damaged in this strike, but he managed to repair it and continued his task; he only evacuated his post when the Gordons he was supporting were relieved. His dogged determination and courage were rewarded with the award of the Military Cross.

On 10 December 1944, Major Clapham and his escort delivered Major David Shepherd, MC, who commanded 266 Battery of the 67th Field Regiment, Royal Artillery to his observation post at Rovine on Monte Calderaro. Major Shepherd subsequently left the observation post alone to return to the Gordons HQ but was never seen again. When it was discovered that he had not arrived at his destination, the Gordons sent out a search party, but all that was found was his helmet. With no evidence of a body, it was presumed that he had been captured. David Shepherd had supported the 6th Battalion Gordon Highlanders all through Italy and played a crucial role at Anzio. It was subsequently learned that he had been ambushed by a German patrol, during which he was wounded. Sadly, he had died of his wounds in hospital on Christmas Day 1944 while prisoner of war.

The support members of the Battalion were kept busy in the mountains. Resupply of the forward positions was only possible at night while it was pitch black, when the rations could be manhandled up slippery, muddy, steep slopes, which was dangerous and exhausting work. The positions they had taken over from American units had poorly recorded mines planted in front of the positions and it was decided it was safer to locate and remove these and replace them with flares. With the ground being frozen, this was a difficult and precarious activity assigned to the Pioneers of the Battalion. During this operation, an incident occurred which could have had tragic consequences but in retrospect it was not without some comedy. As warning flares were being attached to trip wires, one flare was accidentally triggered, leaving Captain James Low and his party spotlighted out in the open. This errant flare had to be dealt with urgently, as there was no immediate cover, but someone had the bright idea of covering it with their steel helmet and then they beat a hasty retreat.

On 3 January 1945, the 6th Gordons were relieved once again and returned to Borgo San Lorenzo, where they held a combined Christmas and New Year celebration. Some leave to Florence was also possible, but by this time the 6th Battalion Gordon Highlanders were severely weakened after almost twelve months of continuous action since landing at Anzio. For example, in the months of November and December 1944, the 6th Battalion casualties amounted to eighteen killed, fifty-seven wounded and eleven missing, totalling eighty-six for all ranks. It came therefore as somewhat of a relief when they learned that their time in Italy was almost over. They left Borgo San Lorenzo three days later, travelling 100 miles south to the central-Italian city of Perugia. It was somewhat perplexing for the 6th Gordons to find themselves in this location and there was no information as to the purpose of their move, which most thought would be a short rest to resupply and take in reinforcements before a return to the front in the north of Italy. It was somewhat of a surprise therefore when they learned they were to reorganize and prepare their equipment for their sea voyage to Palestine. After a slow train journey lasting most of the day, they arrived at Taranto, where they embarked on the SS *Duchess of Richmond*. They sailed on 24 January, arriving at Haifa three days later, which was the beginning of their final chapter as a proud distinct unit.

# Chapter 11

# The Argenta Gap

After leaving Anzio, the 1st Battalion London Scottish had spent almost four months in Egypt, regrouping and training with reinforcements to bring them back to strength before rejoining the fight in Italy. As July began, it was clear that it would not be long before they were back in action and so it came to pass that on 11 July they boarded the troop ship HMT *Batory* in Alexandria and sailed in convoy for Tartanto. Events moved apace and by the end of July, they were engaged in some final training based around Tivoli, 10 miles east of Rome. Officers and men were given the opportunity to go into Rome to take in the sights and it was a great occasion when the drums and pipes played with the drums and pipes of the 6th Battalion Gordon Highlanders in a massed pipe band. This was a spectacle that was greatly appreciated by soldiers and Italians civilians alike.

The Germans had now been pushed back to the north of Italy and the 56th Division was ordered to move north. The emphasis of the next phase of the battle to liberate the whole of Italy would concentrate on the eastern side of the country, while pressure would still remain elsewhere. A reorganization of the Division meant the 1st Battalion London Scottish were now part of 167 Brigade. The eastern coastal belt was less mountainous, and if a breakthrough could be made into the Lombardy Plain, this would be much more difficult for the Germans to defend. First it was necessary to cross the mountains to Tolentino, then north, eventually reaching the front line near Morciano on 5 September. This was just 10 miles south of the tiny independent republic of San Marino. After making good progress, having travelled over 100 miles in two weeks, the enormously long column of vehicles came to a halt as the forward troops came into contact with the enemy holding Croce. It was soon discovered how vulnerable their situation was. The Division was strung out along the road which snaked along the valley of the river 'Torrente Conca'. Without warning, German artillery in the hills above the road brought their guns to bear on the convoy and created chaos as trucks tried to turn and move back or at least get off the road. Men jumped out of vehicles and scrambled for any available cover. Inevitably, there were a number of casualties, which included two London Scottish men killed. They were Captain James Hollebone, the brother of the Adjutant, Captain Derek Hollebone, and Private Arthur Baxter, who was not just mourned by his family but by the many football supporters both north and south of the Scottish border.

Once the situation was brought under control, orders were received for the 1st London Scottish to attack the ridge with the hilltop village of Il Palazzo which the enemy was holding. At a height of almost 250 metres, this position gave the Germans commanding views of the valley below. This was part of the Gothic Line, effectively almost the Germans' last line of defence in the north of Italy, where the Apennine Mountains were used to their advantage. It was almost a rerun of their previous battles in the Gustav Line, where the Germans held the high ground and were difficult to dislodge from their carefully pre-planned defensive positions, preventing any advance by the Division. The 1st London Scottish attack was begun in the early hours of 7 September and was preceded by an artillery barrage. The initial attack was successful, passing the village of Croce on the lower slopes where Sergeant Douglas Scott distinguished himself while he was responsible for his company's flank which was open to enemy action. His position was continually subjected to sniping, continual machine-gun fire and the attention of a high-velocity artillery piece, which were all concealed on the wooded slopes above him. With this level of harassment, his platoon was reduced to just eleven men, but he was determined their position would be secured. Showing great leadership and courage, he led his men to beat off the enemy counter-attacks. Two days later, he was wounded in the head and deafened by a blast, but he remained on duty, encouraging his men, and only sought medical attention when the action was complete. The attacking companies reached their objective on the hilltop very quickly, but the overall plan had not succeeded; their position on the Croce-Il Palazzo Ridge became precarious when the supporting units from the brigade were not able to secure their flanks at Ca' Menghino. This left the London Scottish forward companies in a salient exposed to attack from three sides. With Menghino dominating the 1st London Scottish positions in Il Palazzo, it could not be allowed to remain in the enemy's hands. Lieutenant Fred Forbes, who commanded a platoon of B Company, was ordered to attack it. Leading his attack through a hail of machine-gun fire, he pressed home the attack with great determination against stiff resistance. He achieved the objective, killing many of the enemy, and captured eight others together with their equipment, including their anti-tank gun, depriving the Germans of a weapon which was capable of delivering devastating fire against any target.

Around dawn the next day, the Germans launched a ferocious counter-attack with heavy artillery, mortars and withering machine-gun fire. Although this was beaten off, the London Scottish remained isolated and continual attacks against their positions took place all that day and the next. On the

9th, several direct artillery strikes on the building being used by C Company's HQ caused it to collapse and buried several men under the rubble. Despite being wounded two days earlier, when he had insisted on remaining at duty, Colour Sergeant John Thom reacted instantly and organized the survivors to assist him in digging out the men under the fallen masonry while they were still under enemy fire. Their efforts successfully rescued three men in the process, but it was discovered that the Company Commander, Major Bruce Robertson, had been killed. There were no other officers available, so John Thom did not hesitate to take control of the remnants of his Company and reorganize their defence. He was exposed to enemy fire while he led a counter-attack to drive the German attackers back and successfully held his position. The fierce fighting resulted in all of the commanders of all the forward companies becoming injured, except Captain Neil Will, who was the second-in-command of B Company. Naturally he assumed command of his own Company, then became aware he was the only surviving senior officer of the forward companies and realized that the other companies also required leadership. He made contact with the other companies and ordered Sergeant Thom to move the survivors of C Company into the defensive perimeter he had organized at Il Palazzo. Captain Will then maintained his communication with them, moving between all of the positions, apparently without regard for his own safety, coordinating the defence by all the surviving men. He ensured the men understood his orders and kept encouraging and inspiring them. On at least three occasions, the enemy had some success in infiltrating the defensive perimeter, and on all these occasions, Neil Will organized and personally led counter-attacks against these incursions to eliminate these threats. Over thirty Germans were captured in the process. Neil Will was slightly wounded in these actions but refused to be evacuated. One of Captain Will's platoon commanders, Lieutenant Fred Forbes, also showed great leadership and courage in this episode of the battle. He led a number of patrols, both by day and during the hours of darkness, to reconnoitre the enemy positions. He did so successfully without casualties, despite encountering fierce Spandau machine-gun fire on virtually every excursion. The information he was able to bring back ensured that there were no surprises on the defensive perimeter around Il Palazzo. While he and his platoon were taking cover in a house, it received two direct artillery hits, but his men's natural anxiety was averted by Fred Forbes maintaining calm during this extremely hazardous time.

During these four days, casualties were heavy and many required evacuation to the Regimental Aid Post (RAP) while there was still a need for resupply with rations and ammunition. In addition to organizing the defence, Captain Will had to be mindful of these concerns and was able to coordinate all of these activities. The RAP was dealing with the high number of casualties under the extremely difficult situation that it was also under constant fire. Captain (Doctor) James Pugh, the Medical Officer, worked tirelessly during this period despite the constant danger and saved many lives. His work continued unchecked even after the RAP took a direct hit on 8 September, a gallant action which was rewarded by him being awarded the Military Cross. The Battalion HQ was also under continuous fire and casualties resulted, but Captain Derek Hollebone put the grief of losing his brother aside and calmly and courageously ensured that the Battalion HQ functioned efficiently, even when this meant he had to expose himself to enemy fire to ensure his duties as Adjutant were fully discharged. This was made all the more difficult when the Battalion HQ was engaged in rifle fire exchanges. He too was awarded the Military Cross for his coolness that inspired those around him. The situation deteriorated as the day went on after several determined attacks by the enemy. The London Scottish were effectively cut off but still held their position. An attack was made by the 1st Welch Fusiliers to rescue the situation; after a hard fight, they managed to retake the flanking positions on the ridge, finally allowing the London Scottish to withdraw.

The obliteration of the London Scottish positions on the top of the hill at Il Palazzo was prevented by the courageous actions and leadership of Captain Neil Will, Lieutenant Fred Forbes and Colour Sergeant John Thom. These men were Territorial Army volunteers who were all civilians before the war. Neil Will (the brother of Major Ian Will, MC) was from Edinburgh and a trainee accountant; Fred Forbes, from Arbroath, worked in the office of a consultant engineer in Edinburgh; and John Thom, from Huntly, Aberdeenshire, worked in the Post Office Savings Bank in Aberdeen. For their bravery, Captain Will received the Distinguished Service Order and Colour Sergeant Thom was awarded the Distinguished Conduct Medal. Both of these decorations were, for the men's rank, the tier of gallantry award immediately below the Victoria Cross and widely considered a 'near miss' for a VC. Lieutenant Forbes's prize for his conspicuous gallantry under fire was the award of the Military Cross. This gallantry award for John Thom was the third major decoration awarded to the members of the original Number 9 Platoon of A Company. The platoon commander was Lieutenant John Gillan, who was awarded the Military Cross in July 1943. Also serving in that platoon was George Mitchell, who was awarded the Victoria Cross in January 1944. George Mitchell's brother, David Mitchell, was also a member of that same platoon. Military Medals were also awarded to Sergeants George Harley and Douglas Scott for their courageous deeds during this battle.

Over the preceding few days, the London Scottish had taken very heavy casualties with twenty-seven men killed and 218 wounded. Among the men who died in this battle for Il Palazzo was Captain J.P.O. (Pat) Russell. The tragedy for families back in Britain is illustrated by his parents' experience. While at home in Markinch, Fife, they received a telegram informing them that their second son, Pat, had died of his wounds, which was obviously a time of great sorrow. In their moment of grief their spirits were depressed by a further burden when, later that same day, they received a second telegram to inform them that Pat's older brother, David, had been wounded and was dangerously ill. Major David Russell, who was serving with the Black Watch, had previously been wounded four times, the first at El Alamein, where he was also awarded the Military Cross. Private James (Hamish) Mcleod's death was also a double blow for his family back in Aberdeen. His brother Ronald, who was serving with the 1st Battalion Gordon Highlanders, was killed in Normandy just two months earlier. Deaths on the battlefield on the Croce and Il Palazzo area did not unfortunately end after the Battalion had withdrawn from the feature. On 16 September, a week after the battle on the slopes had ended, the Battalion's Padre, Reverend Robert Macpherson, was supervising the recovery of the Battalion's dead. Despite this being believed to be a quiet area not under enemy attack, an artillery shell exploded unexpectedly and he was killed. Before the war and joining the Battalion as their Padre, Reverend Robert Macpherson had been the Church of Scotland Minister at St Adrian's Church, Pittenweem, Fife, after following his father into the Ministry.

The 56th Division pressed ahead to maintain the momentum against determined German resistance; the next objective was another hilltop village, Mulazzano, where Germans had managed to reinforce the ridge north of their next barrier, the Marano River. The river was crossed in darkness during the early hours of 16 September and they soon reached Mulazzano, which had already been captured. Private Archie Miller was in position at Casa Tramontana, a few miles north of Mulazzano, when, on 19 September, the Germans launched a counter-attack to retake the village with infantry supported by tracked vehicles. Quietly observing the scene, he noticed eight Germans enter a nearby house and he resolved to take action before they came to him. He dashed across the road, which was being swept by Spandau machine-gun fire, and burst into the house, surprising the enemy. He struck the first German with his rifle butt and broke his arm, which brought him down screaming in agony. He fired his rifle and killed another two Germans, then tossed a grenade at the others and retreated quickly to escape the blast. His quick thinking and brave action allowed the position to be restored; the German's counter-attack was beaten off and the village held. Archie had acted entirely alone and completely on his own initiative with complete disregard for his own safety. For his courageous action, he was awarded the Military Medal. The award was, however, delayed, as Archie was captured less than two weeks later and he spent the last six months of the war in Stalag VIIA (Moosburg), Bavaria.

The 1st London Scottish pressed ahead with tank support and good progress was made across the mountains, but casualties were beginning to mount up with taking the successive mountain ridges beyond Mulazzano. One of those killed in these actions was Private Tom Lyon, who was wounded at Anzio and had returned to duty after five months in hospital. In his civilian life before the war, he was a member in the Aberdeen 'Lads Club', where he was an important figure in organizing various sports competitions. The numerous casualties relied on the stretcher bearers getting them to safety and medical attention, but this also put the stretcher bearers in a dangerous situation. George Hingston, one of the Battalion's stretcher bearers, was also killed.

The Battalion pressed on as far as the small town of Savignano sul Rubicone, which was entered on 30 September, where they were greeted by heavy shelling. Further progress was impeded by the river which was swollen by the heavy rains, which had been exploited by the Germans to perform their withdrawal. The prize for the Allies was the flatter terrain beyond the river which was less easy for the enemy to defend and tanks could operate more effectively. The 1st London Scottish was ordered to cross the river and establish a bridgehead on the western side of the River Rubicone (also referred to as the River Fiumicino). The enemy shelling, sniping and high water flow made this a formidable task which had only limited success. With the river level rising constantly, the forward troops became isolated and subject to German counter-attacks. There were not enough men across the river to repel these, with the result that many men were killed or captured. Among those killed was Lieutenant Fred Forbes, whose Military Cross for his actions just a few weeks earlier at Il Palazzo had to be awarded posthumously.

The advances to this point had taken their toll, but great successes had been achieved, not least in the large numbers of prisoners taken. In their weakened state, the whole 56th Division moved into reserve positions. The 1st London Scottish travelled almost 200 miles south and were based in the small town of Puerto San Georgio on the Adriatic coast, where they remained for almost two months resting, regrouping and assimilating reinforcements to build up their numbers for a return to the battle in December. This was a pleasant interlude for the men, with free time to swim in the sea and leave being granted to visit Florence and Rome, which were now firmly in Allied hands.

It was only a matter of time, however, until the Battalion would have to rejoin the war. There was a short period of training to integrate the new recruits and ready the men for battle. The men were certainly as ready as they could be physically but inevitably there were those who were apprehensive about what lay ahead. For the new reinforcements, it was the thought of the unknown, but for even some veterans of previous conflicts, there was always a nagging worry. George Fletcher, known to his friends as 'Gat' from his forenames George Anthony Tolson, confided in his friend Keith Spooner than he had a premonition that he would not make it through the next battle. The battalion moved the 130 miles north, up the east coast of Italy, to south of Faenza in mid-December 1944. This town was located at the edge of the Lombardy Plain which, although much flatter, was intersected by many rivers draining the mountains to the south and north into the mighty River Po. The history of flooding which had created this vast alluvial plain had forced previous generations to construct high flood banks, which were now being used by the Germans as key defensive positions. The rivers, already swollen by the incessant winter rains, initially made progress with the imperative to cross the rivers slower than had been anticipated. These embankments were also a barrier to the progress of Allied tanks.

The first attack which involved the 1st London Scottish was supporting the New Zealanders along the Lamone River. It was during these operations that there was another tragedy for Colour Sergeant John Thom, DCM, when, on 22 December, he was seriously wounded by a mine, resulting in him losing his leg. A very brave soldier's war had come to an end. On the afternoon of Christmas Day 1944, two signalmen, George Fletcher and Jim Rennie, MM, went forward to lay a telephone line between D Company's HQ and a forward platoon in the hamlct of Pila di St Andrea, on the banks of the Naviglione Canal. This was a regular task for the signallers, who had to continually repair lines damaged by artillery or mortar fire. Although routine, it could be a dangerous operation as it involved going forward where there was little cover and tracing the line until the break could be located and then a repair effected by rejoining the wires. On this occasion, the line extended some 600 metres, and before the work had been completed, the two men were caught by a mortar strike. George Fletcher was struck in the back of his head by shrapnel and died almost instantly. Jim Rennie was hit in his hip and ankle but ignored his wounds and managed to finish laying the line and setting up a field telephone in the platoon's position. On testing he found that the new line had been severed by enemy fire, so he retraced it back and made the necessary repairs before retreating to safety. He was then evacuated to hospital for treatment. George (Gat) Fletcher's premonition had been realized, but there was still great sadness among his fellow signallers. Keith Spooner was allowed to attend his burial service, conducted at Forli Cemetery by the Battalion's new Padre, who curiously shared the same surname, the Reverend John Fletcher, a Church of Scotland Minister whose parish was in Lockerbie. One small consolation was the news that Jim Rennie had been awarded a bar to his Military Medal, the only man of the London Scottish to be distinguished in this way. This was well deserved for his devotion to duty in restoring communications at a critical time, while he himself had been wounded.

As the year turned, the weather became more settled with bright weather and hard frosts firming up the ground, meaning the country was now ideally suited for the use of tanks. An offensive with a tank assault began on the night of 3 January with infantry support. An advance of several thousand metres was achieved, with numerous Germans taken prisoner; the 1st London Scottish came to a halt just short of the River Senio. The river remained a barrier to any further advance and, except for occasional rest breaks out of the line, this remained their position for the next two months. There was active patrolling by both sides, which sometimes created violent clashes. During this period, Corporal David Bruce led over thirty such patrols. On 23 February, his platoon was part of an attack to reach the river when his sergeant was wounded and he had to take charge. He reorganized the men and arranged to have a tunnel dug into the riverbank for cover. They were subjected to grenades being thrown from the enemy positions only about 20 metres away and they were fully aware these could collapse the tunnel and bury them at any time. They, however, had a supply of grenades themselves, and Corporal Bruce distributed these among his men. They were all used in their own defence during the thirty-six hours they were pinned down in their position. On another patrol, on 11 March 1944, which was led by Lance Corporal Edward Erskine-White, they boldly raided a German forward post and seized a prisoner, who it was hoped would give up valuable intelligence on the deployment of the Germans behind the river. Attacks by divisional troops successfully achieved a crossing of the River Senio. The nature of war meant that catastrophe could strike at any time; exactly one month later, on 11 April, Corporal Erskine-White was killed along with eight others in an attack across the River Reno, near Lake Comacchio.

Lake Comacchio lay close to the coast of the Adriatic Sea, from which it was separated by a 6-mile-long, 1-mile-wide spit of land. This area was seen of strategic significance as it lay just north of where the River Reno flowed into the sea. This position was held by a significant number of German troops and supplies, and so presented a threat to the right flank of the Allied advance. As part of a larger combined Commando force, No. 9 Commando was tasked with eliminating the enemy from a part of this area. The operation took place over the period from 1–4 April 1945. This was no easy task. To get into position for their attack, the Commandos had to cross the shallow brackish lake in small boats which had to be paddled and pushed for a distance of over 1 mile before the attack could be launched. As a result, the men were exhausted even before the battle had begun. Colour Sergeant George Reace was a London Scottish man who was attached to the Commandos and played a significant part in the success of this operation. In the initial advance, the troop HQ was heavily mortared and George was seriously wounded in his groin. Although in considerable pain, he carried on, fearing that if he made his injury known the advance would be stalled while unit responsibilities were re-allocated. This would allow time for the Germans to regroup, with the element of surprise being lost. Initially the operation went well; numerous Germans were taken prisoner and much of their equipment destroyed. While other sections of the force dealt with the remaining enemy points of resistance, Sergeant Reace was left with two other men to guard around eighty prisoners. The enemy then attacked his position with mortars and mounted a counter-attack to liberate his captives. Keeping a cool head, he organized their defence, kept control of their prisoners and drove off the attack, with the operation netting 100 prisoners of war in total. Even after the operation was almost at an end, he had to be ordered to report himself wounded so that he could be evacuated for medical treatment, but he refused as there was no other senior NCO to replace him. Such was his devotion to duty, skill, and daring of his actions that he was awarded a Distinguished Conduct Medal.

On the night of 5–6 of April 1945, the 1st Battalion London Scottish undertook a crossing of the River Reno in rafts. There was a difficulty almost immediately with an insufficient number of rafts. Once the first wave was across the river, the second wave was hampered as their boats had not been brought up to the riverbank in case they would hinder the first wave's embarkation. Speed was of the essence and it was essential that the second wave cross the river quickly to support the initial wave. Colour Sergeant John Duncan immediately recognized the problem and, without any hesitation and on his own initiative, dived into the freezing cold water and swam across some 60 metres of open water to the other side of the river to retrieve a raft from the first wave. He achieved this successfully but not without difficulty, as the boat had no paddles. Unperturbed, he returned, just pushing the raft in front of him. The river was continually under mortar and small-arms fire, but this did not deter him in any way. Once the men were on board, he entered the river again and pushed them across, returning to the south bank and making three such crossings while the crossing point was under fire. He then turned his attention to assisting in the deployment the rest of the Company, using the boats which had been initially held back. As was to be expected in an attack such as this, the initial assaulting troops suffered many casualties and the stretcher bearers who had crossed the river were overwhelmed trying to treat and evacuate the wounded and called for support. Sergeant Duncan was on the task immediately and organized a party of men to assist and personally supervised the evacuation of a dozen men and tended to other wounded men while he waited for more stretcher bearers. Unbelievably, his sterling work didn't stop there, and he continued to assist in ferrying ammunition and rations over the river to the forward troops. CSM John Duncan was awarded a Distinguished Conduct Medal for his devotion to duty, inspiring all around him and a complete disregard for his own safety to ensure the operation was successful. John Duncan was not only an excellent swimmer but also had other talents, being a proficient musician. He was the Bass Drummer in the Battalion Pipe Band and had played the cornet in the Salvation Army Band in Renfrew before the war.

The NCO who was nominally in charge of the raft crossings was Sergeant Reginald Low, but his orders were changed. In the confusion of the battle and the urgency of his new role, the importance of the organization of the boat supply had been overlooked. Reg Low was instructed to assist in neutralizing another threat to the river crossing. Although, by the morning of 6 April, infantry were firmly established across the river, an enemy strong point remained on the far side of the River Reno; this was still shelling and mortaring the crossing site and the location where the sappers were endeavouring to erect a temporary bridge. The bridge was seen as essential to allow significant reinforcements and armour to cross. To eliminate the threat this remaining enemy position posed, tanks were summoned, but the high flood-prevention embankment obscured their view of the target and they had no way of directing their fire effectively. Reg Low was ordered to go and act as their forward observer. He had to climb up the embankment, which meant he was exposed to enemy fire, to observe where the tanks' shells were landing, then communicate this to the tank commanders so that they could redirect their fire onto the enemy position. Sergeant Low did this without question and got into position on top of the bank, despite being sprayed with Spandau machine-gun and small-rocket fire from *panzerschrecks*. These were a relatively light anti-tank rocket launcher, similar to the American bazooka, used to good effect by the German infantry. His spotting was so good that the enemy position was soon subjected to a heavy, accurate bombardment by the tanks and the Germans surrendered. For his actions this day and previous gallant service in forward positions, Reginald Low was awarded the Military Medal.

Over on the northern side of the river, hard fighting was taking place. On 7 April, there was still a point of significant enemy resistance, situated in a bulge in the flood bank, which had been unsuccessfully attacked four times, resulting in numerous casualties to D Company. Lieutenant Arthur Fraser was ordered to take his platoon and make a fifth attempt. The platoon moved forward on foot along the base of the flood bank, where they were subjected to attacks with grenades and a *panzerschreck*. Lieutenant Fraser was slightly wounded by grenade shrapnel and their advance was stalled. John McElroy, who had been promoted to sergeant, leading the platoon HQ and reserve section, identified that the position which was the focus of their attack was being backed up by several supporting positions. To counter these, he immediately ordered his reserve section to attack and silence them. Ignoring the danger, Corporal David Hoy was then able to lead his section forward under the murderous fire. He charged up the steep embankment alone and into the enemy position, attacking them in their dugouts with his Tommy gun and grenades. He was almost immediately joined by Lieutenant Fraser also storming the position while firing from the hip. Sergeant McElroy then moved to the main objective, joining in the hand-to-hand fighting. The rest of the men were then motivated to follow up and take the position, killing two Germans, wounding ten and capturing over thirty others, including their officer. They also captured numerous automatic weapons, a *panzerschreck* and a mortar. Lieutenant Arthur Fraser shrugged off his wound until the next day when it became apparent, even to him, that treatment had become necessary. For their courageous actions, Lieutenant Arthur Fraser was decorated with the Military Cross, while Sergeant John McElroy and Corporal David Hoy received the Military Medal.

The fighting to take control of the north bank of the River Reno continued for several days. On the afternoon of 11 April 1945, the Germans were still holding a stretch of the river embankment and several houses which formed fortified strong points. Despite the German position dominating the area, B Company were ordered to put in an attack over the open ground. Accurate artillery, mortar and Spandau machine-gun fire resulted in the section under the command of Corporal John Rubie being pinned down. There was a total lack of cover and some men tried to occupy some abandoned German positions, but these were booby trapped and several casualties resulted. John Rubie reorganized his section and they returned fire, giving some respite, but it was impossible to move in the absence of cover and they knew they had to hold on until nightfall. However, in order to keep the Germans' heads down, they were using a considerable amount of ammunition and their supply was running short. John Rubie volunteered to rush back across the 500 metres of open ground, which was being continually swept by lethal fire, to fetch ammunition and deliver messages on the situation to the Company HQ. He did this twice until darkness allowed them all to withdraw, but they had taken heavy casualties. Some thirty men were evacuated through the aid post where Private John Broadley undertook to carry the casualties; Jeeps were waiting to get the men away for treatment. Each evacuation entailed a journey on foot of 1500 metres, across ground where enemy fire was still a danger, to the waiting Jeeps. His diligence and courage was recognized with a Military Medal. John Rubie was also awarded with the Military Medal for his coolness under fire and courageous acts to save his men. These eight men, one officer, six NCOs and a private were all recognized for their significant contribution to the success of the operation on the banks of the River Reno. Their decorations were all well-deserved and entirely in the finest traditions of the regiment of the Gordon Highlanders and of the British Army. However, these were just exemplars of the many individual brave acts which were undertaken to achieve eventual victory, including the selfless actions of the many stretcher bearers, but many others went unrecognized and unrecorded.

The war in Italy continued for only a short period after the Allies had achieved access to the flatter land where the Allied air forces could exact a terrible toll on German units caught in the open, fleeing north. The River Po was the last major obstacle for the Allies to cross, but by this time, the Germans were a beaten army. Almost all of the bridges across this wide river had been demolished which, although intended to impede the advance of the Allies, meant the Germans were also unable to cross with their own heavy weapons. The Germans surrendered in droves, and it was obvious it was all but over. The battalion crossed the mighty River Po, the largest river in Italy, in amphibious DUKWs on 27 April 1945. By this time, the war had moved on and the crossing was uneventful, but the colossal carnage of German troops and machines was in evidence everywhere.

# Chapter 12

# 'In the Bag' (Prisoners of War)

As a consequence of their circumstances during the course of a battle, soldiers were liable to be captured and become prisoners of war (PoWs). This was generally very far from their thoughts going into battle and the obvious outcomes such as wounding or death would be uppermost in their minds. Few ever thought they would end up in enemy hands as PoWs. The 6th Battalion Gordon Highlanders had, by a quirk of a decision of the army high command, been dealt a 'get out of jail card' in March 1940 when they were transferred out of the 51st (Highland) Division. Just three months later, the 6th Battalion Gordon Highlanders were evacuated at Dunkirk as part of Operation Dynamo with most of the rest of the British Expeditionary Force (BEF). However, the entire 51st (Highland) Division, which was under French Army command and detached from the rest of the BEF, was forced to surrender at St Valery-en-Caux on 12 June 1940. These men were ordered to surrender and there was little choice, although a tiny number did make escape attempts. The majority of the men of the 1st and 5th Battalions spent the next five years in German PoW camps: Oflags for officers and Stalags for the other ranks. There were some exceptions such as Walter Philips who did not surrender at St Valery but got away before being rounded up.

Walter Philips managed to evade capture at St Valery and got to Caen. He joined forces with some other escapers from Royal Army Service Corps (RASC) but they were all captured trying to get away by boat. They were taken to join hundreds of other captured British and Allied soldiers who the Germans had assembled to transport to PoW camps. While they were being marched towards Rouen, Walter and two friends waited until the guards were distracted, then jumped into a roadside ditch and hid until the rest of the column passed by. Unfortunately, shortly afterwards, Walter fell ill, probably from drinking ditch water, but was helped by some local civilians and stayed with a French family for three months, working on a farm near Camembert, the area of Normandy world-famous for the production of a distinctive soft cheese. His presence was known to the local French authorities and Gendarmes visited him regularly. One day, men from the French Resistance came from Paris to take his photo to arrange false identity papers, but before these were available, he was betrayed and rounded up by the Germans. He was taken to Trun a few miles away, where he was interned for a year. His friends at Camembert did not abandon him and they contacted the resistance movement in Paris. He was subsequently visited by a girl from an escape organization and taken to Paris, where he was hidden, then joined two RAF flight sergeants who were also evaders. With false papers, they were guided by a resistance courier by train to Marseilles, then on to Nimes and Perpignan. This journey was very dangerous both for the escapers and the resistance guide. The last leg of the journey in France was by car to the foothills of the Pyrenees, where a guide took him and four others over the mountains to Figueras, Spain. Spain was officially a neutral country during the Second World War, but the Fascist Government of General Francisco Franco was sympathetic to the Germans and was anti-British. Fortunately, the recent Spanish Civil War meant that not all of the Spanish people were of the same mind, and this was particularly the case in northern Spain. The escape line extended down through Spain and they boarded a train to Barcelona, where the guard allowed them on the train even though he knew they were British servicemen escaping from the Germans. They travelled to Madrid, where they stayed for six weeks while the British Consul organized their travel to Gibraltar. Once a berth aboard a Royal Navy ship bound for Britain was available, Walter sailed from Gibraltar and returned to Gourock on 7 March 1942. After the war, on the 10th anniversary commemoration by the 51st (Highland) Division of the surrender at St Valery-en-Caux, Walter Philips went back to Normandy and met up with Mademoiselle Gemaine Charpinno, who, with her friends, helped to hide him from the Gestapo in 1940. It was a happy and an emotional reunion.

Private William Donald was captured at St Valery-en-Caux, Normandy, on 12 June 1940. Like the thousands of other men captured there, he was marched up through northern France towards Belgium and Holland on their way to PoW camps in Germany and Poland. After eleven days of marching, the column of men was approaching St Pol, Normandy. Bill Donald was with his friend, Jimmy Beattie, who he had trained with when they both joined the army. They were also determined to escape and as they marched Jimmy suggested a bend in the road up ahead of them where there was thick hedging running at right angles away from the road. As they reached the bend, where the guards behind could not see them and the guards in front had their backs to them, they ran down the side road, their dash for freedom being obscured by the roadside hedge. They later made significant progress south on stolen bicycles all the way to the Demarcation Line, which separated the German-occupied France from Vichy France, nominally free France, but in reality a puppet state answerable to the Germans. They eventually got to Spain but had several bad experiences with the Spanish police; with the intervention of the British Consul, they too returned to Britain in August 1942, with Bill Donald receiving a mention in dispatches for his valiant adventures escaping from the enemy.

However, not all of the men of the 6th Battalion were evacuated from Dunkirk. The 6th Battalion were fully engaged in fighting the German Army in Belgium and there were the inevitable casualties of killed and wounded, but some were also captured. The German offensive on 10 May 1940 plunged the British Expeditionary Force (BEF) into an unequal struggle. They were outnumbered and equipped with inferior and outdated weapons and were quickly overwhelmed by the German Blitzkrieg. On 16 May, following an air raid on the 6th Gordons' position on the Dyle, Private George Thomson was posted missing. His family were notified but had the anxious wait for almost three months until they were notified he had been captured and was a prisoner of war at Stalag XXA (Thorn), Poland.

The encounter with the Germans at Hem, the scene of the abortive patrol, resulted in some men captured as well as those killed and wounded. One of the men captured here was Private Thomas Gray, whose twin brother, Leslie, was also serving with the 6th Battalion. Leslie continued to serve with the battalion until he too was captured at Anzio, in February 1944. Tom Gray was taken to Stalag 344 (Lamsdorf) where he spent the next five years as a PoW. William (Wally) Milton was also captured and taken to Lamsdorf. After his capture at Hem on 24 May 1940, 2nd Lieutenant Harry Shand's injuries were treated and he was transferred to Oflag VIIB (Eischstatt), where he remained for the duration of the war. Robert Frame, who was wounded more seriously when captured with Lieutenant Harry Shand, had a remarkable experience. After he was captured, he was taken by the Germans to a Red Cross *lazarette* in a Jesuit monastery at Maastricht. He was treated there and given good care along with other wounded British and German soldiers. He was then transferred to Calvarienberg Hospital, Maastricht, on 28 September 1940. During his time in the Red Cross *lazarette*, Robert made a great impression on some of the nurses, including a volunteer trainee nurse, Hendrien Julicher, and a local priest, Father Peters. This led to them continuing to write letters to him while he was in Calvarienberg Hospital. One nurse even arranged to visit him and give him sweets. Naturally he was also receiving correspondence and gifts of cigarettes, etc., from his family back in Shotts, Lanarkshire. He was also visited twice a week by a young nurse, Antoinette, who bought him sausage rolls as her father was a baker. In December 1940, he became the last British PoW remaining in the hospital and was grateful for a stream of letters from his family and local people, including Sister Klynen, who sent chocolates and mints and promised to send him books in English. News spread about him being the last British soldier who was a patient in the hospital and local people, including many children, sent cards and fruit. Sadly, Robert Frame died of his wounds on 5 June 1941, just two days before his twenty-third birthday. The German commander, Hauptman (Captain) Diett, decided that, 'friend or foe', Robert should be given a dignified funeral with full military honours. This met with the mood of local people who lined the streets of Maastricht as his cortege drove to the local cemetery. Robert was buried on his birthday. The Germans did not allow any civilians into the cemetery to witness the funeral but Antoinette ordered a wreath from a local florist and asked that it should be placed on his grave. Although requested not to do so, the florist put a card with her name on the wreath and she was interviewed by the Gestapo asking why she would do such a thing for an enemy soldier. She replied she would have done it for anyone, Dutch, British or German. The Gestapo officer concluded his questioning by saying, 'You are an international one sister, you can go', and she was released.

Remarkably, after the war, in February 1946, Robert's family back in Scotland received a letter from Vienna written by a former German soldier, Karl Ihl, who explained he was stationed in Maastricht in 1940 and 1941 and was involved in arranging the military funeral for Robert. He too had also been touched by Robert's situation, being ill in hospital for so long, and took the trouble to obtain his home address so he could write to his family. He knew he would be in serious trouble with the Gestapo if he had tried to write during the war, so would have to write after the war. To Robert's family's great delight, Karl enclosed photos of the funeral ceremony with his letter. Unfortunately, Robert's mother had died in 1944 so did not hear the full circumstances of her son's fate but the letter and photographs were gratefully received by his father and the rest of the family. Antoinette, the young nurse who visited him, also wrote to the family after the war and invited them to visit her in Belgium and this friendship continued for many years afterwards.

In December 1941, the Japanese bombed Singapore and Pearl Harbor virtually simultaneously, signalling the start of the war in the Pacific. The Japanese advance down the Malayan Peninsula stunned the British and just a mere ten weeks after they invaded Thailand and Malaya, Singapore surrendered. It is perhaps somewhat ironic that the men of the 6th Battalion who were posted to the 2nd Battalion had been evacuated from Dunkirk, escaping capture by the Germans, were taken prisoner by the Japanese when the colony capitulated on 15 February 1942.

The Japanese were a cruel and uncaring enemy and chose to totally ignore the provisions of the Geneva Convention, which they had signed but failed to ratify. Their prisoners had a horrific time. All of the former 6th Battalion men who were transferred to the 2nd Battalion were forced to work on the Thai-Burma Railway. There they were fed insufficient rations that invariably caused malnutrition; suffered various tropical diseases, such as malaria, dysentery and typhoid; and were regularly subjected to brutal beatings at the hands of callous guards. After completion of the railway in October 1943, some men were transported to Japan in filthy, overcrowded ships, appropriately known as 'hellships', on which many died when these were torpedoed by American submarines or carrier based planes. The ships carried no markings, so the Americans had no knowledge these ships were carrying Allied PoWs. Seventy-two Gordon Highlanders died in this way, although many more were transported on these vessels but were rescued from the sea after their ship was sunk. William Davidson from Insch, Aberdeenshire was en-route to Japan on the *Hofuku Maru* when it was sunk on 21 September 1944 by US planes. In August 1942, while a PoW in Singapore, William had selflessly donated blood, when his own health was somewhat precarious under the control of the Japanese, to assist in the treatment of Lieutenant Derek Stewart who had been wounded during an operation, demanded by the Japanese, to defuse land mines. Men were not only sent to Japan after their ordeal in Thailand. Of the survivors, some, including Robert Anderson, were sent to Saigon, in what was then known as Indo-China. Although only one of the former 6th Battalion men sent to Singapore died, almost 400 of the 2nd Gordons died at the hands of the Japanese, mostly while they were their PoWs, when they were expected to protect them.

Prior to the Japanese attack on Singapore and Pearl Harbor, Britain, with its Empire and Commonwealth, stood alone against the twin threat of the Germans and Italians. The war was being prosecuted in North Africa, initially with stunning success against the Italians until they were reinforced by the German Afrika Corps. In the Mediterranean, the war in Europe was still largely being prosecuted by hit-and-run raids, such as the Commando Raid on the Messina–Palermo Railway Bridge in Sicily in August 1941.

After their capture in Sicily in September 1941, Robert Brown and John Fergusson were taken to PoW camps on the Italian mainland. They were held in Campo PG (*Prigione di Guerra*, or 'Prison of War') 78 (Sulmona) located in a rural mountainous area in Abruzzo, just outside the town of Fonte d' Amore, which is about 100 miles east of Rome. This camp was originally built during the First World War to hold German PoWs and had very tight security as it held many men who had previously escaped from other PoW camps. It was a sort of Italian version of Colditz, housing what they considered were the 'difficult' prisoners. When Italy capitulated to the Allies on 8 September

1943, the Italian guards left their posts and the camp commander told his inmates that they were no longer PoWs and were free to leave. Initially the PoWs assumed they had just to sight tight and wait for the Allies to arrive and liberate the camp. However, it soon became clear that the Germans had other plans. They immediately rushed to occupy the country and prevent the wholesale return of Allied PoWs to the war. When this news reached the camp, there was a mad rush to escape before the Germans arrived. This was, perhaps, the largest PoW breakout during the whole of the Second World War. With only a few hours to spare, thousands started to climb Mount Moroné behind the camp. This mountain was all loose shale and boulders rising steeply to a summit of 2,500 metres, which meant climbing was arduous and it took many hours to complete the ascent. The Germans arrived while many men were still climbing, and it was terrifying as the Germans started shooting at them from below. Many PoWs surrendered and were recaptured quickly. John Ferguson was able to evade recapture and made it back to Allied lines where he was repatriated. Unfortunately for Robert Brown, he was recaptured and sent to Stalag IVB (Muhlberg) Germany and then to Stalag 344 (Lamsdorf) Poland, in Military District VIII (Breslau), where he remained until the end of the war in Europe.

Escape was generally the only way men were saved from years of incarceration. However, for some lucky soldiers, being captured was not a sentence to the rest of the war behind barbed wire. For example, Leslie Tromans was among the 6th Battalion Gordon Highlanders who had been listed as 'missing' on 19 April 1943. He had been taken prisoner during one of the fighting patrols which were undertaken prior to the main offensive on 23 April. His period of captivity was, however, short, as he was liberated from enemy hands during the Allied drive for Tunis and the final collapse of the Axis forces in North Africa. Irrespective of the length of time in enemy hands, it was never an appealing proposition as the PoW's treatment and fate were uncertain and completely at the discretion of his captors. However, Leslie's experience was not altogether typical; the ebb and flow of war could result in men from both sides being captured and liberated depending on the success of their comrades. His return to the battalion was marked by the honour of being one of only twenty-eight representatives of the 6th Battalion to take part in the victory parade in Tunis, marching within the ranks of the whole 1st Division, where the salute was taken by American General Dwight D. Eisenhower, Supreme Allied Commander. Leslie proudly wrote home to tell his parents that they might be able to spot him in the newsreel shown in their local cinema.

During the attack on the enemy positions over the River Simeto in Sicily in mid-July 1943, a number of men of the 1st London Scottish were captured. Their experiences were varied, with some having better luck than others. Lieutenant Colin Duff and Private David Dalrymple were both wounded when they were captured. After some interrogation, they were taken for medical treatment in a German-run military hospital in Messina. When the Germans started to withdraw across the Straits of Messina to the Italian mainland, they were hidden by a sympathetic Italian doctor and were subsequently able to escape and return to the Battalion in mid-August. It was recognized that they were still not fully recovered from their wounds and they were immediately sent off for further medical treatment. Corporal Ferdinand Townsley and Lance Corporal James Cowie were held as PoWs in Italian hands, and were liberated by the Allies before they could be moved off the island; so they were also able to return to duty with the battalion fairly quickly. Corporal Ian Walker and Private James Lockerbie were not so fortunate and were transferred to Germany as PoWs. Corporal Walker was held at Stalag 344 (Lamsdorf), but he had been wounded and as a consequence he was repatriated back to Britain, being unfit for further military service. This was a process governed by the Geneva Convention where men who were determined to be medically unfit for further military service were examined by a 'mixed medical board' and certified as such. There were some obvious examples such as men with amputated limbs who would never serve again, but it was not always as clear cut; some men may have had a chronic illness. These men were usually repatriated as part of a prisoner exchange through a neutral country, such as Sweden. Ian Walker was subsequently discharged from the army on 24 April 1945, i.e., before the defeat of Germany. His comrade James Lockerbie was the least fortunate of those captured that day. He remained a PoW in Stalag 18A (Wolfsberg) Germany until the end of the war. The camp was liberated on 11 May 1945 by British forces. The PoWs had already taken control of the camp three days earlier, on the day of the German surrender, when the camp commander handed over control of the camp to the senior British officer. The PoWs disarmed their guards in a peaceful transition.

The objective of an operation by the 1st Battalion London Scottish on 11 January 1944 was to eliminate German forces from the south bank of the River Garigliano. This was codenamed Operation Haybag and involved attacking a German fortified farm. The attack was initially successful, but the casualties were so high that only a small force was holding the position when the Germans counter-attacked and it was retaken, with further casualties resulting. Among these were a group of eight men captured. After their capture, these men also had mixed fortunes. Robert King and Victor Berryman both succumbed to their injuries and died in German hands within two days. John Keith was also seriously injured; after treatment, the German doctor considered him well enough to be transferred to Stalag IVB (Muhlberg) in Saxony, the largest PoW camp in Germany. Unfortunately, he died five months after his capture and was initially buried in the cemetery in Neuburxdorf, where there were many burials from the camp. After the war his remains were reinterred in the Military Cemetery in Berlin.

Leslie Ireland was uninjured when he was captured; while he was being taken on a train to a PoW camp, it was attacked by the RAF. In all the confusion, he managed to escape and found his way to Rome, which was still under German occupation. Unluckily, he was recaptured and taken to a prison at Laterina, south of Florence, then held at Feldpost 31979. On 18 July 1944, when the PoWs were being marched through the town to the railway station and bound for PoW camps in Germany, he slipped out of the column and hid in a doorway. After the column had passed by, he checked his surroundings and when the coast was clear, he got away. He managed to link up with partisans in the area and fought with them until Allied forces reached him in Quota, 40 miles south of Florence, on 28 August 1944. He was mentioned in dispatches for his courage and devotion to duty. Five of his comrades, Privates John Kydd, Robert Park, J. Devin, W. Donnely and H. Purdie, were all transported to various PoW camps in Germany where they remained until liberated by the Allies in April 1945.

Anzio, 4 February 1944, was almost certainly the worst day in the history of both the 6th Gordons and 1st London Scottish during the Second World War. Hundreds of men were killed, wounded and captured, but casualties continued to mount during the many battles to hold and expand the bridgehead at Anzio. One of the best accounts of a Gordon Highlander captured at Anzio comes in a letter that was written after the war by Corporal William Duncan of the 6th Gordons and is now part of the collection of the Gordon Highlanders Museum.

Corporal Willie Duncan was a section leader in B Company and so was one of the 6th Battalion survivors of the battle of the Campoleone salient at Anzio which took place on 3–4 February 1944. Like the rest of his Company he was detached to assist a squadron of the 1st Recce Regiment. The night of 7 February was clear, with bright moonlight. The company moved forward to a position north of Padiglione and were easily observed by the enemy; when they attempted to dig in, their position was heavily shelled. In the early hours of the next morning, Corporal Duncan was ordered to take some men and collect the platoon's rations and some ammunition which had been brought up to their vicinity by Bren gun carriers. They used the natural ditches and drainage channels to give them cover and successfully collected the rations and returned to their position; to their horror, they found the entire platoon had been captured and there were Germans occupying their trenches. Willie

Duncan was carrying a box of 'compo' rations on his shoulder, so when he was surprised by the Germans, he was unable to do anything but surrender. The platoon commander was Lieutenant Norman Deboys who, in civilian life, was a well-known sportsman and musician in his hometown of Carnoustie, Angus. He worked for the D.C. Thomson Newspaper Group in Dundee as a reporter on the *Sunday Post,* but on this occasion, he became the news when his capture was reported in the newspaper he worked on.

With his remaining comrades, Corporal Willie Duncan was led away down a ditch towards the German lines. On the way there, they found a wounded German, a wounded corporal of the Queen's Royal Regiment and a badly wounded major of the Recce Regiment, as well as several dead bodies. They carried the wounded with them to get them some medical attention. On their journey came under fire from British artillery that was targeting German tanks in a nearby wood. They all dived for cover, except the men carrying the wounded, who just carried on as if nothing had happened. Luckily none of the shells fell on the road and nobody was hurt. The Queen's Regiment corporal died en-route but they eventually they did come to a German first aid post and handed over the two wounded for treatment. Sadly, after a short time, both were declared dead.

The prisoners were then taken up to a quarry in the Alban Hills and held there for two days. They were thoroughly dispirited in the cold and wet with no shelter from the incessant rain. The Germans did not provide any food until the second day and even forbade them from opening their own compo rations, as they were suspicious they might contain explosives. On the third day, they were loaded onto open lorries, taken further up into the hills and held in an abandoned film studio. Here they were mixed with some men of the Guards Brigade and a number of American Texas Rangers. After a relatively short period of time, they were transported to a railway station and given a small loaf of bread and a tin of bully beef which they were told had to last them two days; being already very hungry, most men ate this on the first day. They were then herded onto cattle waggons, forty-five men to a waggon, and taken in this to Germany.

The journey was very uncomfortable as they were overcrowded, with no toilet facilities except a small barrel in the middle of the waggon, which stank before long. The train did stop briefly once, where they were given a bowl of millet gruel and a cup of coffee, which did a little to improve their situation as they were very stiff with lack of movement and the cold. This was particularly severe as they crossed from Italy into Austria through the Brenner Mountain Pass, which is at an altitude of 1370 metres. The temperature was sub-zero, resulting in some of the men getting frost bite. On the third day, 2 March

1944, they arrived at their destination, the guards ordered them out of the waggons and they marched to Stalag IVB (Muhlberg) in Saxony. At this camp, they were processed. After giving their name, rank and number, they were photographed and given a PoW number, which replaced their British Army service number and was used in all correspondence with the PoW's family or for German administration and Red Cross purposes to identify them. Willie Duncan only spent a few weeks here and at the end of March 1944 was moved to Stalag XXA (Thorn) in Poland. However, as he was an NCO, he was not required to work as all lower ranks were compelled to do, so was transferred to a camp for NCOs. One of the first people Willie Duncan encountered after he marched through the gates of Stalag 357 (Fallingbostel) was Sergeant Willie Ogg, a man he knew well and who was also from the Banffshire town of Keith. Sergeant Ogg had been attached to the brigade HQ when the 6th Battalion was still with the 51st (Highland) Division in France in 1940. He had remained with the Highland Division when the 6th Battalion was transferred to the 1st Division in March 1940, so was captured at St Valery-en-Caux when the Division was stranded there on 12 June 1940. While in Stalag 357 (Fallingbostel), Willie Ogg was not the only familiar face. Willie Duncan associated with Sergeant Bobby Mitchell and Corporal Charlie Gillies, who were also captured at Anzio. Both were serving with the 1st London Scottish when they were captured. Charlie Gillies was from Buckie, Banffshire, where Willie Duncan was born, and they had both joined the 6th Battalion Gordon Highlanders (TA) in April 1939; they already knew each other well. Charlie was transferred to the London Scottish during the war.

Another man captured at Anzio was Buckie-born Lieutenant William (Bill) Dallas who, prior to joining the army in 1941, was a school teacher living in Stirling. On 3 February, Lieutenant Dallas was ordered to make a night patrol to ascertain where the Germans were. His patrol was ambushed and apart from himself, every soldier in his patrol was killed. The Germans had thrown hand grenades at them and in one of these explosions he was wounded in the back and thigh by shrapnel. His injuries were to such an extent that he could not move and he lay in a ditch all night. In the morning of 4th February, while he was still lying immobilized, a German Tiger tank bore down upon him and he was sure this was the end as he thought it would run over him. Fortunately, the driver evaded him and he was taken prisoner by the infantry soldiers following behind the tank. They took him to a German aid post where a German military surgeon operated on him to remove the shrapnel. While immensely grateful for the medical attention, the experience was quite harrowing as the procedure was undertaken without anaesthetic; with the large number of casualties on both sides, they had run out. After time to recover enough to talk, Bill Dallas was interrogated by a German officer, who showed some empathy as it turned out he too was a school teacher in civilian life.

Just three days later, his wife, Mairi, received the unwelcome, but inevitable, notice from the War Office informing her that her husband had been posted missing, but this could mean he was wounded, a PoW, both or, even worse, killed. She immediately wrote to the Reverend Robin Gilmour, the 6th Battalion Gordons Padre and a personal friend, to ask him if he was able to provide any further details about the circumstances concerning her husband's fate. He answered her on 25 February, writing, 'The Gordons had a terrible night and day and had losses that nearly broke our hearts. I found out Bill's company had gone…the information was that the company had been surrounded and captured entire…I reckon his chances of being a prisoner are good.' This was reassuring news, but better news came shortly afterwards as an announcement was heard on the German-controlled Radio Rome, 'Lieutenant William Davidson Dallas, 267307, Stirling, Scot was a prisoner.' This message was heard by Mr. J. Robertson who was a pharmacist in St Andrews, where Bill Dallas's mother then lived. He recognized the name and telephoned her to give her the good news, which was immediately passed on to Bill's wife. Another radio message also reported that Private Vernon Ross was also a prisoner. Vernon was also a 6th Battalion soldier, from Aberdeen, who was reported missing on 4 February at Anzio. Like Mairi, his family were also relieved and delighted but they were cautioned by the War Office that these enemy-controlled radio messages could not be wholly relied on. However, Vernon's parents were wholly convinced the communication had been dictated by their son, as in his message he had said, 'My love to the kiddies.' Shortly afterwards, Mairi Dallas received a postcard from Bill, in his own handwriting, stating, 'I am a prisoner – slightly wounded in German captivity but in perfect health.' At last she could breathe a sigh of relief. Vernon Ross's family also received a similar message giving confirmation that he was alive, safe but a PoW. Although Radio Rome was broadcasting information as propaganda, several other families were still very pleased to hear the news about their relative. It was through such a broadcast that Arthur McKenzie recorded a message for his parents confirming his capture but they were also surprised to hear that he also mentioned that his cousin, John (Ian) Longmore was with him.

This was not the end of Lieutenant Bill Dallas's adventures. He was transported from Italy by train, passing through Rome, on 15 March 1944; he could only see the iconic sights of the 'Eternal City' through the slits in the horse box he travelled in. With the Allies having almost total control of the skies, his train presented a tempting target for an American P-38 Lightning fighter bomber. Without knowing Allied PoWs were on board, the pilot streaked down and strafed the train. The train crashed, and in the scramble to get out of the wreckage, Bill broke his glasses, leading to his later idle jest that the Americans came closer to killing him than the Germans. He eventually arrived in Germany at Stalag VIIA (Moosburg, Isar) Bavaria, a transit camp, on 17 March 1944, where his details were registered. He was subsequently transferred some 350 miles north to the officer camp, Oflag 79 (Braunschweig), near Hanover, Saxony. He remained there until the camp was liberated by Americans on 12 April 1945. This merited great rejoicing and his family still have a photograph of the celebrations with some of the camp inmates holding jugs of beer, singing along to a piano accordion played by Lieutenant William G. Vandersen, a former Fleet Street press photographer. He was also a prisoner at the camp, and like Bill Dallas, also captured in Italy. He had been serving with the Army Film and Photographic Unit (AFPU).

Also liberated by the Americans, after being captured at Anzio, was Douglas Harding. He was initially held at Feldpost 31979 in northern Italy before being transported to Stalag 4D (Torgau), which is also in Saxony. He was forced to work in a copper mine for four months; the work was exhausting, exacerbated by the meagre diet the PoWs were fed. Torgau is famous as the place where the American troops linked with the Red Army on the River Elbe on 25 April 1945. As the Soviets advanced through Poland and eastern Germany, the PoWs were marched westwards. The Germans tried to march them back east, towards the camp, as they began to come close to the advancing Americans. In the confusion among the guards, Douglas managed to escape and hid outside the camp until he was picked up by Americans. He was extremely grateful to be with them, as they gave him cigarettes and much-needed food. He was repatriated soon afterwards and welcomed home by his family in Kirkcaldy.

After being wounded and captured at Anzio, Charles Melrose was destined for Stalag IXC (Maulhausen). Due to his wounds, he was first being treated in the Reserve-Lazaret, Obermassfeld, a hospital serving the camp. At this hospital there were two officers of 5th Battalion Gordon Highlanders who had been captured at St Valery-en-Caux in June 1940. Under the Geneva Convention, officers and NCOs were not required to work, but it was inevitably boring being held prisoner for years with nothing to occupy their time. Captain William Lawrie and Lieutenant James Sinclair were both keen to do something positive to improve the welfare of other PoWs, such as Charlie Melrose. They volunteered to work at the hospital and from August 1942 until May 1945 they assisted the German and British medical staff treating injured Allied PoWs. Bill Lawrie's civilian profession was a physical education teacher at Bucksburn Academy, Aberdeen, and with his knowledge of physiology he took charge of the departments dealing with massage, physiotherapy and physical training. Jim Sinclair was an engineer in Fraserburgh, Aberdeenshire, so was good at solving technical problems. He was ingenious at inventing apparatus to facilitate the rehabilitation work using the only materials he could beg, borrow or steal, such as string from Red Cross parcels, cotton reels and old pieces of wood. Even artificial limbs were fashioned and fitted to some of the amputees by Lieutenant Sinclair, utilising his engineering skills. Both conducted exercise classes and in addition to the physical assistance they provided, they gave encouragement and sympathy to ease the mental burden of disabled men, which played a significant role in maintaining their morale at a time when their spirits were low. After the war, their humanitarian efforts were honoured by each being made a Member of the British Empire (MBE). They had treated some 450 British and American patients who, without their help, would have returned home partially or completely crippled.

Whilst Captain Bill Lawrie and Lieutenant Jim Sinclair were using their technical and craft skills to fabricate ingenious devices for physiotherapy, other PoWs were also creative while they had time on their hands. This was largely limited to officers and NCOs as the other ranks were often just glad to relax after hard work in mines, factories or farms. Corporal Andrew Haldane was held at Stalag VIIA (Moosburg) in Bavaria after being captured at Anzio when serving with the 1st Battalion London Scottish. He came up with the idea of making a chess set, with which he and his fellow prisoners could play to pass the time and keep their minds sharp. Using wood taken from his bed boards, his project turned into a labour of love. He carved extremely fine, intricate chess pieces with fantastic detail, creating the two opposing sets of chessmen by blackening one set with charcoal. The pieces are all different, exhibiting a terrific imagination and quality of workmanship. The detail is extraordinary. The white king looks pious, clutching his orb and sceptre, while his queen has her hands clasped in prayer. In contrast, the black king has a long, flowing beard and is leaning on his broadsword, alongside his queen, who strikes a austere pose with her hands crossed in front of her. The knights' horses are rearing up, while the rooks are in the Scots baronial style and the black bishop is wearing a hooded monk's habit. Another Gordon Highlander captured at Anzio while serving with the 6th Battalion was Sergeant William Graham. He was also at Stalag VIIA (Moosburg), where similarly he spent time in fabricating items from unneeded material he could acquire within the camp. His craft skill was turned to a less aesthetic purpose when he made a metal trunk using over forty discarded large Maple Leaf butter tins from Canadian Red Cross parcels. He cleaned and flattened these and joined them together by turning over the edges and interlocking each tin to form larger metal sheets. The corners had to be mitred and the sharp edges were all covered by folded strips of metal which also gave extra strength. All of the exteriors of the tins were inside the box so that the exterior was a plain gilt colour concealing all the red Maple Leaf branding inside. He had to fabricate hinges, lid fasteners and a handle, and he strengthened the edges further with thin wooden batons which he fixed along the top of the inside edges. He created a useful and secure container for his personal belongings as well as giving himself an interesting project requiring a great deal of thought and craftsmanship. This metal box is now part of the collection of the Gordon Highlanders Museum.

Unfortunately, after a fierce battle like that at Anzio, it was inevitable that men would be seriously wounded. When their position was overrun, they were captured, but both the Allies and enemy made serious attempts to treat these men to save their lives. Regrettably, not every wounded soldier could be saved, despite the efforts of enemy medics. After being wounded and captured at Anzio on 4 February 1944, both Thomas Smith and Gavin Clarkson ended up being treated by German medics in Rome. Sadly, they died and were buried in the Campo Verano Cemetery in Rome. This is now a famous tourist attraction due to the many magnificent monuments to the many prominent Italians, including artists, politicians and entertainers who have been buried there over the last 200 years. These include Claretta Petacci, who was a mistress of the Italian dictator Benito Mussolini. After the war, the Imperial War Graves Commission reinterred his remains, along with those of other Allied soldiers, burying them in the War Cemetery in Rome.

Also captured on 4 February 1944 at Anzio was Lance Corporal Charles Graham, a Londoner serving with the 6th Battalion Gordon Highlanders. He was held in Stalag 344 (Lamsdorf) and made eight escape attempts but was always recaptured. His two most successful attempts took him to Munich and Prague. The last escape was made in the company of Royal Artillery Sergeant John Boyce from Maidford, Northamptonshire, who had been captured in Crete in June 1941; he had spent a long time in captivity. When they reached Prague they were arrested. Since Charles Graham was a serial escaper, he was turned over to the SS, who were in command of a concentration camp where he was treated very badly.

Despite their fearsome reputation, the SS in Prague had not bargained for the audacity of William (Bill) Greig from Aberdeen, who was a 1st Battalion Gordon Highlander who had been captured at St Valery-en-Caux in June 1940. He was held at Stalag 344 and Stalag VIIIC (Gorlitz). In a strange repetition of history, Bill's father had also been a PoW during the First World War. In Military District VIII (Breslau) where Lamsdorf and Gorlitz were located, the PoWs were forced to do hard labour at a quarry at Konigswalde, which was only 20 miles from the Czechoslovakian border and 80 miles from Prague. Bill had made friends with Tommy Vokes, a fellow Scot from Kilmarnock, who was captured at Anzio on 24 February 1944 while serving with Queens Royal Regiment.

One day, early in 1945, while being marched to work in the quarry, the two men seized an opportunity to hide under some bushes before rolling into a ditch to escape. While on the run, they foraged for food, spending several nights sleeping rough in a cemetery until they were befriended by the Mužík family. It was this family that, at great risk to themselves, fed them and gave them civilian clothes before taking them to a railway station and putting them on a train to Prague. Here the two escaped men were looked after by another family. While in Prague, which was occupied by the Germans, Bill Greig volunteered to work with the Resistance as a courier. He carried messages between groups, which was extremely dangerous work, particularly as he didn't speak Czech, although he had picked up some German while a PoW. The war was almost over but a unit of fanatical SS troops in Prague refused to surrender. The local partisans, aided by many of the population, tried to liberate their city, but they were only lightly armed. On 5 May 1945, they gained control of the Cesky Rozhlas radio station, but it didn't take long for German forces outside Prague to rally to the aid of their Nazi comrades in the city. It seemed that the historic city would become a battleground involving the destruction of many historic buildings.

Bill Greig and Tommy Vokes were both involved in guarding the radio station. The broadcasting equipment was kept in a small room along a tunnel where they spent many hours lying flat with their rifles pointing at the door at the tunnel's entrance. Bill Greig, being a native English speaker, agreed to broadcast an appeal to the Allies for assistance. Bill was certainly not accustomed to public speaking so was extremely nervous when the microphone was placed in front of him, his mouth suddenly dry. He stiffened himself, cleared the frog in his throat and spoke; fully mindful his broadcast could save one of Europe's most iconic cities and thousands of its citizens. He began: 'Prague is in great danger. The Germans are attacking us with tanks and planes. We are calling urgently our allies to help. Send immediately tanks and aircraft. Help us defend Prague. At present, we are broadcasting from the broadcasting station and outside there is a battle raging.' Fortunately, Bill's appeal was heard by the American military, which sent planes to destroy a column of German panzer reinforcements heading into the city. Bill's broadcast was even heard in Britain and when Bill's mother, in Aberdeen, heard it, she recognized his voice.

This, however, was not the boldest of the intrepid two's adventures in Prague. The SS were in the Na Smetance primary school, just a couple of streets away from the radio station; they were still refusing to surrender and successfully resisting a number of the Czech partisans whose ammunition was almost exhausted. Here Bill Greig and Tommy Vokes took on an even more dangerous role. Dressed as smartly as they could in their British Army uniforms, they volunteered to speak to the SS commander. They pretended they were the vanguard of a much larger British force and threatened that his unit would be crushed and the only way for them to survive was for the German commander to surrender. The boldness of this approach was too much for the Germans to disbelieve and it worked, with the SS troops surrendering to Bill and Tommy. They gave up their weapons in return for safe passage towards the town of Beroun, about 20 miles west. The bonus for the Germans was that they could possibly remove their uniforms and evade capture or surrender to the Americans, rather than the Russians. On 9 May, the Red Army entered Prague and the city was saved, but the knowledge that the Russians were also just outside the city may also have influenced the German commander's decision. To mark Tommy Vokes and Bill Greig's critical part in saving the city in its hour of utmost danger, the Government of Czechoslovakia awarded them the country's Military Cross for this brave and significant action. Following a generous donation by his family, William Greig's Czech Military Cross now forms part of the collection of the Gordon Highlanders Museum. The honours did not end there. On 5 May 2021, a memorial plaque was unveiled at the Na Smetance primary school in Prague's 2nd District of Vinohrady, commemorating the two brave British soldiers who fought with the Czechs during the Prague Uprising exactly 76 years earlier.

Sergeant Robert (Bob) Louis Souter was a pre-war Territorial soldier with the 1st Battalion London Scottish. He was a prolific artist. Before the war, he was a regular contributor to the *London Scottish Regimental Gazette*. In addition, the recruiting poster seen in London by Michael Burge was almost certainly designed by Robert Souter. He served with the 1st Battalion London Scottish in Iraq and Sicily, and had used his free time to continue his passion for sketching what he saw around him, sometimes using a caricature style to give a small degree of humour. When he was captured in the Anzio Bridgehead on 27 April 1944, his sketches were still on his person and were eagerly examined by the German intelligence officer, who anticipated the drawings would provide some valuable information. However, all of his sketches were returned to Bob with the terse comment, 'of no military importance'. Bob Souter was initially held as a PoW in Stalag VIIA (Moosburg, Isar) but later transferred to Stalag 383 (Hohen Fels), as he was an NCO. He continued sketching during captivity and in one instance captured a fine caricature of another Gordon Highlander sergeant at Stalag 383 (Hohen Fels) who had been captured at St Valery. Bob Souter noted in his caption that the five years of hardship, waiting and hoping for liberation was etched on his face, but he was still able to smile.

A smile was brought to the face of Thomas Gray, who had also been languishing for many years after his capture at Hem, Belgium in 1940. He was being held in Lamsdorf when, one day in 1944, his twin brother, Leslie, arrived at the camp. Thomas and Leslie had joined the army together with their army numbers being consecutive. Leslie Gray was captured at Anzio on 4 February, arriving at Lamsdorf in the company of William Fyfe, who was from the small village of Craigellachie, Banffshire. William's hometown was just a couple of miles from the Gray twins' home in Aberlour, and both villages were famous for their single malt whiskies and salmon fishing on the River Spey. Tom Gray was a founder member of the Lamsdorf Loons Club, which was formed secretly on 21 October 1943 in Barrack Room 16A of Stalag 344 (Lamsdorf). The members were all from the north-east of Scotland, choosing the alliterative club title from the camp name and the Doric term 'loon', meaning 'boy or young man'. At its height, the club had around fifty members, the majority being Gordon Highlanders, who met and entertained each other with stories and songs; Bill Barclay would play his mandolin, accompanied by George Forsyth on his guitar. Naturally, both Leslie Gray and Willie Fyfe joined the club.

While being held as a PoW, there were many challenges, not least that their incarceration was not time limited and the PoWs also knew that their captors could be fickle. Their treatment often depended on the circumstances in which they found themselves. For example, working on farms could be tolerable, especially if this mirrored the PoWs' civilian employment, and in some circumstances the farmer's family would treat the PoW as one of their own. However, some jobs were much more unpleasant, like being forced to work down in salt or coal mines, where not only were the working conditions unpleasant, accidents leading to serious injury were not uncommon. In addition, there was always the attitude of the guards to be mindful of, although in general the Germans treated the PoWs reasonably fairly. It was therefore disturbing that in addition to all of these worries, they were sometimes inadvertently placed in danger by their own side. The Allied air forces were not only targeting cities, but also factories and other infrastructure such as bridges and railways. Although the Geneva Convention expressly prohibited requiring PoWs to work in any industry which aided the German war effort, there were many grey areas which the Germans were not slow to exploit.

Edward Wild, like so many others, had been captured on 4 February 1944 while serving with the 6th Battalion Gordon Highlanders at Anzio. He was being held at Stalag VIIA (Moosburg). On 20 October 1944, the first of a series of air raids was carried out on the railway station and the railway tracks at Rosenheim, which was an important transportation hub between Munich, Salzburg and Innsbruck. This was a daylight mass air attack by 100 American bombers dropping 1,000 bombs around lunchtime, leaving twenty-seven civilians dead and fifty-nine wounded. In addition, Edward and six other British PoWs were killed. This was just eight months after Edward's capture. He was initially buried at Rosenheim Civil Cemetery prior to being reinterred at Durnbach War Cemetery in Bayern, Germany.

Another danger faced by the PoWs came as the war was coming to its conclusion. In January 1945 the Russian 'Red' Army was advancing into Poland and threatening to liberate the PoW camps. The Germans were determined this would not happen, as they did not want their PoWs to be liberated and return to active duty against them. For this reason, they started to evacuate the camps and move the PoWs westwards, away from the advancing Russians. The conditions were harsh, as the weather was bitterly cold, and the men, in large groups of about 600, had to live off the land and often spent the nights without shelter. Archie Mochrie, who had been captured at Anzio, was originally held at Stalag VIIIC (Sagan) when he was forced by the German guards to evacuate the camp in freezing conditions. His group marched for over 600 miles in thirty-eight days with a daily ration of a small piece of bread and a tiny portion of cheese. At night, the men had to sleep in the open, without blankets; their physical condition deteriorated, with no washing or medical facilities provided during the whole march. He was eventually liberated on Good Friday at Stalag IXB (Bad Orb) by the 6th American Armoured Division.

After crossing Luneburg Heath, where later Field Marshal Bernard Montgomery took the German surrender, Willie Duncan's group came to a small hamlet and were each issued with a Red Cross parcel. Willie took his to a small area of woodland to open and enjoy some of the contents when he spotted a flight of six Typhoon fighter planes circling overhead. They then started to line up in an attacking formation and started to dive on the column of men, which they assumed was a column of Nazi troops. The men scattered and dived for any cover, but the attack did kill around fifty men and wounded many others, including some German guards. It was a tragedy so near to their liberation, which actually took place the next day, when they saw some British tanks travelling along the road in the valley below them. They waved to attract the attention of the soldiers; a Bren gun carrier came to investigate and they were free at last. The German guards gave up without a fight, smashing their rifles against a wall as soon as they saw the tanks, and were apparently pleased that, for them also, the war was over.

John Bowman, from Pittenweem in Fife, had been serving with the 1st Battalion London Scottish when he was captured at Anzio on 24 February 1944. Like thousands of others, he was force-marched westwards from Stalag 8C (Sagan). He died at Wurzen, Liepzig, Germany some 120 miles west of Sagan. It is believed he died on 25 March 1945, but the circumstances of his death are unclear. He was originally buried in the civil cemetery of Wurzen before being reinterred in the War Cemetery in Berlin. It is possible he was killed trying to escape or died through exposure.

Vernon Ross had been held at Stalag VIIIC (Sagan) on the German-Polish border, but after his forced winter march away from the Russian Army, he was liberated by American forces in April 1945 at Stalag IXB (Wegschelde Bad Orb), which is over 300 miles west of his original PoW camp. On 2 April 1945, an American task force broke through the German lines and drove north almost 40 miles through enemy-held territory to Bad Orb. They liberated Stalag IXB, where the GIs were shocked to find the PoWs in a poor state of health and suffering from malnutrition. Archie Mochrie, another 6th Gordon, from Falkirk, who had been captured at Anzio, was also liberated here. He complained bitterly about their treatment by the German guards and the lack of food, claiming they would have starved without the Red Cross parcels. He saw one PoW shot for stealing a turnip from a passing cart. With the approaching American forces, the camp commandant attempted to get the PoWs to go on another forced march, but the men refused to move, so he threatened them with a firing squad. Fortunately, the camp welfare officer persuaded him that very few of the men were fit enough to march, so he relented.

If the PoWs were liberated by the western Allies, British or Americans, their future was fairly straightforward. Their immediate needs were seen to and they were quickly evacuated and arrangements made to get them home as soon as possible. Liberation by the Russians could be much more problematic. George Thomson had been captured at Hem in May 1940 and was held at Stalag XXA (Thorn), Poland. He escaped from the marching column of PoWs in February 1945. He found his way to the Russian lines, being one of the first Gordon Highlanders to overcome the dangers of no man's land and make it successfully to friendly Allied forces. He was sent east to Odessa, on the Black Sea, where he arrived on 12 March and handed over to the British authorities a week later. He arrived back in Britain on 19 April. His army record was appended with the note, 'Escaped PoW, duties restricted to the UK until the cessation of hostilities with Germany.' He was given seven weeks leave, then stationed at No. 95 Polish Repatriation Camp, Burrowhead, Whithorn,

Wigtown. During this time he married his fiancée, who he met before he was posted to France in January 1940; she had waited for him. Although they were both from Aberdeen, they married in Glasgow.

When the Red Army arrived to liberate Stalag IVB (Muhlberg), Saxony, on 23 April 1945, Fred Lowe and John Warren, two 6th Battalion Gordons captured at Anzio, were overjoyed. However, the Russians were mainly only interested in their own soldiers, who they led away from the camp immediately and were then treated harshly as they were considered to have given up too easily. Although the British and American prisoners were treated well by the Russians, the food was terrible and they were held in the camp, which was little better than being under the German regime. This was part of a strategy demanded by Joseph Stalin to ensure that Russian PoWs liberated by the western Allies would be handed over to the Red Army and not allowed to melt away into western countries after the war. The British and American PoWs were being used as bargaining chips to ensure he had men to exchange for the men he wanted back in Russian hands.

After three days, Fred and John decided they'd had enough of being PoWs so made a successful escape by just walking out of the camp, with the guards assuming they were coming back. They hoped to be able to reach the British or American lines but this proved to be dangerous and difficult, so they decided to return to the camp but on their return it was virtually deserted. The PoWs had been moved back towards Russia, where they would eventually be repatriated through Odessa after Stalin had the assurances regarding Russian PoWs which he had demanded. John and Fred stayed at the camp for a few days, but there was nothing for it but to set off again. This time they were apprehended by some Russian Frontier guards and thrown into a cellar at Furstenwalde, about 100 miles north-east of the camp and just south-east of Berlin. They were kept there without food for three days, so at the first opportunity they made another escape from the clutches of the Russians and went back south to Saxony, where they were befriended by some German civilians who gave them food and civilian clothes. By June, the war in Europe was over and they knew that British troops had entered Berlin, so they started to make their way north again, but they were still in Russian-controlled East Germany where they again fell foul of some Russian soldiers who mistook them for Germans. After stealing their watches, the Russians arrested them again and took them to Doberlug, where they were held for a month and were still barely halfway towards Berlin where their hope of repatriation could be realized. When they were eventually released, they made their way back to Saxony, where they had at least found some friends, and decided to remain there for another two months until a railway connection with Berlin opened and they were able to take the train. They finally reached Berlin and were able to make it through to the British sector; arrangements were made to get Fred back home to his family in Wigan and John to his in London. By this time, it was mid-November, seven months after their initial liberation, with their comrades repatriated through Odessa back home before them and with a great deal fewer hair-raising exploits. They were possibly the last of the able-bodied PoWs to return to Britain. Even their 6th Battalion comrades who had become prisoners of the Japanese in the Far East came home at the end of October. Japan finally surrendered unconditionally, on 15 August 1945, after the Americans dropped atomic bombs on Hiroshima and Nagasaki.

# Chapter 13

# The Epilogue

The 6th Battalion Gordon Highlanders arrived in the port of Haifa, Palestine (now Israel) on board the SS *Duchess of Richmond* on 27 January 1945. They then journeyed the 100 miles south by train, in cattle truck carriages, to a camp just outside Gaza where they were based for six months. Their future role was uncertain and although the outcome of the war was not in doubt, the fighting was still far from over, with Germany still holding firm and the crossing of the Rhine still a little way off; meanwhile, the Japanese were also far from defeated.

Their time in Gaza was initially quiet and pleasant with chances to have a rest and the luxury of a bath, which was rarely available when in an active theatre of the war. There were also chances to enjoy sport, visit the army cinema or visit Cairo on a short leave. With their front-line service behind them, when there was no opportunity to spend their pay, the men accumulated it as a credit. Like most of his comrades, Walter Lindley had thirty pounds credit when he went to Cairo, which equates to over £1,000 in current value. It is not surprising therefore that, on his five days leave with the rest of B Company, he said he had the best holiday of his life. They all knew that it couldn't last forever and inevitably, normal training continued, which also included exercising with tanks.

On 29 April, after secret negotiations, the formal surrender of German forces in Italy was signed at a ceremony in the eighteenth-century Palace of Caserta, just north of Naples. The surrender was, however, only formally effective from 2 May 1945. Although the Italian Government had surrendered in September 1943, after the conquest of Sicily, troops who remained loyal to the Italian Fascist dictator, Benito Mussolini, had fled north, with Marshal Rodolfo Graziani, who had accepted the role of his Minister of Defence. Mussolini was captured and executed on 28 April 1945 by Italian partisans in the small village of Giulino di Mezzegra, on the shores of Lake Como in northern Italy, 50 miles north of Milan. The following day, German forces in Italy surrendered, and Graziani's own surrender was negotiated and accepted by (now) Major Hamish Henderson. The war in Italy was over. Adolf Hitler committed suicide the next day, Monday, 30 April 1945, but Germany tried to continue the war under Admiral Karl Donitz in a futile effort to avoid unconditional surrender to the Allies.

When the war in Europe finally came to a conclusion, the 6th Battalion marked the occasion with a thanksgiving service on 8 May 1945; the pipe band played in Jerusalem. The following day was treated as a holiday and a celebratory dinner was served to all ranks, with the officers performing their traditional role for such occasions.

Following the end of the First World War, the British held a League of Nations mandate to govern the territory of Palestine and, although at that time there was only a small Jewish population there, the British Government had previously supported the concept that Palestine could form the basis of a Jewish state. This encouraged the mass immigration of displaced Jewish people at the end of the war while enraging the indigenous Arab populace. The country was unstable, with Arab and Jewish factions displaying considerable hostility to each other, with the Gordons often ending up in the middle of the trouble. After the war ended, there was a large influx of displaced Jewish families who were determined to settle in Palestine. The Battalion spent two weeks in Haifa assisting with the control of Jewish migrant ships and trying to stop them from landing, but this proved largely unsuccessful.

From Gaza, the Battalion went to central Palestine, south of Jerusalem, then up north to Tiberius, which were both fairly quiet with little terrorism; they did spend a short time in Jericho and Jaffa, which were trouble spots. The Battalion also spent some time in Lebanon and Syria where some peace-keeping work was also required. News came in May 1945 that the 6th Battalion Gordon Highlanders was to be disbanded, but this bitter blow was tempered with a War Office promise that they would travel home to Keith, from where they had mobilized at the start of the war, and be disbanded there. It was, therefore, a great disappointment that this promise was not honoured, and the Battalion was disbanded in Cairo at the end of November 1946. Before this, the men who did not qualify for demobilization had to be transferred to other units. Willie McHardy was promoted to the rank of Lieutenant Colonel and given the task of making all the arrangements, which he considered was important to ensure his men were posted to appropriate units. This approach was demonstrated to be best when a General Headquarters officer randomly posted some 6th Battalion Gordon Highlanders to an English regiment based in Suez. Seeing this was a mistake, Lieutenant Colonel McHardy arranged to have the men returned and he phoned his opposite number of this English regiment and thanked him for sending his men back. The English CO replied that he had been very impressed with the Gordons sent to him, who he thought were very clean, smart and efficient but nobody could understand a word they said!

On 8 April 1945, a party of 6th Battalion Gordon Highlanders returned to Anzio and assembled in a glade overlooking Peter Beach to commemorate their fallen comrades. A service was held which was led by the Reverend R.B.R. Anderson, who was the Church of Scotland Padre in Rome for Allied Area Command. Lieutenant Colonel James Peddie unveiled the memorial of white marble which had the Gordon Highlanders' regimental crest on one side with the inscription: 'The 6th (Banffshire) Battalion The Gordon Highlanders, To The Memory Of Those Who Gave Their Lives On The Anzio Beachhead, 22 January – 4 June 1944, Bydand.' The names of the sixty-eight men who died at Anzio are inscribed on the reverse. After the service, a piper played a lament. The memorial stands at the crossroads which was the B Echelon area of the battalion during the battle and is now in the centre of the small town of Lavinio, just 4 miles up the coast road from Anzio.

When the Italian surrender became effective on 2 May 1945, the 1st London Scottish was still in Italy, across the River Adige. They moved forward to Dolo, on the outskirts of Venice. Almost immediately they were ordered forward to Gorizia, on the Italian-Yugoslavian (now Slovenian) border to make a show of strength to some Yugoslavian partisans who wished to dispute the position of that border with the aim of increasing the Yugoslavian territory. On 13 May, the Battalion held a thanksgiving service to commemorate their fallen and give thanks for the end of the war in Europe. Shortly afterwards, the battalion made their final move of the war to Pula, at the tip of the Istrian peninsula, in what is now modern-day Croatia.

There were, however, some local tensions here with the ethnic population of Slavs and Italians making claims on the area, but the London Scottish took control of the transport routes and ensured that there were no marked changes to the resident make-up of the population. Men were given leave to visit Venice, where the tourist hotspots of St Mark's Square and the picturesque canals were popular spots to have souvenir pictures taken. A hostel was also set up in Techendorf, Austria for the men visiting that country, which was named the 'Glenmoriston Hotel' after the Scottish connections of the commanding officer, Lieutenant Colonel Ian Grant. Techendorf was almost 200 miles north on the shores of the lake Weißensee, in the southern Alps, a world away from the war. Shortly after the move to Pula, there was a tragic accident involving Ian Grant. He was killed when he was involved in trying to recover a German motor launch which had been sunk in Pula Bay. He had taken over command of the 1st Battalion London Scottish in March 1945 and had previously served with the Queen's Own Cameron Highlanders and was wounded in Tunisia, in March 1943, while serving in their 5th Battalion.

At Pula there were facilities for sport and recreation, but the task of demobilization began. For those with the longest service, this was carried out over the remainder of the year, eventually leading to the disbandment of the Battalion in September 1946, but it was reformed back in London in March 1947. There were, however, a number of special occasions prior to this. In February 1946, the Battalion moved some 70 miles north, back over the Italian frontier, to Trieste to carry out border guard duties. While here, the Battalion colours were sent out from London and a ceremonial colour parade was arranged to receive them, believed to be the first such parade in Italy after the war. This was held on 29 March 1946 and was a splendid spectacle, with a large gathering of representatives from other Allied units and civilian spectators, including local dignitaries. The inspection was carried out by Lieutenant General Sir John Harding, who at that time commanded XIII Corps. He was a highly decorated, distinguished soldier who had joined the London Regiment as a Territorial Army soldier in 1914 and went on to be awarded a Military Cross during the First World War. During the Second World War, he was awarded the Distinguished Service Order in 1941 for his actions in the Western Desert and a Bar to his DSO in 1942. Another parade was held on 2 May 1946 to commemorate the first anniversary of the surrender of the German forces in Italy.

After this parade, the colours were sent back to London so they could be carried at the victory parade in London, which was held on 8 June 1946, the largest parade ever seen in the capital, with the salute being taken in The Mall by King George VI. This parade involved some 20,000 of the men and women of armed and emergency services from the Empire and Commonwealth and other Allied nations, which naturally included representatives of the Gordon Highlanders. The whole parade was led by the massed pipe bands of the Scottish and Irish regiments and included hundreds of military vehicles and a fly past of over 300 aircraft led by the celebrated Battle of Britain pilot, Douglas Bader. As might be expected for such a special event, the route was lined by millions of cheering civilians.

Sadly, although equally deserving of such a ceremony, the 6th Battalion's colours did not receive such a celebration. This was just one of the sad aspects of the disbandment of the 6th Battalion as the colours were not paraded. As the disbandment neared in November 1946, they were packed up and shipped back to the Battalion Headquarters at Keith, where they were laid up for the last time.

The men of the 6th Battalion and the 1st London Scottish had been overseas for around three years and when the war had ended, the postings back to Britain and demobilization took place. When this occurred depended to an extent on the man's age, length of service, health and whether or not they had any special skills in civilian life required by the country to assist the post-war recovery. The men's return home brought all sorts of issues, but predominantly there were many happy reunions. Naturally there was an enormous relief that a loved one had survived the war but there was an inevitable period of readjustment for both the family and the soldier, with children having grown older, even some born after the soldier's posting overseas. Single men had lost a significant part of their adolescence and were now able to be their own person, rather than continually having to obey orders. Before the Japanese surrendered, there was great frustration for some men who were given a few weeks leave and then ordered to report back to holding units for training and a possible posting to the Far East. For many, there were differing degrees of post-traumatic stress after the long periods of action in extremely challenging situations. This was often acutely felt by the PoWs, who had been under the control of the enemy, some for five years, and was particularly heightened for those who survived captivity under the Japanese.

Some of the first men to get home were the PoWs held in German-occupied Europe, many of whom were liberated in April 1945 before the Allied victory in Europe. Desmond Miller was captured at Anzio in February 1944. He arrived back home in Aberdeen in mid-April 1945, after being held in Stalag XIA (Altengrabow), Germany. Having served in the 6th Battalion Gordon Highlanders, he was unusual in his family as his father, twin brother and elder brother all served in the Merchant Navy while even his sister was a WREN in the Women's Royal Naval Service. Another Gordon Highlander captured on the same day at Anzio who had also spent time at Stalag XIA was Peter Fallon from Glasgow. He was serving with the 1st Battalion London Scottish. On his return home, his employers, James Aitken & Co at the Falkirk Brewery, organized a social function for all of their employees who had been PoWs. They were entertained and given a gift of money from the firm and their former workmates of the brewery. Major James Williamson, MC, last saw his wife, Dorothy, when he had embarkation leave around the festive period in 1942. When he came home to Aberdeen, he had the joy of his first meeting with his young son, who was born after he left for North Africa, in February 1943. There were also private gestures of generosity. John Barrowman was captured at Anzio; after his liberation and return home to Bellshill, Lanarkshire, the residents of the street where he lived took up a collection to give his family a gift of money. This prompted his wife to place an announcement in the local newspaper to thank them.

In early December 1945, Private John Bruce was on his way back to Scotland after serving with the 6th Battalion in Italy and Palestine. His route took him by train through France, which was full of other soldiers who were also on their way home. They had appreciated that the French Railway Company (SNCF) had taken the trouble to decorate the engine with Union Jacks and the British coat of arms but were unaware of what lay in store. When the train arrived at Dieppe, John Bruce was stunned as he stepped off the train to be personally greeted by Major General John Halsted, the Assistant Quartermaster General, who had travelled over from Whitehall to France especially for the occasion. It was almost like winning the lottery as Private Bruce was declared as the 500,000th British soldier to be repatriated through France by the British Army Repatriation Department. He was the guest of honour at a lunch, where General Halsted presented him with a clock.

Walter Lindley described the process of being 'demobbed.' He travelled home from Palestine through Egypt, by sea from Port Said to Toulon, then by train to Marseilles, Amiens and Dieppe, took the ferry to Dover and finally the train to Victoria Station in London. From here he was taken to Inkerman Barracks in Aldershot where the military formalities of discharge were taken care of. The next day he was taken to a warehouse in Woking in Surrey, which Walter described as being like a large Marks and Spencer's store. Here there were counters with all manner of clothing, suits, shoes, hats, raincoats, etc. Walter chose a blue suit, a raincoat and a hat which were all parcelled up for him and he was discharged; he got the train home that evening.

The war was over, but the effects were still felt by many and those that survived were thankful. They remembered their fallen comrades with sadness and pride. The two Gordon Highlander battalions that had served in Italy had suffered greatly in the number of casualties taken, but the courage of the men was reflected in the numerous gallantry awards bestowed on them. The Americans also saw fit to honour some of the men, with Lance Corporal James Agnew receiving the Silver Star, while Major Duncan M. Annand, Lieutenant Joseph Lynam and CQMS George Melville received the Bronze Star.

On 20 August 1949, the City of Aberdeen also honoured the regiment by bestowing the freedom of the city on the Gordon Highlanders, an honour shared by the London Scottish. The parade comprised of over 300 officers and men of both Regular and Territorial battalions. Among them were three officers and fifty other ranks of the London Scottish.

# Appendix

# Casualties and Gallantry Awards

This table lists many of the men who served with the 6th Battalion Gordon Highlanders and the 1st Battalion London Scottish during the Second World War. Those included are those who received gallantry awards or suffered as a casualty. The names which are written in capitals are those who were killed in action, died of wounds or were accidentally killed while in service. Unfortunately, there is no definitive nominal roll for these two battalions, so the table was compiled from numerous sources. This included archive material from the Gordon Highlanders Museum, family records, contemporary newspapers, the Commonwealth War Graves Commission, the National Archives and various miscellaneous sources. Only the man's surname and first forename are shown, except where more than one man shared these names or he was known by his middle name. Every effort has been made to make this list as accurate as possible but it is not exhaustive and there are, unfortunately, possible omissions. If any has occurred, I apologize in advance. If available, a photograph of the soldier concerned has been included. Where appropriate, gallantry awards appear in brackets after the soldier's name and the type of casualty the soldier suffered is shown in the fifth column.

A number of abbreviations have been used in the table. These are as follows:

**General**
Bn. – Battalion
6th – 6th Battalion Gordon Highlanders
1LS – 1st Battalion London Scottish (Gordon Highlanders)
GH – served in more than one battalion
RA – Royal Artillery
RAMC – Royal Army Medical Corps
RACD – Royal Army Chaplains Department
N/a – Not available
N/k – Not known

**Fate (Casualty Type)**
W – Wounded
W+W – Wounded more than once

PoW – Prisoner of war
PoWJ – Japanese prisoner of war
KIA – Killed in action
DoW – Died of wounds
AK - Accidentally killed
Died – Died of illness, etc.


**Gallantry Awards**
VC – Victoria Cross
DSO – Distinguished Service Order
MC – Military Cross
DCM – Distinguished Conduct Medal
MM – Military Medal
MID – Mentioned in Dispatches

| Army Number | Name | Photo | Bn. | Fate |
|---|---|---|---|---|
| 14383835 | ABERCROMBIE, ROBERT | N/a | 1LS | KIA |
| 1078067 | Abrams, Thomas | N/a | 1LS | W |
| 2880579 | Adam, Robert | N/a | 6th | W + PoW |
| 2886480 | Adams, Alexander | N/a | 6th | PoW |
| 278578 | ADAMSON, RORY | N/a | 1LS | KIA |
| 3194362 | Adamson, William | N/a | 6th | W + PoW |
| 3320161 | ADAMTHWAITE, FRED | | 6th | KIA |
| 2883139 | ADDISON, ALBERT | N/a | 6th | KIA |
| 2886483 | Addison, John | N/a | 6th | PoW |
| 2879562 | ADDISON, WILLIAM | N/a | 1LS | KIA |
| 14636295 | Adsmead, Donald | N/a | 6th | W |
| 3130988 | Agnew, James (MID + US Silver Star) | N/a | 6th | W+W |
| 7021564 | Aiken, Samuel | N/a | 6th | PoW |
| 14626023 | AILSBY, RONALD | N/a | 1LS | KIA |
| 14540637 | AIRD, HUGH | N/a | 1LS | KIA |
| 2824705 | Aitchison, James | N/a | 6th | PoW |
| 3195574 | Aitken, Alexander | N/a | 6th | W+W |
| 268218 | AITKEN, RAMSEY | N/a | 1LS | KIA |
| 2829384 | Aitken, Robert | N/a | 6th | PoW |

| Army Number | Name | Photo | Bn. | Fate |
|---|---|---|---|---|
| 3253214 | Alexander, Thomas | N/a | 1LS | W |
| 2765784 | Allan, A. | N/a | 1LS | W |
| 14540642 | ALLAN, DAVID | N/a | 1LS | KIA |
| 2191355 | Allan, John | N/a | 6th | W |
| 14433322 | Allen, Henry | N/a | 6th | W+W |
| 14503661 | Anderson, A. | N/a | 6th | PoW |
| 2766372 | Anderson, Alexander | N/a | 6th | PoW |
| 14427163 | Anderson, Charles | N/a | 1LS | W |
| 3130574 | ANDERSON, EBENEZER | N/a | 6th | AK |
| 14649019 | Anderson, G. | N/a | 6th | W |
| 2885416 | Anderson, George | N/a | 6th | W |
| 7889136 | Anderson, Jack | N/a | 1LS | PoW |
| 3249964 | Anderson, John | N/a | 1LS | W+W |
| 14382619 | Anderson, John | N/a | 1LS | PoW |
| 2884829 | Anderson, Matthew | N/a | 1LS | W |
| 2882177 | Anderson, Robert | | GH | W + PoWJ |
| 2880207 | Anderson, Sidney George (MID) | | 6th | W + PoW |
| 274816 | ANDERSON, SIDNEY LYNE | N/a | 1LS | DoW |
| 14205279 | Anderson, W. | N/a | 1LS | W+W |
| 2881607 | Andrew, John | N/a | 6th | PoW |
| 6215479 | Andrews, James | N/a | 1LS | W |
| 2886485 | ANGUS, ARTHUR | N/a | 6th | KIA |
| 3195785 | Angus, William | N/a | 6th | W + PoW |
| 70632 | Annand, Duncan Mathieson (MBE, MID, US Bronze Star) | | 6th | N/a |
| 28031 | ANNAND, DUNCAN STEWART | | 6th | KIA |
| 6288395 | Apps, S. | N/a | 1LS | W |
| 2890171 | Archer, Albert | N/a | 1LS | W |

| Army Number | Name | Photo | Bn. | Fate |
|---|---|---|---|---|
| 2883660 | Archer, Colin | N/a | 6th | PoW |
| 14563481 | Archibald, John | N/a | 6th | W |
| 3247866 | ARMIT, DONALD | N/a | 6th | KIA |
| 2757798 | Armit, Robert | N/a | 6th | W + PoW |
| 1823039 | ARMSTRONG, ALEXANDER | N/a | 1LS | KIA |
| 3053580 | Armstrong, George | N/a | 6th | W |
| 2885956 | Armstrong, Robert | N/a | 1LS | W |
| 2615646 | Armstrong, H. | N/a | 6th | PoW |
| 2760369 | Arnot, D. | N/a | 6th | W+W |
| 5621031 | ARSCOTT, SIDNEY | N/a | 1LS | KIA |
| 2763291 | Arthur, Robert | N/a | 1LS | PoW |
| 14412411 | ASHBURNER, JOHN | N/a | 1LS | KIA |
| 2934389 | ASHLEY, JACK | N/a | 1LS | KIA |
| 3602289 | Ashton, S. (MID) | N/a | 6th | PoW |
| 14251126 | ASTLEY, LOUIS | N/a | 6th | KIA |
| 14640956 | Atkins, Bernard | N/a | 6th | W |
| 2885419 | Atkinson, William | N/a | 6th | W + PoW |
| 2878692 | Attfield, Reginald | N/a | 1LS | PoW |
| 4468554 | ATTWELL, ALBERT | N/a | 6th | KIA |
| 137918 | Attwooll, Hugh (MC) | | 1LS | PoW |
| 14629955 | AVERALL, FRANCIS | N/a | 6th | KIA |
| 2890320 | Bain, John | N/a | GH | W+W |
| 2829460 | Bain, John M.C. | N/a | 1LS | N/a |
| 176431 | Bain, Robert (MID) | | 6th | N/a |
| 5955092 | BAIN, WILLIAM | N/a | 1LS | KIA |
| 14587259 | BAINBRIDGE, DENNIS | N/a | 6th | KIA |
| 7047661 | Baker, Harold | N/a | 1LS | W + PoW |
| 14201486 | BALL, CHARLES | N/a | 6th | KIA |
| 2764679 | Ball, H. | N/a | 1LS | W |
| 14503837 | Ballantyne, John | N/a | 1LS | W+W |
| 14206059 | Ballinger, C. | N/a | 6th | PoW |
| 14401013 | Balmforth, Sydney | N/a | 6th | W |

| Army Number | Name | Photo | Bn. | Fate |
|---|---|---|---|---|
| 3318360 | BALSILLIE, GEORGE | N/a | 6th | KIA |
| 4124876 | Bamford, E. | N/a | 6th | W+W |
| 3065041 | Banks, P. | N/a | 1LS | PoW |
| 4920172 | Bannister, R. (MID) | N/a | 1LS | N/a |
| 14002538 | Banton, F. | N/a | 1LS | W |
| 2888817 | Barclay, George | N/a | 6th | PoW |
| 3320324 | Barker, A. | N/a | 6th | PoW |
| 3322174 | Barker, G. | N/a | 6th | W |
| 14420211 | Barker, Richard | N/a | 1LS | W |
| 3196374 | Barkham, J. | N/a | 6th | W |
| 14612511 | BARLOW, JOHN | N/a | 1LS | KIA |
| 4621172 | BARNES, ARTHUR | N/a | 1LS | KIA |
| 14636361 | BARNES, HARRY | N/a | 6th | W + KIA |
| 2885270 | Barr, Hugh | N/a | 1LS | W |
| 2930345 | BARR, ROBERT | N/a | 1LS | KIA |
| 14605184 | Barratt, R. Kenneth (Kennett) | N/a | 1LS | PoW |
| 3327327 | Barrett, J. | N/a | 1LS | W |
| 14642602 | BARRETT, MATTHEW | N/a | 6th | KIA |
| 14644404 | BARRIE, JAMES | N/a | 6th | KIA |
| 3325684 | BARRISKELL, DONALD | N/a | 1LS | KIA |
| 14540656 | Barron, G. | | 1LS | PoW |
| 2885616 | BARRON, JAMES | N/a | 1LS | KIA |
| 2884349 | Barrowman, John | N/a | 6th | W + PoW |
| 2980174 | Barton, Ronald (MID) | N/a | 1LS | W |
| 58564 | Baucher, Jack | | 6th | N/a |
| 2888493 | BAXTER, ARTHUR | | 1LS | W + KIA |
| 2889375 | Baxter, William | N/a | 6th | PoW |

| Army Number | Name | Photo | Bn. | Fate |
|---|---|---|---|---|
| 3247882 | Beadie, Henry | | 6th | N/a |
| 5732592 | BEAMAN, WILLIAM | | 6th | KIA |
| 2883308 | BEATON, ANDREW | N/a | 6th | KIA |
| 3247803 | Beaton, J. | N/a | 6th | PoW |
| 2766540 | Beattie, J. | N/a | 1LS | W |
| 14595399 | Beattie, Patrick | N/a | 6th | W |
| 2879307 | Beauchamp, George | N/a | 6th | W |
| 2890502 | Begg, Andrew | | 1LS | PoW |
| 2934771 | Belcher, William | N/a | 1LS | PoW |
| 2890321 | BELCHER, WILLIAM | N/a | 6th | N/a |
| 2878324 | Bell, David | N/a | 6th | W |
| 3601702 | Bell, H. | N/a | 6th | PoW |
| 14205291 | Bell, R.M. | N/a | 6th | W + PoW |
| 14348728 | BELL, ROBERT | | 1LS | DoW |
| 2886335 | Bell, Thomas | N/a | 1LS | W+W |
| 3602410 | Bell, W. (MID) | N/a | 6th | N/a |
| 2871998 | Bennett, Alexander | | 6th | PoW |
| 2877845 | Bennett, Malcolm | N/a | 1LS | W |
| 2825598 | Bentley, David | N/a | 6th | PoW |
| 3316706 | BERRY, GILBERT | N/a | 6th | KIA |
| 109572 | BERRYMAN, GRAHAM | N/a | 6th | KIA |
| 14410665 | BERRYMAN, VICTOR | N/a | 1LS | PoW + DoW |
| 6097835 | BEVAN, SIDNEY | N/a | 1LS | KIA |
| 3060416 | Beveridge, T. | N/a | 1LS | W |

| Army Number | Name | Photo | Bn. | Fate |
|---|---|---|---|---|
| 2890655 | Beverley, David | N/a | 6th | PoW |
| 2890720 | BICKLE, RICHARD | N/a | 6th | KIA |
| 7014158 | BINGHAM, JAMES | N/a | 1LS | KIA |
| 2764435 | Binnie, A. | N/a | 1LS | W |
| 14616379 | Binns, Jack | N/a | 1LS | PoW |
| 14219776 | BINNS, REGINALD | N/a | 1LS | KIA |
| 3601703 | Birney, J. | N/a | 1LS | W |
| 2885042 | Birnie, William | N/a | 6th | PoW |
| 14656743 | BIRRELL, JAMES | N/a | 1LS | W |
| 2890323 | BISSET, DOUGLAS | N/a | 6th | KIA |
| 2879817 | BISSET, ROBERT | N/a | 6th | KIA |
| 2890469 | Bissett, Adam | N/a | 1LS | W |
| 2883077 | BISSETT, GEORGE | N/a | 1LS | N/a |
| 2879657 | Bissett, John (MM) | N/a | 1LS | W |
| 14427198 | Black, A. | N/a | 6th | N/a |
| 2823574 | Black, Allan | N/a | 6th | W |
| 2886493 | BLACK, JOHN | N/a | 6th | KIA |
| 14554384 | Black, P. | N/a | 1LS | N/a |
| 2879636 | Blackett, Matthew | N/a | 1LS | W+W |
| 14588151 | Blackie, Alfred | N/a | 1LS | PoW |
| 14414310 | BLACKSHAW, CLEMENT | N/a | 1LS | KIA |
| 14208979 | Blackshaw, Hugh | N/a | 6th | PoW |
| 3909668 | Blackwell, Albert | N/a | 1LS | PoW |
| 2879820 | Blackwood, Douglas | N/a | 6th | W |
| 14207659 | Blades, P. | N/a | 6th | PoW |
| 2760379 | BLAIR, ALEXANDER | N/a | 6th | KIA |
| 2888728 | Blair, James | N/a | 1LS | PoW |
| 14588153 | BLAIR, THOMAS | N/a | 1LS | KIA |
| 3134084 | BLAIR, WILLIAM | N/a | 1LS | KIA |
| 239418 | Blamey, Edward (MC) | | 1LS | PoW |
| 4867533 | Blanchard, Richard | N/a | 6th | PoW |
| 155738 | BLANDY, JOHN | N/a | 6th | KIA |
| 2940078 | BLEASBY, HAROLD | N/a | 1LS | KIA |
| 14612969 | Blumenstock, L. | N/a | 6th | W |

| Army Number | Name | Photo | Bn. | Fate |
|---|---|---|---|---|
| 2881639 | Boardman, George Keith | | 6th | N/a |
| 3602288 | Boardman, R. | N/a | 6th | PoW |
| 14515695 | BOATH, RONALD | N/a | 1LS | KIA |
| 14201986 | Boden, F. | N/a | 6th | W + PoW |
| 14607141 | Boland, Chester | N/a | 1LS | W + PoW |
| 3133577 | BOND, THOMAS | N/a | 1LS | DoW |
| 2890324 | BONNYMAN, JOHN | N/a | 6th | KIA |
| 14646938 | Booth, Andrew | N/a | 1LS | PoW |
| 14376381 | Borsberry, W. | N/a | 1LS | PoW |
| 73992 | Borthwick, Algernon Malcom (MC) | | 1LS | W |
| 14607691 | Borthwick, Robert | N/a | 1LS | PoW |
| 14636492 | Bowers, Colin | N/a | 6th | W |
| 14383001 | Bowles, J. | N/a | 6th | W |
| 14595192 | BOWMAN, JOHN | N/a | 1LS | PoW + Killed |
| 14595588 | Boyce, E. | N/a | 1LS | PoW |
| 2883134 | Boyce, Robert | N/a | 6th | W |
| 2890326 | BOYCE, WILLIAM | N/a | 6th | KIA |
| 14515192 | Boyd, John | N/a | 1LS | W |
| 2871353 | Boyd, William | | 6th | N/a |
| 2890327 | Boyes, James | N/a | 6th | W+W |
| 3191896 | BOYLE, JOHN | N/a | 1LS | KIA |
| 2868324 | Boyne, James | N/a | 6th | N/a |
| 2756087 | BRACCINI, A. | N/a | 1LS | KIA |
| 14402150 | Bradford, D. | N/a | 1LS | PoW |
| 5350145 | Brading, Percy | N/a | 6th | PoW |
| 14204666 | Bradley, F. | N/a | 6th | PoW |
| 3317754 | Bradley, W. | N/a | 6th | W |

| Army Number | Name | Photo | Bn. | Fate |
|---|---|---|---|---|
| 665 | Bradshaw, Humphrey Ivan | | 6th | N/a |
| 14621415 | Brady, Patrick | N/a | 1LS | KIA |
| 3136021 | Braithwaite, John | N/a | 1LS | W |
| 3602293 | BRAMMER, ERIC (MM) | N/a | 6th | KIA |
| 2888731 | Brand, George | N/a | 1LS | N/a |
| 2890328 | Brandie, Alexander | | 6th | W |
| 14557748 | Branigan, William | N/a | 6th | W |
| 3602420 | Branthwaite, Cyril | N/a | 6th | PoW |
| 2889082 | Brechin, George | N/a | 1LS | W |
| 2886402 | Brechin, William | N/a | 6th | PoW |
| 3062067 | Bremner, James | N/a | 1LS | W |
| 3252713 | Brennan, J. | N/a | 1LS | W |
| 1790798 | BRERETON, JAMES | N/a | 1LS | KIA |
| 105772 | Bridgman, Robert, Lindsay (MC) | | 6th | N/a |
| 14648255 | Brightling, Donald | N/a | 6th | W |
| 2884998 | Brittan, George | N/a | 1LS | W |
| 14410529 | Broadhurst, James | N/a | 1LS | PoW |
| 3315970 | Broadley, J. | N/a | 1LS | N/a |
| 14403373 | Broadley, John (MM) | N/a | 1LS | N/a |
| 14202046 | Broderick, J. | N/a | 6th | PoW |
| 4621198 | Brook, Leonard | N/a | 1LS | W |
| 14201489 | Brooks, H. | N/a | 1LS | PoW |
| 2879827 | BROOKS, PHILIP | N/a | 1LS | KIA |
| 2874478 | Brooks, William | N/a | 6th | W |
| 2767088 | Brotherstone, David | N/a | 6th | W |
| 14554913 | Brough, Peter | N/a | 1LS | W+W |
| 2987622 | BROWN, ALEXANDER | N/a | 6th | KIA |
| 2884982 | Brown, Andrew | N/a | 1LS | W |
| 3316210 | Brown, C. | N/a | 1LS | W |

| Army Number | Name | Photo | Bn. | Fate |
|---|---|---|---|---|
| 2890064 | Brown, Charles | N/a | 6th | PoW |
| 1816314 | Brown, D.F.R. | N/a | 1LS | W |
| 14208987 | BROWN, DONALD | | 6th | DoW |
| 14203527 | Brown, F. | N/a | 1LS | W + PoW |
| 2888633 | Brown, Gilbert | N/a | 1LS | W |
| 3602210 | Brown, J. | N/a | 6th | W |
| 2764535 | Brown, J. | N/a | 1LS | W |
| 14206062 | Brown, J.F. | N/a | 1LS | PoW |
| 2766383 | Brown, R. | N/a | 1LS | PoW |
| 2821878 | Brown, R. | N/a | 1LS | W |
| 2885190 | BROWN, ROBERT | N/a | 6th | KIA |
| 2886404 | BROWN, ROBERT | N/a | 1LS | KIA |
| 2879761 | Brown, Robert Hall (MM) | N/a | 1LS | PoW |
| 2885282 | Brown, Thomas | N/a | 1LS | W |
| 1738908 | Brown, W. | N/a | 1LS | W |
| 14204667 | Browne, J. | N/a | 6th | PoW |
| 2756946 | Bruce, David (MM) | N/a | 1LS | W+W |
| 288260 | BRUCE, DONALD | N/a | 1LS | KIA |
| N/k | Bruce, John | | 6th | N/a |
| 2878513 | Bruce, Ronald (MID) | N/a | 1LS | N/a |
| 2869745 | Bruce, Thomas (MID) | N/a | 6th | N/a |
| 2767090 | Brunton, J. | N/a | 1LS | W |
| 3059464 | BRYCE, JAMES | N/a | 1LS | KIA |
| 14208991 | Bryce, Robert | N/a | 6th | PoW |
| 6665107 | BRYDEN, JOHN | N/a | 1LS | KIA |
| 137915 | Buchanan, Alexander (MC) | N/a | 1LS | N/a |
| 3054603 | Buchanan, Charles | N/a | 1LS | W |
| 2188486 | Buchanan, George | N/a | 6th | W |
| 2883481 | BUCHANAN, HENRY | N/a | 1LS | KIA |
| 6985765 | Bull, Thomas | N/a | 1LS | W |
| 14642348 | Bullen, J. | N/a | 6th | W+W |
| 14203315 | Bullimore, E. | N/a | 1LS | N/a |

| Army Number | Name | Photo | Bn. | Fate |
|---|---|---|---|---|
| 14587851 | Bulloch, D. | N/a | 1LS | W |
| 14626056 | Bullock, Raymond | N/a | 1LS | PoW |
| 7951288 | Bunt, T. | N/a | 1LS | PoW |
| 5343573 | Burdon, George | N/a | 6th | PoW |
| 315252 | Burge, Michael | N/a | GH | N/a |
| 11256975 | Burgess, A. | N/a | 1LS | W |
| 6209522 | BURGESS, RICHARD | N/a | 6th | KIA |
| 2888140 | Burnham, Arthur | N/a | 6th | W |
| 2888653 | Burns, David | N/a | 1LS | PoW |
| 2879957 | Burns, George | N/a | 1LS | W |
| 2824456 | Burns, John | N/a | 1LS | W |
| 3325438 | Bushell, W.J. | N/a | 1LS | PoW |
| 2756564 | Butler, Henry C. | N/a | 6th | PoW |
| 14397910 | Butler, R. | N/a | 6th | W |
| 14614758 | Byrne, George | N/a | 6th | W |
| 2886992 | Byrne, Nicholas | N/a | 6th | PoW |
| 2879677 | Byrne, Ronald | N/a | 1LS | W |
| 2884866 | CADDELL, THOMAS | N/a | 1LS | KIA |
| 2940201 | Cadzow, Robert | N/a | 1LS | PoW |
| 14620854 | CAIRNCROSS, JOHN | | 1LS | KIA |
| 14620855 | CAIRNCROSS, THOMAS | | 1LS | KIA |
| 3196047 | Cairns, Francis | N/a | 1LS | W |
| 2886115 | Cairns, John | N/a | 6th | W |
| 1826543 | Cairns, William | N/a | 1LS | W |
| 3318181 | Calder, John | N/a | 1LS | W+W |
| 2888503 | Cameron, Charles | N/a | 6th | N/a |
| 2755897 | Cameron, Donald | N/a | 6th | W |
| 2875701 | Cameron, John | N/a | 6th | W |
| 3060150 | Cameron, Peter | N/a | 1LS | W |
| 1545362 | CAMERON, ROBERT | N/a | 1LS | PoW + DoW |
| 2758174 | Cameron, William | N/a | 6th | N/a |
| 3247905 | CAMPBELL, ANDREW | N/a | 6th | DoW |

| Army Number | Name | Photo | Bn. | Fate |
|---|---|---|---|---|
| 2878280 | Campbell, David Alexander (MID) | N/a | 1LS | N/a |
| 2885339 | Campbell, David Ramsey | N/a | 1LS | W |
| 2879723 | CAMPBELL, IAIN | N/a | 1LS | W + KIA |
| 2880308 | Campbell, James | N/a | 6th | W + PoW |
| 2885347 | Campbell, James Laird | N/a | 1LS | W |
| 14297078 | Campbell, James T. | N/a | 1LS | W + PoW |
| 2883278 | CAMPBELL, JOHN AITKEN | N/a | 1LS | KIA |
| 14425528 | Cannaford, Thomas | N/a | 6th | W |
| 3195612 | CANVESS, JOHN | N/a | 6th | KIA |
| 3321196 | Carle, Andrew | | 6th | PoW |
| 2878319 | CARMICHAEL, JAMES | | 6th | KIA |
| 14390391 | Carolan, Patrick | N/a | 1LS | W |
| 3061154 | CARRICK, JAMES | N/a | 1LS | KIA |
| 14002869 | Carroll, D. | N/a | 1LS | PoW |
| 14423564 | Carroll, George | N/a | 1LS | W |
| 2883715 | Carter, Edward | N/a | 6th | PoW |
| 14201381 | Cartledge, J. | N/a | 1LS | W |
| 14648270 | Cartwright, Frank | N/a | 6th | W |
| 2823587 | Cassels, D. | N/a | 1LS | W |
| 2886406 | CAULFIELD, PATRICK | N/a | 1LS | KIA |
| 2886150 | Cavanagh, William | N/a | 1LS | W |
| 14641914 | Chaderton, W. | N/a | 1LS | W |
| 2890335 | Chalmers, George | N/a | 6th | W + PoW |
| 2763473 | CHALMERS, JAMES | N/a | 1LS | KIA |
| 2881608 | Chalmers, John | N/a | 6th | W |
| 14547189 | Chalmers, P. | N/a | 1LS | W |
| 14201567 | Chalmers, R. | N/a | 6th | PoW |
| 14201383 | Chambers, C. | N/a | 6th | W + PoW |
| 2879607 | CHANDLER, HAROLD | N/a | 1LS | DoW |
| 2881102 | CHANDLER, NORMAN | N/a | 1LS | KIA |
| 3254757 | Chilton, Arthur | N/a | 1LS | W |
| 2890721 | Chisholm, George | N/a | 6th | W |

| Army Number | Name | Photo | Bn. | Fate |
|---|---|---|---|---|
| 264642 | Christie, A.M. (MID) | N/a | 1LS | N/a |
| 2890336 | Christie, John | N/a | 6th | W |
| 14595601 | Christie, L. | N/a | 6th | W |
| 273841 | Christie, Reginald | | 6th | N/a |
| 2824498 | Christison, John | N/a | 6th | W+W |
| 14206076 | Cinderby, William (MM) | N/a | 1LS | W |
| 5111957 | CLACK, CHRISTOPHER | N/a | 6th | KIA |
| 62892 | Clapham, John Brian | | GH | N/a |
| 2890337 | Clark, Alexander | N/a | 6th | PoW |
| 2878133 | Clark, Alister | N/a | 6th | W |
| 2882543 | CLARK, ANDREW | N/a | 6th | Died |
| 2883718 | Clark, Arthur | N/a | 6th | W |
| 1545402 | CLARK, DANIEL | N/a | 1LS | KIA |
| 3056857 | Clark, G. | N/a | 1LS | W |
| 2890339 | CLARK, JAMES | | 6th | KIA |
| 2886407 | CLARK, JOHN | N/a | 1LS | KIA |
| 2889384 | Clark, John Michael | N/a | 6th | PoW |
| 2884933 | Clark, Stephen Henry | N/a | 1LS | W |
| 3602484 | Clark, T.S. | N/a | 6th | PoW |
| 3133449 | CLARK, THOMAS | N/a | 1LS | DoW |
| 5349601 | Clark, William | N/a | 6th | W |
| 2886120 | Clark, William | N/a | 6th | PoW |
| 2829035 | CLARKSON, GAVIN | N/a | 6th | PoW + DoW |
| 3325226 | Clarkson, Harry | N/a | 6th | PoW |
| 2888739 | Clarkson, Thomas | | 6th | PoW |
| 3191404 | Cleghorn, Robert | N/a | 6th | W |
| 14595604 | CLELAND, ROBERT MCKENZIE | N/a | 6th | KIA |

| Army Number | Name | Photo | Bn. | Fate |
|---|---|---|---|---|
| 3322317 | Clelland, A. | | 6th | PoW |
| 2886341 | Coates, Robert | N/a | 1LS | W |
| 2877718 | COBBAN, IAN (Jock) (MID) | | 6th | KIA |
| 2883222 | Cochran, Samuel (MID) | N/a | 6th | W + PoW |
| 2890341 | Cochrane, William | N/a | 6th | W |
| 14003082 | Cocks, G. | N/a | 1LS | W |
| 14201491 | COLCLOUGH, ARNOLD | N/a | 6th | KIA |
| 2933510 | COLEMAN, THOMAS | N/a | 6th | KIA |
| 3597856 | COLLINS, JAMES | N/a | 6th | KIA |
| 2932394 | Colquhoun, G. | N/a | 6th | W |
| 3189843 | COLVINE, ANDREW (Dan) | N/a | 1LS | KIA |
| 14554235 | Conlin, J. | N/a | 1LS | W + PoW |
| 1545351 | Conn, William | N/a | 1LS | W |
| 2883208 | CONNAR, JOHN | N/a | 1LS | DoW |
| 1105607 | Connell, Andrew | N/a | 1LS | W |
| 2889514 | Connell, William | N/a | 1LS | PoW |
| 2762407 | Connelly, J. | N/a | 1LS | W + PoW |
| 167553 | CONNER, FREDERICK | N/a | 6th | KIA |
| 14423693 | Connor, Bernard | N/a | 1LS | PoW |
| 5194225 | COOK, ARTHUR | N/a | 6th | KIA |
| 14432212 | Cook, Charles | N/a | 1LS | PoW |
| 4864306 | COOK, JAMES | N/a | 6th | W + KIA |
| 3247845 | Cook, T. | N/a | 6th | W |
| 2878600 | Cooke, Arthur | N/a | 1LS | W |
| 2886707 | COOKE, AUSTIN | N/a | 1LS | N/a |
| 14649231 | Cooper, Frank | N/a | 6th | W |
| 2888237 | Cooper, John | N/a | 1LS | W+W |
| 14405096 | Cooper, R. | N/a | 1LS | PoW |
| 1460115 | Cooper, William | N/a | 1LS | W |
| 14206070 | Cope, H. | N/a | 6th | W |
| 5347450 | Cope, Ted | N/a | 6th | PoW |

| Army Number | Name | Photo | Bn. | Fate |
|---|---|---|---|---|
| 14607470 | Corbett, Albert | | 1LS | PoW |
| 2873914 | Cormack, George Hall | N/a | 6th | PoW |
| 2874996 | CORMACK, GEORGE KITCHENER | | 6th | KIA |
| 14410767 | Corney, M. | N/a | 1LS | PoW |
| 5344870 | Cottrell, F. | N/a | 1LS | W |
| 2882262 | Coull, Robert | | 6th | PoW |
| 2885101 | Coulter, Charles | N/a | 1LS | PoW |
| 2760477 | Coutts, A. | N/a | 1LS | W |
| 2885265 | Cowan, Ian | N/a | 1LS | W |
| 14210531 | Cowie, A. | N/a | 1LS | W |
| 2878827 | Cowie, George | | 6th | PoW |
| 2890205 | COWIE, JAMES | N/a | 1LS | KIA |
| 4278895 | COX, ARTHUR | N/a | 6th | PoW |
| 3715911 | Coyne, John | N/a | 1LS | PoW |
| 14201989 | Cragg, A. (MID) | N/a | 1LS | N/a |
| 2888742 | CRAIB, JAMES | | 6th | KIA |
| 2824726 | Craig, Peter | N/a | 6th | W |
| 14644478 | Craig, Robert | N/a | 1LS | W |
| 14201327 | CRAKE, THOMAS | N/a | 1LS | DoW |
| 2879904 | Crawford, Douglas | N/a | 1LS | W |
| 14608128 | Crawford, James | N/a | 1LS | W+W |
| 2827693 | CREEK, ARTHUR | N/a | 1LS | KIA |
| 5052369 | Cresswell, Clement | N/a | 1LS | PoW |

| Army Number | Name | Photo | Bn. | Fate |
|---|---|---|---|---|
| 158880 | Crewdson, John | | 6th | N/a |
| 2763494 | CRIGHTON, DAVID | N/a | 1LS | DoW |
| 2890659 | Crighton, James | N/a | 6th | PoW |
| 4347496 | Croll, Sidney | N/a | 6th | PoW |
| 3137724 | Cromack, William | N/a | 1LS | W |
| 14410993 | Crook, F. | N/a | 6th | PoW |
| 3602332 | Crook, John | N/a | 6th | W + PoW |
| 2885424 | Crossan, George | N/a | 1LS | W |
| 14624377 | CROW, JOSEPH | N/a | 1LS | KIA |
| 1571123 | CROWSTON, RONALD | N/a | 6th | KIA |
| 2890342 | CRUICKSHANK, ARTHUR | | 6th | AK |
| 2883084 | Cruickshank, Charles | N/a | 6th | W |
| 2886518 | Cruickshank, Norman | | 6th | PoW |
| 14633728 | Cruickshanks, William | N/a | 1LS | W+W |
| 2933494 | CRUISE, PETER | N/a | 1LS | KIA |
| 2878314 | Cumming, James | | 6th | W |
| 2886171 | CUMMING, THOMAS | N/a | 1LS | KIA |
| 3131417 | CUMMING, WILLIAM | N/a | 6th | KIA |
| 2888608 | Cummins, Thomas | N/a | 1LS | W+W |
| 2873125 | Cunnigham, James | N/a | 6th | PoW |
| 14420652 | Cunning, Robert | N/a | 1LS | W |
| 2884802 | CUNNINGHAM, JAMES | N/a | 1LS | KIA |
| 1545348 | Currie, L. | N/a | 1LS | W |
| 2888745 | CURRIE, MARK | N/a | 6th | KIA |
| 14211598 | CUSACK, FRANCIS | N/a | 6th | KIA |
| 1823094 | Cusick, William | N/a | 1LS | W |
| 2884991 | Cuthbert, David | N/a | 1LS | W+W |
| 2888512 | Dailly, James | N/a | 1LS | W |

| Army Number | Name | Photo | Bn. | Fate |
|---|---|---|---|---|
| 2889085 | Dalby, James | N/a | 6th | W |
| 2075086 | Dalgarno, Alfred | | 1LS | PoW |
| 2890345 | Dalgarno, John | N/a | 6th | W |
| 2879443 | Dalgleish, Peter | N/a | 6th | PoW |
| 267307 | Dallas, William | | 6th | PoW |
| 2879982 | Dalrymple, David | N/a | 1LS | W+W |
| 14407223 | Dalton, Stanley | N/a | 1LS | W |
| 2023603 | Dalziel, John | | 1LS | W |
| 5347924 | Dance, A. | N/a | 1LS | W |
| 316789 | DANIEL, GEOFFREY | N/a | 1LS | W + KIA |
| 2884801 | Darroch, Charles | N/a | 1LS | W |
| 14419353 | Daubney, Francis | N/a | 1LS | PoW |
| 3131204 | DAVERS, JOHN | N/a | 1LS | KIA |
| 14624663 | Davey, Noel | N/a | 1LS | W |
| 2884305 | Davidson, Alexander | N/a | 1LS | W |
| 820934 | Davidson, Andrew | | 1LS | PoW |
| 14634048 | Davidson, Charles | N/a | 1LS | W |
| 2882931 | DAVIDSON, DOUGLAS | N/a | 6th | KIA |
| 2884985 | DAVIDSON, FRANCIS | N/a | 1LS | KIA |
| 2890346 | Davidson, George | N/a | 6th | W + PoW |
| 2763200 | Davidson, James | N/a | 6th | W |
| 2880333 | Davidson, John | N/a | 1LS | W |
| 1460201 | DAVIE, JOHN | N/a | 1LS | KIA |
| 2880119 | Davies, Geoffrey | N/a | 1LS | PoW |
| 14204676 | DAVIES, THOMAS | N/a | 1LS | DoW |
| 1545460 | Davitt, John | N/a | 1LS | W+W |
| 2933637 | DAW, PERCY | N/a | 1LS | KIA |
| 2885587 | Dawson, Robert | N/a | 6th | W |

| Army Number | Name | Photo | Bn. | Fate |
|---|---|---|---|---|
| 11277219 | Deans, J. | N/a | 1LS | W |
| 2881919 | Deans, James | | 6th | W |
| 235396 | Deboys, Norman | N/a | 6th | PoW |
| 6028183 | DEMPSEY, JAMES | N/a | 1LS | KIA |
| 2880263 | Dermit, William (MID) | N/a | 1LS | W+W |
| 2825213 | Devlin, J. | N/a | 1LS | PoW |
| 2758977 | Devlin, W. | N/a | 1LS | W |
| 3247843 | Dewar, J. | N/a | 6th | PoW |
| 3602383 | Dewhurst, A. | N/a | 6th | W |
| 2881578 | Dey, Alexander | N/a | 6th | N/a |
| 420060 | Dick, Alexander | N/a | 1LS | W |
| 2934006 | Dick, R. | N/a | 6th | W |
| 3323428 | Dickson, D. | N/a | 1LS | W |
| 1630480 | DICKSON, WALTER | N/a | 1LS | KIA |
| 14595426 | Dickson, William | N/a | 1LS | W |
| 2889232 | Dickson, William | N/a | 6th | PoW |
| 14201391 | Dilkes, C. | N/a | 1LS | W |
| 6985776 | DINES, JOHN | N/a | 1LS | KIA |
| 2881787 | DINGWALL, JAMES | | 6th | KIA |
| 2876118 | Dinnie, Allie | | 6th | W |
| 1772288 | Dinsley, George | N/a | 6th | W |
| 2886680 | DIXON, ARTHUR | N/a | 1LS | KIA |
| 2889796 | Dobbie, James | N/a | 1LS | W+W |
| 2889763 | Dobson, John | | 1LS | W |
| 2764983 | Docherty, J. | N/a | 1LS | PoW |
| 2935252 | Docherty, T. | N/a | 1LS | W |
| 2880571 | Dodd, Alfred | N/a | 1LS | W |
| 14607481 | Doherty, Thomas | N/a | 1LS | W |

| Army Number | Name | Photo | Bn. | Fate |
|---|---|---|---|---|
| 2885405 | Donachie, John | N/a | N/a | Anzio |
| 3318293 | DONACHY, DANIEL | N/a | 1LS | KIA |
| 2886415 | DONALD, JAMES | | 1LS | DoW |
| 14209044 | DONALD, JAMES | N/a | 6th | KIA |
| 2880305 | Donald, William (MID) | | 6th | PoW |
| 2886344 | DONALDSON, THOMAS | N/a | 1LS | W + KIA |
| 1467032 | DONLAN, MARTIN | N/a | 1LS | KIA |
| 14408936 | Donneley, M. | N/a | 6th | PoW |
| 3314577 | Donnelly, D. | N/a | 1LS | W |
| 14563549 | Donnelly, W. | N/a | 1LS | PoW |
| 14211821 | Doran, W. (MM) | N/a | 1LS | W+W |
| 3136051 | Dorian, J. | N/a | 1LS | PoW |
| 14217812 | DORRINGTON, JOHN | | 6th | KIA |
| 3318793 | DOUGLAS, GEORGE | N/a | 6th | KIA |
| 1485180 | Douglas, Peter | N/a | 1LS | W |
| 3133583 | Doull, William | N/a | 6th | PoW |
| 1494730 | Dow, D. | N/a | 1LS | W |
| 1545379 | Dowdles, William | N/a | 1LS | PoW |
| 2890228 | Dowie, George | | 6th | W + PoW |
| 2885962 | Downs, Alexander | N/a | 6th | W+W |
| 14201570 | Downs, W. | N/a | 1LS | W+W |
| 14607175 | Drever, J. | N/a | 1LS | W |
| 2889818 | Drew, John | N/a | 1LS | W+W |
| 14204685 | Driffield, L. | N/a | 6th | PoW |
| 2886525 | Duddy, Hugh | N/a | 1LS | W |
| 4920244 | Dudley, F. | N/a | 1LS | W |

| Army Number | Name | Photo | Bn. | Fate |
|---|---|---|---|---|
| 239414 | Duff, Colin | | 1LS | W |
| 3601907 | DUFF, DONALD | N/a | 6th | AK |
| 2888863 | Duff, Henry | N/a | 6th | W |
| 2759356 | Duffy, Patrick (MM) | N/a | 1LS | N/a |
| 2884073 | Duffy, Thomas | N/a | 1LS | W |
| 2878819 | Duguid, Evander | N/a | 6th | W |
| 2896939 | Duguid, William | N/a | 6th | W |
| 2885331 | DUKE, ANDREW | N/a | 6th | KIA |
| 14344157 | Dunbar, C. | N/a | 6th | W |
| 2881317 | Dunbar, George | | 6th | N/a |
| 2884022 | Duncan, Dennis | N/a | 1LS | W+W |
| 2873979 | Duncan, Frederick | N/a | 6th | PoW |
| 14633741 | Duncan, G. | N/a | 6th | W |
| 2890229 | Duncan, George Anderson | N/a | 6th | PoW |
| 2877732 | Duncan, George Marnoch | N/a | 6th | W |
| 2883783 | Duncan, James (MID) | | GH | W+W |
| 2886417 | Duncan, James Walker (MID) | N/a | 1LS | N/a |
| 2880114 | Duncan, John (DCM) | N/a | 1LS | N/a |
| 2890662 | Duncan, Patrick | | 6th | PoW |
| 2880520 | Duncan, Thomas | | 6th | PoW |
| 2881088 | Duncan, William | N/a | 6th | PoW |
| 2890508 | Duncan, William James | N/a | 6th | W + PoW |
| 2890231 | Dunsmuir, Walter | N/a | 6th | PoW |

| Army Number | Name | Photo | Bn. | Fate |
|---|---|---|---|---|
| 3254735 | Duris, James | N/a | 1LS | PoW |
| 2761011 | Dyce, A. | N/a | 1LS | W |
| 14226128 | Dyer, G. | N/a | 6th | W |
| 5054222 | DYKE, ROBERT | N/a | 1LS | KIA |
| 2883751 | Eagles, Ernest | N/a | 1LS | W |
| 5889627 | Eames, H. | N/a | 1LS | W+W |
| 798542 | Eastwood, Robert | N/a | 1LS | W |
| 3602362 | Eatock, Jack | N/a | 6th | W |
| 6291605 | Ebsworth, W. | N/a | 6th | W |
| 3050900 | Eckford, George | N/a | 1LS | W |
| 3602189 | EDEN, HORACE | N/a | 6th | DOW |
| 1566145 | Edgar, R.T. | N/a | 1LS | W |
| 2879886 | Edgar, Robert Robertson | N/a | 6th | PoW |
| 2889849 | Edge, William | N/a | 6th | W + PoW |
| 2888865 | Edmonds, Alexander | N/a | 6th | PoW |
| 2886419 | Edward, Ernest (MID) | N/a | 1LS | W |
| 2878665 | Edward, Robert | N/a | 1LS | W |
| 2889397 | Edwards, James | | 6th | W + PoW |
| 289721 | Elgood, Douglas | N/a | 1LS | PoW |
| 1749773 | Elliott, J. | N/a | 1LS | W+W |
| 14640963 | ELLIOTT, JAMES | N/a | 6th | KIA |
| 14648305 | Elliott, Maurice | N/a | 1LS | W + AK |
| 3137624 | ELLIOTT, THOMAS | N/a | 1LS | KIA |
| 14641937 | ELLIS, WILFRED | N/a | 1LS | KIA |
| 1494762 | Ellison, J. (MID) | N/a | 1LS | N/a |
| 14607728 | Ellison, P. | N/a | 6th | N/a |
| 2928914 | Elrick, Allan | N/a | 6th | W + PoW |
| 903787 | EMMANUEL, FRANK | N/a | 6th | AK |
| 14203319 | Ennor, W. | N/a | 6th | PoW |
| 228655 | Erskine, J. | N/a | 6th | W |
| 2981217 | Erskine, S. | N/a | 1LS | W |
| 2878458 | ERSKINE-WHITE, EDWARD | N/a | 1LS | KIA |
| 14200429 | Etherridge, S. | N/a | 6th | PoW |
| 14421086 | EVERETT, WILLIAM | N/a | 1LS | DoW |

| Army Number | Name | Photo | Bn. | Fate |
|---|---|---|---|---|
| 2886420 | Ewen, Charles | N/a | 1LS | PoW |
| 5833435 | EWEN, GLENALBINE | N/a | 1LS | KIA |
| 2879746 | EWING, ROBERT WATSON | N/a | 1LS | KIA |
| 14620872 | Fairweather, John | N/a | 1LS | W |
| 2992081 | Fallon, Peter | N/a | 1LS | W + PoW |
| 1678878 | FARGHER, WILLIAM | N/a | 1LS | W + KIA |
| 14383208 | Farmer, E. | N/a | 1LS | W |
| 105769 | FARQUHARSON, IAN | N/a | 6th | KIA |
| 14656762 | FARRELL, JOHN FERRIER CURRIE | N/a | 1LS | KIA |
| 14281044 | FARRELL, JOHN JOSEPH | N/a | 1LS | KIA |
| 3134734 | FAULKNER, HARRY | N/a | 1LS | KIA |
| 2877661 | FAUTLEY, BERNARD | N/a | 1LS | KIA |
| 14206086 | Fenton, G. | N/a | 6th | W |
| 1838729 | FERGUSON, ARCHIBALD | N/a | 1LS | KIA |
| 2988040 | Ferguson, James | | 1LS | PoW |
| 811144 | Ferguson, John | N/a | 1LS | W |
| 2880192 | Ferguson, John Ronald (MM) | N/a | 1LS | PoW |
| 2829043 | Ferguson, Stewart | N/a | 1LS | PoW |
| 14621419 | Ferguson, William | | 1LS | W |
| 2829276 | Ferris, John | N/a | 1LS | W |
| 2890723 | Findlay, Duncan | N/a | 6th | PoW |
| 172397 | Findlay, James (DSO) | | 1LS | W |
| 2763529 | Finlayson, Gilbert | N/a | 6th | PoW |
| 2870606 | Finnie, Andrew | N/a | 6th | W |
| 14596071 | Finnigan, Peter | N/a | 1LS | W |
| 3602174 | Fisher, John | N/a | 6th | PoW |
| 3195023 | Fisher, W. | N/a | 6th | W |
| 14616454 | FITTON, RONALD | N/a | 6th | KIA |
| 14567626 | Fitzgerald, John | N/a | 1LS | PoW |

| Army Number | Name | Photo | Bn. | Fate |
|---|---|---|---|---|
| 14636530 | Flack, Frederick | N/a | 6th | W+W |
| 14003021 | Flaherty, J. | N/a | 1LS | W |
| 14632121 | Flaherty, William | N/a | 6th | W |
| 2879801 | Flannagan, John | N/a | 6th | PoW |
| 41296 | FLEMING, A.G. INNES | | 6th | DoW |
| 14419358 | Flesher, Henry | N/a | 1LS | W |
| 2878677 | FLETCHER, GEORGE (GAT) | N/a | 1LS | N/a |
| N/k | Fletcher, John | | RACD | N/a |
| 2879845 | FLETT, FREDERICK | N/a | 1LS | Died |
| 14637307 | Flynn, C. | N/a | 1LS | W |
| 5773144 | Flynn, H. | N/a | 1LS | PoW |
| 3192470 | FOGO, EDWIN | N/a | 1LS | KIA |
| 7945463 | Follis, Peter | N/a | 1LS | W |
| 2879712 | Forbes, Alexander (MID) | N/a | 1LS | W |
| 927153 | FORBES, CHARLES | N/a | 1LS | KIA |
| 6212141 | Forbes, D. | N/a | 1LS | W |
| 320429 | Forbes, Fred (MC) | | 1LS | KIA |
| 2886423 | Forbes, James | N/a | 1LS | W |
| 14410492 | Forbes, Robert | N/a | 1LS | W |
| 3192800 | Ford, William | N/a | 1LS | W |
| 14634073 | Fordyce, John | N/a | 1LS | W |
| 240324 | Fordyce, William | N/a | 6th | W + PoW |
| 2882488 | Forsyth, Robert | N/a | 6th | W+W |
| 2890725 | Foster, Alfred | N/a | 1LS | W |
| 4758458 | Foster, M. (MID) | N/a | 1LS | N/a |
| 14634074 | FOSTER, RICHARD | N/a | 1LS | KIA |
| 2886351 | Foster, William | N/a | 1LS | W+W |
| 2885499 | Fotheringham, George | N/a | 1LS | W |
| 14613097 | FOULDS, JOSEPH | N/a | 6th | N/a |
| 14624531 | Foulstone, J. | N/a | 6th | W |

| Army Number | Name | Photo | Bn. | Fate |
|---|---|---|---|---|
| 3247895 | Fox, J. | N/a | 6th | PoW |
| 2890236 | Fox, Robert | N/a | 6th | W |
| 2934646 | Frame, James | N/a | 1LS | W |
| 3247891 | FRAME, ROBERT | | 6th | DoW |
| 3130509 | France, John | N/a | 1LS | W |
| 2890474 | Franklin, Henry | N/a | 1LS | W |
| 197587 | Fraser, Arthur (MC) | N/a | 1LS | N/a |
| 2885379 | Fraser, George | N/a | 1LS | W |
| 2890239 | Fraser, Robert Douglas | N/a | 6th | W |
| 87181 | Fraser, Robert McNeill Hart | | 1LS | N/a |
| 2877393 | Fraser, Vernon (MM) | N/a | 1LS | N/a |
| 14587597 | Fraser, William | N/a | 1LS | PoW |
| 3247889 | Frew, James | | 6th | N/a |
| 14206087 | FROST, JAMES | N/a | 6th | KIA |
| 14640964 | Fry, William | N/a | 1LS | W+W |
| 2765843 | Fulton, Albert | N/a | 6th | PoW |
| 14439832 | FULTON, DAVID | N/a | 1LS | KIA |
| 14524543 | Fussell, Bernard | N/a | 6th | W |
| 2880408 | Fyfe, William | | GH | PoWJ |
| 2889047 | Fyffe, David | N/a | 1LS | PoW |
| 14217582 | Galbraith, J. | N/a | 6th | PoW |
| 2882661 | Galbraith, Malcolm | N/a | 1LS | W |
| 14595627 | GALLACHER, EDWARD | N/a | 1LS | KIA |
| 2824521 | Gallacher, Edward | N/a | 6th | PoW |
| 2879620 | GALLACHER, JOHN | N/a | 1LS | N/a |
| 2873248 | Gallow, Daniel | N/a | 1LS | W |
| 2889821 | Galloway, Ernest | N/a | 6th | PoW |

| Army Number | Name | Photo | Bn. | Fate |
|---|---|---|---|---|
| 2886352 | Gamblin, William | N/a | 1LS | W |
| 6022479 | GAMMAN, JOHN | N/a | 1LS | KIA |
| 14607734 | Gannon, Jack | | 1LS | PoW |
| 7047683 | Garbutt, Robert | N/a | 1LS | W |
| 2766784 | Gardiner, G. | N/a | 6th | W |
| 2759698 | GARDINER, ROBERT | N/a | 1LS | KIA |
| 329769 | Gardiner, S. (MID) | N/a | 1LS | N/a |
| 2879224 | Gardner, Daniel | N/a | 1LS | W |
| 282276 | Garioch, Henry George | | 6th | PoW |
| 3192884 | Garrett, Hugh | N/a | 1LS | W |
| 2890478 | Garven, Ian | N/a | 1LS | W + PoW |
| 3324569 | Gaughan, Henry | N/a | GH | W |
| 3247855 | Gavin, William | N/a | 6th | PoW |
| 14554741 | Geary, William | N/a | 1LS | W |
| 2877091 | GEDDES, ALEXANDER | N/a | 6th | KIA |
| 2884994 | GEDDES, ANDREW | N/a | 1LS | KIA |
| 2880088 | GEDDES, ROBERT | N/a | 6th | DoW |
| 3252990 | Gee, Albert (MM) | N/a | 1LS | W |
| 14644417 | George, John | | 1LS | PoW |
| 4750851 | George, Roy | N/a | 1LS | W |
| 1794876 | GERRARD, JOHN | N/a | 1LS | KIA |
| 2890241 | Gerrie, Peter | | 6th | PoW |
| 2881617 | Gibb, George | N/a | 1LS | W |
| 14202051 | Gibbon, A. | N/a | 6th | W+W |
| 2823983 | Giblin, James | N/a | 6th | PoW |
| 2888029 | Gibson, Charles | N/a | 6th | W + PoW |
| 14574905 | Gibson, J. | N/a | 1LS | PoW |
| 2883058 | Gibson, John Loban | N/a | 1LS | PoW |

| Army Number | Name | Photo | Bn. | Fate |
|---|---|---|---|---|
| 2889550 | GIBSON, WILLIAM | N/a | 1LS | KIA |
| 3323504 | Gifford, H. | N/a | 1LS | W+W |
| 7047681 | Gilbert, Arthur | N/a | 1LS | PoW |
| 2819258 | Gilchrist, J. | N/a | 1LS | W |
| 2889337 | Gilchrist, James | N/a | 1LS | W |
| 6985783 | Gill, Walter | N/a | 1LS | W |
| 239416 | GILLAN, JOHN (MC) | | 1LS | W |
| 2829488 | GILLANEY, JOHN | N/a | 1LS | W + KIA |
| 2885939 | GILLIES, ALEXANDER | N/a | 1LS | KIA |
| 2880507 | Gillies, Charles | N/a | 6th | PoW |
| 2882504 | Gillies, Robert | N/a | 6th | W |
| 2883092 | Gilmore, James | N/a | 6th | PoW |
| 3596257 | GIRLING, WILLIAM | | 6th | W + AK |
| 2829304 | GLACKEN, DANIEL | N/a | 1LS | KIA |
| 14363851 | Glaister, John | N/a | 1LS | W |
| 2763207 | Glass, James | N/a | 6th | W |
| 2885942 | Gleave, Edward | N/a | 1LS | W |
| 1819086 | Glen, David | N/a | 1LS | W+W |
| 184629 | GLOVER, I. (MID) | | 1LS | N/a |
| 14388192 | Godsir, T. | N/a | 1LS | PoW |
| 14648331 | GOLD, GEORGE | N/a | 1LS | KIA |
| 3780603 | Golding, C. | N/a | 1LS | W |
| 3320718 | Goldstone, J. | N/a | 1LS | W |
| 3193267 | Goodall, George | N/a | 1LS | W |
| 2880613 | Goodbrand, James | N/a | 6th | PoW |
| 2869834 | GOODBRAND, WILLIAM | N/a | 6th | AK |
| 14633940 | Goodison, David | | 1LS | W |

| Army Number | Name | Photo | Bn. | Fate |
|---|---|---|---|---|
| 14397924 | Goodson, S. | N/a | 1LS | W |
| 3246990 | Gordon, George (MID) | N/a | 6th | W |
| 2890245 | Gordon, James | N/a | 6th | PoW |
| 2884984 | GORDON, PETER | N/a | 1LS | N/a |
| 239423 | GORDON, RONALD | | 1LS | KIA |
| 2987836 | Gordon, Walter | N/a | 6th | PoW |
| 14205363 | Gordon, William (MID) | N/a | 6th | W |
| 5348962 | Gordon-Crosby, Michael | N/a | 6th | PoW |
| 13022875 | Goudie, John | N/a | 6th | PoW |
| 2766412 | Gourlay, James | N/a | 6th | PoW |
| 14326852 | Gow, Alfred | N/a | 1LS | W |
| 2755204 | Gow, James | N/a | 6th | PoW |
| 3249389 | Gowans, Adam | N/a | 1LS | W |
| 14632147 | Gower, Frederick | N/a | 6th | W |
| 156807 | Grace, Edward (MC) | | 6th | W |
| 2885990 | Gracie, Thomas | N/a | 6th | W |
| 4618017 | Graham, Charles | N/a | 6th | PoW |
| 2750979 | Graham, Christopher | N/a | 1LS | PoW |
| 2888635 | Graham, John | N/a | 1LS | W |
| 3247876 | Graham, William | | 6th | PoW |
| 1439883 | GRANT, ABRAHAM | N/a | ? | KIA |
| 2880282 | Grant, Charles | N/a | 6th | W |
| 40713 | GRANT, IAN PATRICK | | 1LS | W + AK |
| 2082100 | Grant, J. | N/a | 1LS | W |
| 2890247 | Grant, James Richmond | N/a | 6th | PoW |
| 2884920 | Grant, John | N/a | 1LS | PoW |
| 14365284 | GRANT, WILLIAM | N/a | 1LS | KIA |
| 2874400 | Gray, James | N/a | 6th | N/a |

| Army Number | Name | Photo | Bn. | Fate |
|---|---|---|---|---|
| 2886554 | Gray, Joseph | N/a | 1LS | W |
| 2875069 | Gray, Leslie | | 6th | PoW |
| 2882245 | Gray, Robert | N/a | 6th | W |
| 2875068 | Gray, Thomas | | 6th | PoW |
| 14364328 | Gray, William | | 1LS | PoW |
| 2880310 | Green, Donald | N/a | 6th | PoW |
| 3602301 | Green, G. | N/a | 6th | W |
| 2881090 | GREEN, JAMES | | 6th | DoW |
| 3247909 | Greenfield, W. | N/a | 6th | PoW |
| 2886354 | Greensitt, Norman | N/a | 6th | PoW |
| 2764924 | GREENWOOD, JAMES | N/a | 6th | KIA |
| 2881322 | Greig, Allan | | 6th | PoWJ |
| 2888884 | Greig, Herbert | | 6th | PoW |
| 14205366 | Greig, J. | N/a | 6th | W |
| 2880559 | GREIG, JAMES | N/a | 6th | KIA |
| 2890248 | GRIERSON, WILLIAM | N/a | 6th | KIA |
| 4122654 | Griffiths, W. | N/a | 6th | W |
| 14205369 | Grimley, J. | N/a | 1LS | W |
| 3602349 | Grimshaw, Tom | N/a | 6th | PoW |
| 3244797 | Grover, Alexander | N/a | 1LS | W |
| 3318316 | GRUBB, JAMES | N/a | 1LS | KIA |
| 3327633 | Grumley, E. | N/a | 1LS | W |
| 2991179 | Guzuski, Anthony | N/a | 6th | PoW |

| Army Number | Name | Photo | Bn. | Fate |
|---|---|---|---|---|
| 2882226 | Hadden, Alexander (MM) | | 6th | N/a |
| 2881797 | Hadden, James | | 6th | N/a |
| 3195252 | HADDOCK, WILFRED | N/a | 6th | KIA |
| 14202023 | HAGAR, ALFRED | N/a | 1LS | KIA |
| 2990356 | HAGGART, JOHN (MID) | | 1LS | DoW |
| 2884576 | Haggarty, John | | 6th | PoW |
| 3059324 | Haggerty, R. | N/a | 1LS | W |
| 14424113 | HAGUE, JOHN | N/a | 1LS | KIA |
| 2890673 | Haig, Edward | N/a | 6th | W |
| 2823884 | Hainey, John | N/a | 6th | PoW |
| 2885260 | Haldane, Andrew | N/a | 1LS | PoW |
| 3601812 | Hall, J. | | 6th | PoW |
| 5344272 | Hall, T. | N/a | 1LS | PoW |
| 14656251 | Hallett, Herbert | N/a | 1LS | W |
| 14404634 | Hallows, F. | N/a | 6th | PoW |
| 14607738 | Hamill, Alexander | N/a | 1LS | PoW |
| 2767051 | Hamilton, Daniel | N/a | 6th | PoW |
| 2885970 | HAMILTON, JOHN | N/a | 6th | KIA |
| 2880299 | HAMILTON, WILLIAM | N/a | 1LS | N/a |
| 2825434 | HAMPSAY, JOHN | N/a | 1LS | DoW |
| 2982224 | Hampson, J. | N/a | 1LS | W |
| 2889364 | HANCOCK, ROWLAND | N/a | 1LS | KIA |
| 2756637 | HANDY, FRANCIS | N/a | 6th | KIA |
| 2993441 | Hanley, J. | N/a | 1LS | W |

| Army Number | Name | Photo | Bn. | Fate |
|---|---|---|---|---|
| 2890736 | Hannan, John | N/a | 6th | PoW |
| 1494855 | Hannay, Robert | N/a | 1LS | PoW |
| 11265603 | HANNON, ROBERT | N/a | 1LS | KIA |
| 4544631 | Hansborough, Frank | N/a | 6th | W |
| 3254725 | Happenstall, Frank | N/a | 1LS | W |
| 2877114 | Hardie, George (MM) | N/a | 6th | W+W |
| 2763926 | Harding, Douglas | N/a | 6th | PoW |
| 1607055 | Hardman, Arthur | N/a | 6th | W |
| 2821397 | HARKINS, JOHN | N/a | 1LS | KIA |
| 2987845 | Harkness, R. | N/a | 1LS | W+W |
| 2886717 | HARLAND, CLARENCE | | 1LS | DoW |
| 2879634 | Harley, George (MM) | N/a | 1LS | W |
| 1093854 | Harley, James | N/a | 1LS | W |
| 2884309 | Harper, George | N/a | 1LS | PoW |
| 14200483 | Harper, R. | N/a | 6th | W |
| 14602282 | HARRIS, EDWARD | N/a | 1LS | KIA |
| 4128309 | Harrison, E. | N/a | 1LS | W |
| 14620885 | Harrison, Francis | N/a | 6th | W |
| 2889413 | Harrison, Thomas | N/a | 6th | W |
| 2878132 | HARROWER, DOUGLAS | | 6th | KIA |
| 2884980 | Harrower, James | N/a | 1LS | W |
| 3251248 | Hartshorne, Frank | N/a | 1LS | W |
| 14540571 | HARVIE, EDWARD | N/a | GH | KIA |
| 3254711 | Haslam, William | N/a | 1LS | W + PoW |
| 3192680 | HASTIE, ARCHIBALD | N/a | 1LS | DoW |
| 3135447 | Hastings, Robert | N/a | 1LS | PoW |
| 88461 | Hatt, Leslie | | 6th | N/a |
| 2763211 | HAUGHEY, HUGH | N/a | 6th | KIA |
| 5345353 | HAWES, HENRY | N/a | 1LS | W + KIA |
| 14503049 | Hawkins, G | N/a | 1LS | W+W |
| 2877815 | HAY, ALLAN | N/a | 6th | KIA |

| Army Number | Name | Photo | Bn. | Fate |
|---|---|---|---|---|
| 2886557 | HAY, DOUGLAS | | 1LS | W+W |
| 2930360 | Hay, J. | N/a | 1LS | W |
| 2890741 | HAY, JAMES HUNTER | | 1LS | DoW |
| 2880359 | Hay, John McDonald | N/a | 6th | W+W |
| 2879895 | Hay, William Douglas (MID) | N/a | 1LS | N/a |
| 14002675 | Hay, William G. | N/a | 6th | PoW |
| 2933678 | Haydock, Hubert | N/a | 1LS | W + PoW |
| 968893 | Hayes, Charles | N/a | 1LS | W |
| 14002818 | Hayes, J. | N/a | GH | W |
| 2885623 | Hayes, John | N/a | 6th | W |
| 14551492 | HAYNES, ALBERT | N/a | 1LS | DoW |
| 2940112 | Haynes, H. | N/a | 1LS | PoW |
| 1775357 | Haythorne, Albert | N/a | 6th | W |
| 4698317 | Haywood, Cyril | N/a | 6th | PoW |
| 1792980 | HEARD, JAMES | N/a | 1LS | KIA |
| 2890485 | HEASMAN, ERNEST | N/a | 1LS | KIA |
| 4621261 | Hebden, Norman | N/a | 1LS | PoW |
| 896803 | HENDER, GERALD | N/a | 1LS | KIA |
| 2993347 | Henderson, Duncan | N/a | 6th | PoW |
| 2829310 | Henderson, Donald | N/a | 1LS | W |
| 316684 | HENDERSON, EDWARD | N/a | 1LS | N/a |
| 239417 | Henderson, F. (MID) | | 1LS | N/a |
| 2890461 | HENDERSON, JAMES | N/a | 1LS | KIA |
| 2883894 | Henderson, John | N/a | 6th | W + PoW |
| 2883109 | HENRY, NORMAN | | 6th | KIA |
| 2888643 | Hepburn, William | N/a | 1LS | W |
| 3602359 | Hibbert, William | N/a | 6th | PoW |
| 879035 | HICKEY, JAMES | N/a | 1LS | KIA |

| Army Number | Name | Photo | Bn. | Fate |
|---|---|---|---|---|
| 6665902 | HIGGINBOTHAM, CYRIL (MID) | N/a | 1LS | KIA |
| 2888164 | Higgins, Wilfred | N/a | 6th | PoW |
| 2888890 | Hill, Archibald | N/a | 6th | PoW |
| 2765262 | Hill, G. | N/a | 1LS | PoW |
| 14200506 | Hill, N. | N/a | 6th | N/a |
| 14201584 | Hill, Stanley | N/a | 1LS | PoW |
| 14607530 | HILL, WILLIAM | N/a | 6th | KIA |
| 3246830 | Hillan, Hugh | N/a | 1LS | PoW |
| 5346482 | Hills, C. | N/a | 1LS | W |
| 3318995 | Hills, M. | N/a | 6th | PoW |
| 1130617 | HILTON, NORMAN | N/a | 6th | PoW + DoW |
| 2886360 | HINGSTON, GEORGE | | 1LS | W + KIA |
| 14201412 | Hodson, R. | N/a | 6th | PoW |
| 2933638 | HOGAN, DAVID | N/a | 1LS | KIA |
| 14436821 | HOGG, FREDERICK | N/a | 6th | KIA |
| 14644468 | HOGG, JAMES | N/a | 6th | KIA |
| 3132901 | Hogg, John | N/a | 1LS | W+W |
| 3192353 | Hogg, William | N/a | 1LS | W |
| 160786 | Hoggarth, Frank | | 6th | N/a |
| 14632169 | Hollands, Stanley | N/a | 6th | W |
| 96684 | Hollebone, Derek Graham (MC) | N/a | 1LS | N/a |
| 87896 | HOLLEBONE, JAMES | | 1LS | KIA |
| 14201914 | Hollingsworth, F. | N/a | 1LS | PoW |
| 2889621 | Holloway, Horace | N/a | 1LS | PoW |
| 2829312 | Holmes, Alexander | N/a | 1LS | PoW |
| 2879690 | HOLOHAN, LAWRENCE | N/a | 1LS | KIA |
| 2759527 | Holt, Walter | N/a | 6th | PoW |
| 3308064 | Hope, J. | N/a | 1LS | W |
| 2886144 | Horn, George | N/a | 6th | W + PoW |

| Army Number | Name | Photo | Bn. | Fate |
|---|---|---|---|---|
| 3054343 | Horne, Jack | N/a | 6th | PoW |
| 2876984 | Horne, William | | 6th | N/a |
| 2886226 | Hosie, James | | 6th | W+W |
| 11257783 | HOSIE, JOHN | N/a | 1LS | DoW |
| 3602199 | HOSLER, RONALD | N/a | 6th | KIA |
| 14201965 | Hough, D. | N/a | 6th | PoW |
| 2047449 | House, Frank | N/a | 1LS | PoW |
| 3060184 | Hoy, David (MM. MID) | | 1LS | N/a |
| 1820158 | Hoy, Thomas | N/a | 1LS | PoW |
| 7047737 | HUBBARD, HARRY | N/a | 1LS | KIA |
| 2888459 | HUBBLE, HUGH | N/a | 1LS | KIA |
| 4698982 | Huddleston, W. | N/a | 1LS | PoW |
| 14636559 | Hudson, Arthur | N/a | 6th | W |
| 1750970 | HUGHES, ALEXANDER | N/a | 1LS | DoW |
| 2829052 | HUGHES, HENRY | N/a | 6th | KIA |
| 4750880 | HUGHES, HENRY EDWARD | N/a | 1LS | DoW |
| 1484097 | Hughes, R.W.J. | N/a | 1LS | W |
| 14407459 | Hughes, Ronald | N/a | 1LS | W |
| 2884899 | Hume, John | N/a | 1LS | W |
| 2889345 | Humphrey, Jack Douglas | N/a | 6th | PoW |
| 3193184 | HUNT, RAYMOND | N/a | 1LS | KIA |
| 2753216 | Hunter, George | N/a | 1LS | W |
| 2885319 | HUNTER, ROBERT | N/a | 1LS | KIA |
| 105990 | HUTCHEON, DAVID | | 6th | KIA |
| 14272861 | Hutchinson, A.L. | N/a | 6th | PoW |
| 14589533 | Hutchinson, Aubrey W. | N/a | 1LS | W |
| 14207684 | Hutchinson, N. | N/a | 6th | W |
| 2886228 | Hutchison, Alexander | N/a | 6th | PoW |

| Army Number | Name | Photo | Bn. | Fate |
|---|---|---|---|---|
| 2879805 | Hutchison, Angus | N/a | 6th | PoW |
| 14201915 | Hyde, G. | N/a | 6th | PoW |
| 14648372 | HYLAND, PATRICK | N/a | 1LS | KIA |
| 2886563 | Illingworth, Percy | N/a | 6th | N/a |
| 2890253 | Inch, William | N/a | 6th | W |
| 14407432 | Inglis, J. | N/a | 1LS | W |
| 321176 | INGRAM, ALISTAIR (MID) | N/a | 1LS | KIA |
| 2869036 | INGRAM, JAMES | N/a | 6th | KIA |
| 4697767 | Ireland, Leslie (MID) | N/a | 1LS | PoW |
| 3129238 | Irvine, David | N/a | 6th | PoW |
| 1586071 | IRVINE, SMITH | N/A | 6th | KIA |
| 14656774 | Jack, Gavin | N/a | 1LS | N/a |
| 3247789 | Jack, Robert | | 6th | W |
| 5339350 | Jackson, Eugene | N/a | 6th | W |
| 14557115 | JACKSON, JOHN | N/a | 1LS | KIA |
| 2890256 | Jackson, Joseph | N/a | 6th | W |
| 2762490 | Jackson, R. | N/a | 1LS | W |
| 2767122 | Jackson, Wilson | N/a | 6th | W |
| 2875689 | Jaffray, George | N/a | 6th | PoW |
| 14342043 | JAMES, DERRICK | N/a | 1LS | KIA |
| 5512080 | James, E. | N/a | 1LS | PoW |
| 2930979 | James, H. | N/a | 1LS | W |
| 1554366 | JAMES, THOMAS | | 6th | KIA |
| 6857953 | JAMESON, JOHN | N/a | 1LS | KIA |
| 14515870 | Jamieson, R. | N/a | 1LS | PoW |
| 2885030 | Jamieson, Stanley | | 6th | AK |
| 2879859 | JARRATT, CHARLES | N/a | 1LS | DoW |
| 14574926 | JEANS, CHARLES | N/a | 1LS | KIA |
| 2879984 | Jeans, John | N/a | 1LS | PoW |
| 14423012 | Jeffrey, David | N/a | 1LS | PoW |

| Army Number | Name | Photo | Bn. | Fate |
|---|---|---|---|---|
| 14201506 | Jeffs, H. | N/a | 1LS | W |
| 14201507 | JENKINS, DAVID | N/a | 1LS | AK |
| 14648378 | JENKINS, GEORGE | N/a | 6th | KIA |
| 3066869 | Jennings Thomas | N/a | 1LS | W |
| 14626119 | Jennison, George | N/a | 1LS | PoW |
| 1156185 | Jewell, Arthur | N/a | 6th | W |
| 2762492 | Johnson, H. | N/a | 1LS | W |
| 5349612 | Johnson, R. | N/a | 6th | PoW |
| 2940170 | Johnson, Robert | N/a | 1LS | PoW |
| 2888898 | Johnson, Walter | N/a | 6th | W |
| 2882701 | Johnston, James | | 6th | PoW |
| 2886320 | Johnston, John (MM) | N/a | 1LS | N/a |
| 14410343 | Johnstone, A. | N/a | 1LS | N/a |
| 14002602 | Johnstone, J.M.M. (MID) | N/a | 1LS | N/a |
| 3137697 | Johnstone, John (MID) | N/a | 1LS | N/a |
| 2880573 | Johnstone, Peter (MID) | N/A | 1LS | N/a |
| 1743568 | Jolly, Joseph | N/a | 1LS | W |
| 14201510 | Jones, D. | N/a | 6th | PoW |
| 7047697 | JONES, JOHN | N/a | 1LS | KIA |
| 2880828 | Jones, Laurence | N/a | 1LS | PoW |
| 41323907 | Jones, R.E.F. | N/a | 6th | W |
| 6022520 | Jones, Richard B. | N/a | 6th | PoW |
| 7047070 | JONES, RICHARD WILLIAM HENRY | N/a | 1LS | KIA |
| 14403347 | Jones, Robert | N/a | 1LS | W |
| 14201589 | Jones, S. | N/a | 1LS | W + PoW |
| 4278992 | Jones, Terrence | N/a | 6th | W |
| 14602295 | Jones, W. | N/a | 6th | W |
| 2886231 | JORDAN, CHARLES | N/a | 1LS | KIA |
| 14204799 | Jordan, D. | N/a | 6th | PoW |
| 3133591 | JUDGE, JOHN | N/a | 6th | KIA |
| 100295 | Jupp, Kenneth Graham (MC) | N/a | RA | N/a |
| 14563406 | Kane, D. | N/a | 1LS | W |
| 14505701 | Kane, E. | N/a | 6th | PoW |

| Army Number | Name | Photo | Bn. | Fate |
|---|---|---|---|---|
| 3236944 | KANE, ROBERT | N/a | 1LS | AK |
| 2884997 | KAY, SAMUEL | N/a | 1LS | KIA |
| 14412849 | Kaye, William | N/a | 6th | W |
| 14633953 | Keay, David | N/a | 1LS | W |
| 2878141 | Keene, Charles | N/a | 1LS | W |
| 2764419 | Keightley, A. | N/a | 1LS | PoW |
| 2875516 | Keith, Alexander | | 6th | N/a |
| 14253418 | KEITH, JOHN | N/a | 1LS | PoW + DoW |
| 3189864 | Kelly, Alexander | N/a | 1LS | W |
| 2885627 | Kelly, Gerard | N/a | 1LS | W |
| 2934748 | Kelly, Patrick | N/a | 1LS | W |
| 2763610 | Kelly, Thomas | N/a | 6th | W + PoW |
| 2884537 | KEMLO, JOHN | N/a | 1LS | W+W |
| 7047699 | Kendrick, Isaac | N/a | 1LS | W + PoW |
| 165892 | KENILWORTH, DOUGLAS | | 1LS | DoW |
| 2763221 | Kennedy, Andrew | N/a | 6th | PoW |
| 3189842 | Kennedy, J. | N/a | 1LS | PoW |
| 2886569 | Kennedy, Robert | | 6th | W+W |
| 2872504 | Kennedy, Walter (MID) | N/a | 1LS | N/a |
| 14647066 | KENYON, JOHN | N/a | 6th | KIA |
| 3129612 | Kerr, J. | N/a | 1LS | W |
| 1078938 | KERSHAW, JOHN | N/a | 6th | KIA |
| 3195862 | Kerwin, John | N/a | 6th | PoW |
| 2878427 | Kidd, Andrew | N/a | 1LS | PoW |
| 4758483 | Kilburn, F. (MID) | N/a | 1LS | N/a |
| 2890292 | Kilgour, James | N/a | 6th | W |
| 2890290 | Kiloh, John | N/a | 6th | W+W |
| 14629767 | KIMBERLEY, LEON | N/a | 6th | KIA |
| 14206119 | King, F. | N/a | 6th | W + PoW |
| 3324483 | King, R.C. | N/a | 6th | W |

| Army Number | Name | Photo | Bn. | Fate |
|---|---|---|---|---|
| 14563409 | KING, ROBERT | N/a | 1LS | PoW + DoW |
| 2825154 | KINNANE, JOHN | N/a | 1LS | KIA |
| 2940067 | Kinsella, Ronald | N/a | 1LS | W+W |
| 2890291 | Kippen, William | N/a | 6th | W + PoW |
| 14308182 | Kirk, Benjamin | N/a | 1LS | W |
| 14201917 | Kirkby, W. | N/a | 6th | PoW |
| 2880959 | Kirkwood, George | N/a | 1LS | W |
| 6467328 | Kitchen, F. (MID) | N/a | 1LS | N/a |
| 2991909 | Kitching, Richard | N/a | 6th | W |
| 14200537 | KNIGHT, LESLIE | N/a | 1LS | POW + DoW |
| 2880335 | KNIGHTLY, EDWARD | N/a | 1LS | KIA |
| 3128304 | KNIGHTSON, JOHN | N/a | 6th | KIA |
| 2888901 | KNOWLES, JAMES | N/a | 6th | AK |
| 14209121 | Kydd, John | N/a | 1LS | PoW |
| 4456640 | Kyle, Thomas | N/a | 6th | W |
| 14314469 | Lafferty, G. | N/a | 1LS | W |
| 14201512 | Laffey, T. | N/a | 6th | PoW |
| 2764576 | LAIDLAW, PETER | N/a | 6th | W + KIA |
| 2880554 | Laird, Frederick | N/a | 6th | N/a |
| 3137701 | Lamb, Alexander | N/a | 1LS | PoW |
| 2879720 | Lamb, Alfred Haddan | N/a | 1LS | W |
| 14595456 | Lamb, Charles | N/a | 6th | W |
| 3597087 | Lamb, John (MID) | N/a | 6th | W |
| 2890294 | Lamberton, Alexander | N/a | 6th | PoW |
| 1460095 | LAMONT, GEORGE | N/a | 1LS | KIA |
| 14554936 | Lannarelli, Alexander | N/a | 1LS | PoW |
| 2382592 | Launder, Robert | N/a | 6th | W + PoW |
| 2883480 | Lauriston, Henry | N/a | 1LS | PoW |
| 14205391 | Laverty, W | N/a | 1LS | PoW |
| 47260 | Law, Andrew Torrance (DSO, MID) | | 1LS | N/a |
| 68733 | Lawrie, Norman (MC) | N/a | 6th | N/a |
| 65061 | Lawrie, William (MBE) | | 5th GH | PoW |
| 2879571 | LAWSON, ALEXANDER | N/a | 1LS | KIA |

| Army Number | Name | Photo | Bn. | Fate |
|---|---|---|---|---|
| 2890061 | Lawson, Gavin | N/a | 6th | N/a |
| 14573447 | LAWTON, JOSEPH | N/a | 6th | KIA |
| 2762505 | Leaburn, Thomas | N/a | 1LS | PoW |
| 3194109 | Leadbitter, George | N/a | 6th | PoW |
| 193437 | LECKIE, JAMES (MID) | | 6th | KIA |
| 14417402 | Ledicott, Douglas | | 6th | N/a |
| 16293 | Ledingham, John | | 6th | N/a |
| 2878057 | Lee, Basil | N/a | 1LS | W |
| 14002845 | Lee, H. | N/a | 1LS | W+W |
| 105149 | Lee, Ian | N/a | 6th | PoW |
| 14598911 | Leeming, John | N/a | 1LS | W |
| 14518310 | Leff, George | N/a | 1LS | PoW |
| 3130698 | Leighton, Frederick | N/a | 6th | PoW |
| 2890476 | Lennie, Robert | N/a | 1LS | W |
| 4696751 | Leonard, Henry | N/a | 6th | PoW |
| 2889080 | Leslie, John Duncan | N/a | 1LS | PoW |
| 2882383 | Leslie, John Gordon | N/a | 6th | W |
| 2881269 | Lewin, Frederick | N/a | 1LS | PoW |
| 1545223 | LEWIS, ROBERT | N/a | 1LS | KIA |
| 2886572 | Lewis, Samuel | N/a | 1LS | W |
| 2890517 | Leys, William | | 1LS | PoW |
| 4920316 | Liggins, E. | N/a | 1LS | W |
| 4920319 | Liggins, Robert | N/a | 1LS | PoW |
| 1078949 | Lindley, Walter | | 6th | N/a |
| 3250202 | Lindsay, George | N/a | 1LS | PoW |

| Army Number | Name | Photo | Bn. | Fate |
|---|---|---|---|---|
| 14209128 | LINDSAY, JAMES | N/a | 6th | KIA |
| 2760980 | Lindsay, P.C. | N/a | 1LS | W |
| 3247787 | Lindsay, Walter | N/a | 1LS | PoW |
| 2884987 | Lindsey-Clark, Peter | N/a | 1LS | PoW |
| 2879613 | Little, Donald | N/a | 6th | PoW |
| 3185676 | Little, James | N/a | 1LS | W |
| 2890296 | LITTLE, JAMES | N/a | 6th | KIA |
| 2874791 | Littlejohn, David | N/a | GH | W |
| 2871823 | Littlejohn, William | N/a | 6th | PoW |
| 2823798 | Livingstone, H. | N/a | 1LS | W |
| 14632899 | LIVINGSTONE, JOHN | N/a | 6th | KIA |
| 2934538 | Lloyd, Derek | N/a | 6th | W |
| 3325159 | Lobban, A. | N/a | 1LS | W |
| 2881802 | Lobban, James | | 6th | W |
| 2889272 | Lochnell-Campbell, Alasdair | N/a | 1LS | W |
| 3132935 | Lockerbie, James | N/a | 1LS | PoW |
| 2886167 | LOCKHART, DAVID | N/a | 1LS | DoW |
| 14205400 | LOGAN, BARTHOLOMEW | N/a | 1LS | KIA |
| 2829323 | Logan, Charles | N/a | 1LS | W+W |
| 14633799 | Logan, J. | N/a | 1LS | PoW |
| 2882155 | Logan, William | | 6th | PoW |
| 2887516 | Long, Eddie | N/a | 6th | PoW |
| 5435461 | Long, F. | N/a | 1LS | W |
| 2882286 | Longmore, John | N/a | 6th | PoW |
| 14587689 | LONGRIDGE, JAMES | N/a | 1LS | KIA |
| 2890661 | Lord, Alastair | | 6th | W |
| 2882971 | Lorimer, Douglas | | 6th | PoW |
| 2829208 | Louden, S. | N/a | 1LS | PoW |

| Army Number | Name | Photo | Bn. | Fate |
|---|---|---|---|---|
| 2878196 | Lovett, Frederick George | | 1LS | W |
| 2883200 | Low, Alexander | N/a | 6th | PoW |
| 302163 | Low, James | N/a | 6th | N/a |
| 2884814 | Low, Reginald (MM) | N/a | 1LS | N/a |
| 14573450 | Lowe, Fred | N/a | 6th | PoW |
| 4696779 | Lowe, G. | N/a | 1LS | W |
| 4244105 | Lowe, T. | N/a | 1LS | W |
| 14547201 | Lumsden, G. | N/a | 1LS | W |
| 2880107 | Lund, Peter | N/a | 1LS | W |
| 14624541 | Lunn, Ernest | N/a | 6th | PoW |
| 105742 | LYALL-WILSON, THOMAS LESLIE | | GH | AK |
| 14343320 | LYCETT, JOSEPH | N/a | 1LS | KIA |
| 307947 | Lynam, Joseph (US Bronze Star) | N/a | 1LS | W |
| 3715137 | Lynch, David | N/a | 6th | PoW |
| 6607913 | Lynch, John | N/a | 1LS | W |
| 2829325 | Lynn, Joseph | N/a | 1LS | W+W |
| 14575183 | Lynn, Joseph | N/a | 6th | W |
| 2870623 | Lyon, Alexander | N/a | 6th | PoW |
| 2763371 | Lyon, George | N/a | 6th | PoW |
| 13106521 | LYON, THOMAS SLATER | | 1LS | W + KIA |
| 2889864 | Lyons, Leonard | N/a | 6th | PoW |
| 2890309 | MacAllister, John | N/a | 6th | W |
| 2889775 | MacDonald, Donald | N/a | 6th | PoW |
| 14599686 | MacDONALD, HUGH | N/a | 1LS | W + KIA |
| 2890311 | MacDonald, Thomas | N/a | 6th | PoW |
| 2827537 | MacDonald, William | N/a | 6th | PoW |
| 2878299 | MacDOUGALL, WILLIAM | N/a | 1LS | KIA |
| 2882243 | Macduff, Robert | N/a | 6th | PoW |
| 2880468 | MacFarlane, Donald | N/a | 1LS | W+W |
| 13015035 | Macfarlane, W. (MID) | N/a | 1LS | N/a |
| 2878553 | MacGILL, CAMERON | N/a | 1LS | DoW |

| Army Number | Name | Photo | Bn. | Fate |
|---|---|---|---|---|
| 2888554 | MACKAY, ANGUS | N/a | 1LS | KIA |
| 991113 | MACKAY, DONALD | N/a | 1LS | KIA |
| 2890065 | Mackay, Donald Lee | N/a | 1LS | PoW |
| 2884947 | Mackay, George | N/a | 1LS | W + PoW |
| 2890522 | Mackay, Kenneth | N/a | 1LS | PoW |
| 5260136 | MacKENZIE, HECTOR | N/a | 1LS | KIA |
| 2887250 | MACKIE, ARCHIBALD | N/a | 6th | KIA |
| 3326171 | Mackie, George | N/a | 1LS | PoW |
| 14554415 | Mackie, John | N/a | 1LS | W |
| 2882556 | Mackie, William | | GH | PoWJ |
| 2882692 | MacLagan, Alexander (MID) | N/a | 1LS | W |
| 239419 | MacLean, J.B. | | 1LS | W |
| 14644434 | MACLEAN, JOHN NEIL | N/a | 6th | KIA |
| 98599 | MacLEOD, ANGUS | | 1LS | KIA |
| 137921 | Macleod, K.W. (MID) | | 1LS | N/a |
| 102573 | MACPHERSON, ROBERT | | RACD | KIA |
| 2932232 | Madden, D. | N/a | 1LS | W |
| 2829524 | Magee, James | N/a | 1LS | PoW |
| 14217588 | Maiden, W. | N/a | 1LS | PoW |
| 2878287 | MALCOLM, KENNETH | N/a | 6th | AK |
| 2757399 | Malloy, Hugh | N/a | 6th | PoW |
| 13095572 | Malpas, B. | N/a | 6th | W |
| 1694628 | MALTBY, RICHARD | N/a | 6th | KIA |
| 4758036 | Mansfield, A. | N/a | 6th | W |
| 2939946 | MANSFIELD, JAMES | N/a | 1LS | W+W |

| Army Number | Name | Photo | Bn. | Fate |
|---|---|---|---|---|
| 2890690 | Manson, Robert | | 6th | W |
| 2821412 | MARR, WILLIAM | N/a | 1LS | KIA |
| 3974650 | Marsh, R. | N/a | 1LS | PoW |
| 14201971 | Marsh, W. | N/a | 6th | W |
| 2876887 | Marshall, Alexander | N/a | 6th | N/a |
| 2886370 | Marshall, John | N/a | 1LS | W |
| 2886173 | Marshall, Sidney | N/a | 1LS | W |
| 3059811 | Marshall, W. | N/a | 1LS | PoW |
| 14646535 | Martin, Frederick | N/a | 6th | W |
| 6985794 | Martin, George (MM) | N/a | 1LS | N/a |
| 2886591 | Martin, James | N/a | 6th | W+W |
| 1808074 | Martin, P. | N/a | 1LS | W |
| 2890728 | MARTIN, PETER | N/a | 6th | KIA |
| 14218588 | Martin, R. | N/a | 1LS | PoW |
| 201496 | Martin, Stanley | N/a | 6th | W |
| 2762536 | Mason, J. (MID) | N/a | 1LS | W |
| 14409703 | MASON, MATHEW | N/a | 1LS | KIA |
| 14209187 | Massari, B. | N/a | 6th | W |
| 2880611 | Masson, George | N/a | 6th | W |
| 2880253 | MASSON, WILLIAM | N/a | 6th | AK |
| 3325163 | Masterman, J. | N/a | 6th | PoW |
| 11412886 | MASTERS, KENNETH | N/a | 1LS | KIA |
| 2987947 | Matheson, Donald | N/a | 1LS | W+W |
| 2763621 | Mathieson, Robert | N/a | 1LS | PoW |
| 1732359 | Mauchland, James | N/a | 1LS | W |
| 3325164 | Maughan, E. | N/a | 6th | PoW |
| 2824039 | Maxwell, James | N/a | 6th | W |
| 14409151 | MAXWELL, STEPHEN | N/a | 1LS | KIA |
| 3312643 | McAdam, R. | N/a | 1LS | W |
| 3058778 | McALPIN, WILLIAM | N/a | 6th | KIA |
| 3130582 | McAlpine, James | N/a | 1LS | W |
| 3247846 | McArthur, J. | N/a | 6th | PoW |
| 864417 | McARVAIL, HUGH | N/a | 1LS | KIA |
| 3247781 | McAULAY, THOMAS | N/a | 6th | DoW |

| Army Number | Name | Photo | Bn. | Fate |
|---|---|---|---|---|
| 1784994 | McAvoy, J. | N/a | 1LS | W |
| 2879912 | McBay, James William | N/a | 1LS | W |
| 14282129 | McBride, John | N/a | 6th | W |
| 14296976 | McBride, T. | N/a | 6th | W + PoW |
| 14281567 | McCabe, J. | N/a | 1LS | W |
| 2879993 | McCabe, William | N/a | 1LS | W |
| 3316034 | McCafferty, J. | N/a | 1LS | W |
| 1545290 | McCafferty, Thomas | N/a | 1LS | W |
| 3316808 | McCall, John | N/a | 6th | PoW |
| 2882987 | McCALL, JOHN | N/a | 6th | KIA |
| 3247823 | McCALLUM, DUNCAN | N/a | 6th | KIA |
| 7957564 | McCALLUM, IAN | | 6th | KIA |
| 3136077 | McCallum, John | N/a | 1LS | W |
| 2884541 | McCANN, FELIX | N/a | 6th | W + KIA |
| 2885518 | McClements, John | N/a | 1LS | W |
| 4389381 | McCLUSKEY, VINCENT | N/a | 1LS | KIA |
| 14574949 | McClymont, J. | N/a | 1LS | W |
| 3190914 | McClymont, William | N/a | 1LS | W |
| 2880037 | McCONNACHIE, ALEXANDER | N/a | 6th | KIA |
| 3130386 | McConnachie, John | N/a | 6th | W |
| 2888918 | McCONNACHIE, JOHN | N/a | 6th | W + KIA |
| 2889308 | McConnachie, John | N/a | 6th | W |
| 2881819 | McConnachie, John Alexander (MM) | | 6th | PoW |
| 14383246 | McCORMICK, JOHN | N/a | 1LS | KIA |
| 2935905 | McCracken, P. | N/a | 1LS | W |
| 2878190 | McCubbin, Alan | N/a | 1LS | W |
| 2881637 | McCULLOCH, ALEXANDER | N/a | 6th | KIA |
| 2985890 | McCULLOCH, LAWRENCE | N/a | 1LS | KIA |
| 14205408 | McDade, D. | N/a | 6th | W |
| 1819092 | McDERMOTT, PATRICK | N/a | 1LS | KIA |
| 3247900 | McDermott, T. | N/a | 6th | PoW |
| 2939387 | McDonagh, Thomas | N/a | 1LS | W |

| Army Number | Name | Photo | Bn. | Fate |
|---|---|---|---|---|
| 2884879 | McDONALD, ANDREW | N/a | 1LS | W + KIA |
| 2829489 | McDonald, E. | N/a | 1LS | W |
| 2879596 | McDonald, Hector | N/a | 1LS | W |
| 2766521 | McDonald, J. | N/a | 1LS | PoW |
| 2885631 | McDONALD, JAMES | N/a | 1LS | KIA |
| 2888749 | McDonald, Malcolm | N/a | 1LS | PoW |
| 2883482 | McDonald, Neil | N/a | 6th | PoW |
| 1149366 | McDonald, William | N/a | 1LS | W |
| 6026782 | McDougall, P.O. | N/a | 6th | PoW |
| 2885633 | McDougall, Peter | N/a | 1LS | W |
| 3321339 | McDOWALL, ROBERT | N/a | 1LS | N Italy |
| 14648409 | McElduff, Daniel | N/a | 1LS | W |
| 14205415 | McElroy, A. | N/a | 6th | PoW |
| 2878336 | McElroy, John (MM) | N/a | 1LS | W |
| 2755120 | McEwan, T.F. | N/a | 1LS | W |
| 1449665 | McEwan, Thomas Doeherty | N/a | 1LS | W |
| 2889278 | McEwan, George Ruben | N/a | 6th | W |
| 3062081 | McFadden, John | N/a | 6th | PoW |
| 167836 | McFADYEAN, ANGUS (MC) | | 1LS | KIA |
| 2885630 | McGARRITY, JOSEPH | | 1LS | DoW |
| 3247827 | McGarry, D. | N/a | 6th | PoW |
| 917392 | McGill, William | N/a | 1LS | W |
| 203148 | McGillivray, Donald | | 1LS | W |
| 2829505 | McGlinchey, Francis | N/a | 1LS | W |
| 3247910 | McGlynn, F. | N/a | 6th | W |
| 3062087 | McGovern, Henry | N/a | 1LS | W |
| 2883198 | McGowan, William | N/a | 6th | PoW |
| 14564068 | McGregor, A. | N/a | 6th | PoW |
| 3315858 | McGregor, A. | N/a | 1LS | W |
| 14587718 | McGregor, Hugh | N/a | 1LS | PoW |
| 2888300 | McGREGOR, JAMES | N/a | 6th | KIA |

| Army Number | Name | Photo | Bn. | Fate |
|---|---|---|---|---|
| 2760705 | McGuire, J. | N/a | 1LS | W+W |
| 269954 | McHardy, William | | 6th | N/a |
| 14563649 | McHATTIE, ALEXANDER | N/a | 6th | KIA |
| 2878349 | McHATTIE, WILLIAM | N/a | 6th | DoW |
| 13029307 | McInnes, Dugald | N/a | 1LS | PoW |
| 2757659 | McInroy, W. | N/a | 1LS | W |
| 2889222 | McIntosh, Alexander | N/a | 6th | W |
| 2888481 | McINTOSH, ARCHIBALD | N/a | 1LS | W + KIA |
| 127849 | McIntosh, George (MC) | N/a | 6th | W |
| 2880286 | McIntosh, Joseph (MID) | | 6th | N/a |
| 2878828 | McIntosh, Peter | N/a | 6th | W |
| 6213239 | McINTOSH, ROBERT | N/a | 6th | KIA |
| 3326910 | McIntyre, D | N/a | 1LS | W |
| 186410 | McINTYRE, HOODLESS | | 6th | KIA |
| 2877094 | McIrvine, Alexander | N/a | 6th | N/a |
| 14607590 | McIver, N. | N/a | 1LS | PoW |
| 14612412 | McKay, Arthur | N/a | 1LS | PoW |
| 2822226 | McKay, George Gordon (MM) | N/a | 1LS | W + PoW |
| 14214325 | McKay, J. | N/a | 6th | W |
| 2766191 | McKeand, William | | 1LS | PoW |
| 113412 | McKELLAR, ALASTAIR | N/a | 6th | DoW |
| 2889112 | McKenzie, Alexander William | N/a | 1LS | W |
| 2880516 | McKenzie, Arthur | N/a | 6th | PoW |
| 2882695 | McKENZIE, JOHN ADDIE | N/a | 1LS | KIA |
| 2939390 | McKenzie, Neil | N/a | 1LS | W |
| 14634141 | McKENZIE, WILLIAM HAY | N/a | 6th | KIA |
| 2765146 | McKerlie, Alex | N/a | 6th | PoW |
| 14510718 | McKIERNAN, JOHN | N/a | 1LS | KIA |

| Army Number | Name | Photo | Bn. | Fate |
|---|---|---|---|---|
| 2890314 | McKinnell, John | N/a | 6th | W |
| 14564076 | McKINNIE, HUGH | N/a | 1LS | KIA |
| 2885235 | McKinnon, Peter | N/a | 6th | PoW |
| 2882264 | McLAREN, ROBERT | N/a | 6th | KIA |
| 2988103 | McLAUGHLAN, FRANCIS | N/a | 1LS | KIA |
| 2992023 | McLAUGHLIN, ARTHUR | N/a | 1LS | KIA |
| 3196218 | McLAUGHLIN, PATRICK | N/a | 6th | KIA |
| 1656661 | McLAY, JOHN | N/a | 1LS | KIA |
| 14383265 | McLean, A. | N/a | 1LS | W |
| 2821552 | McLEAN, ALEXANDER | N/a | 6th | DoW |
| 2875693 | McLean, Charles | N/a | 6th | PoW |
| 2885346 | McLEAN, CYRIL | N/a | 1LS | KIA |
| 14226516 | McLean, Daniel | N/a | 6th | PoW |
| 2939391 | McLean, Donald | N/a | 6th | W |
| 2875261 | McLean, Donald | N/a | 6th | PoW |
| 3247805 | McLean, James | | 6th | N/a |
| 2883121 | McLean, James | N/a | 6th | W |
| 2883003 | McLean, James Wilson | N/a | 6th | W |
| 4277910 | McLEAN, MALCOLM | N/a | 1LS | KIA |
| 2890315 | McLEAN, ROBERT | N/a | 6th | AK |
| 2875450 | McLean, William | N/a | 6th | PoW |
| 2879838 | McLean, William | N/a | 1LS | W |
| 2885258 | McLean, William Allan Burns | N/a | 1LS | PoW |
| 2885877 | McLeish, John | N/a | 1LS | PoW |
| 2766473 | McLELLAN, ROBERT | N/a | 1LS | KIA |
| 2882176 | McLennan, Roderick | N/a | 6th | PoW |
| 1476298 | McLEOD, DONALD | N/a | 1LS | KIA |
| 14564079 | McLeod, G. | N/a | 1LS | W |
| 14205428 | McLEOD, JAMES (HAMISH) | N/a | 1LS | W + DoW |
| 2890686 | McLeod, Neil | N/a | 6th | W + PoW |
| 2760070 | McLUCKIE, ADAM | N/a | 1LS | DoW |
| 3247907 | McLuckie, W. | N/a | 6th | PoW |
| 1798870 | McMahon, Columbus | N/a | 1LS | W |
| 1798871 | McMAHON, PETER | N/a | 1LS | KIA |
| 3130588 | McMASTER, JOHN | N/a | 6th | DoW |

| Army Number | Name | Photo | Bn. | Fate |
|---|---|---|---|---|
| 2987937 | McMATH, SAMUEL | N/a | 1LS | KIA |
| 2759246 | McMillan, J. | N/a | 1LS | W |
| 2991197 | McMillan, Peter | N/a | 1LS | PoW |
| 14214613 | McMINIGAL, HUGH | N/a | 1LS | KIA |
| 14575211 | McMullen, A. | N/a | 1LS | W |
| 2881814 | McNab, James | N/a | 6th | PoW |
| 2880730 | McNAB, JOHN | N/a | 1LS | KIA |
| 2883694 | McNALLY, WILLIAM | N/a | 1LS | KIA |
| 14212567 | McNaught, William | N/a | 1LS | W |
| 2823294 | McNaughton, Robert | N/a | 6th | PoW |
| 1464705 | McNee, D. | N/a | 1LS | W |
| 2883002 | McNee, William | | 6th | PoW |
| 2981594 | McNeice, W. | N/a | 1LS | W |
| 2993285 | McNicol, J. | N/a | 1LS | W |
| 2991638 | McNicol, J.D. | N/a | 1LS | W |
| 14554413 | McNicoll, D. | N/a | 1LS | W |
| 3136092 | McPeak, John | N/a | 1LS | W |
| 2886030 | McPHERSON, RICHARD (MID) | N/a | 6th | DoW |
| 2877501 | McRae, Charles | | 1LS | PoW |
| 2874482 | McRae, George | | 6th | W |
| 2993472 | McRae, John | N/a | 6th | PoW |
| 2883004 | McRitchie, Robert | | 1LS | PoW |
| 2890688 | McRonald, Douglas | | 6th | PoW |
| 2879535 | McSorley, Francis | N/a | 6th | PoW |
| 2758696 | McStay, W. | N/a | 1LS | W |
| 14209176 | McTaggart, C. | N/a | 6th | PoW |

| Army Number | Name | Photo | Bn. | Fate |
|---|---|---|---|---|
| 2762530 | McTAVISH, ROBERT | N/a | 6th | W + KIA |
| 1465305 | McVicar, A. | N/a | 6th | W + PoW |
| 2881812 | McWilliam, Peter | N/a | 6th | W +W |
| 14648424 | Mead, Dennis | N/a | 6th | W |
| 1690012 | Medway, Harold | N/a | 1LS | W |
| 2933554 | Mee, Joseph | N/a | 6th | W |
| 2885208 | MEIKLE, STANLEY | N/a | 6th | KIA |
| 3247844 | Meikle, T. | N/a | 6th | N/a |
| 2883124 | Melrose, Charles | N/a | 6th | W + PoW |
| 2873902 | Melville, George D. (MID + USA Bronze Star) | N/a | 6th | W |
| 2876677 | Melville, Sinclair | N/a | 6th | W |
| 2890729 | Mennim, Alexander (MM) | | 6th | N/a |
| 14595478 | MENZIES, GERARD | | 1LS | PoW + DoW |
| 2884937 | Menzies, Ian | N/a | 1LS | W |
| 1464713 | Menzies, J.H. | N/a | 1LS | W |
| 2879835 | MENZIES, JOHN CHARLES | N/a | 1LS | DoW |
| 153402 | Methven, James | N/a | 6th | W |
| 14205445 | Middleton, Fred | | 6th | PoW |
| 2882271 | MIDDLETON, GORDON | N/a | 1LS | KIA |
| 2882305 | Middleton, William | | 6th | PoW |
| 2874068 | MILLAR, ARCHIBALD | N/a | 1LS | KIA |
| 2767236 | Millar, David | N/a | 1LS | PoW |
| 14273091 | Millar, J. | N/a | 6th | W |
| 14213674 | Millar, John | N/a | 6th | W |
| 2879760 | MILLAR, JOHN PITCAIRN | N/a | 1LS | KIA |
| 2886597 | Miller, Alfred | N/a | 6th | W |
| 2883233 | MILLER, ANDREW | N/a | 6th | KIA |

| Army Number | Name | Photo | Bn. | Fate |
|---|---|---|---|---|
| 2890173 | Miller, Anthony | N/a | 6th | W |
| 13031125 | Miller, Archibald (MM) | N/a | 1LS | PoW |
| 2890692 | Miller, Desmond | | 6th | PoW |
| 2827653 | Miller, J. | N/a | 1LS | W |
| 2829350 | MILLER, JOHN | | 1LS | KIA |
| 3247483 | MILLER, JOHN | N/a | 1LS | KIA |
| 2758480 | Miller, R.S. | N/a | 6th | W |
| 3192496 | Miller, Thomas | N/a | 1LS | W |
| 2889203 | Mills, William | N/a | 1LS | W |
| 2890480 | Milne, Alan | N/a | 1LS | W |
| 2884127 | Milne, George | | 1LS | N/a |
| 2888663 | MILNE, JAMES | N/a | 6th | KIA |
| 2890299 | Milne, Lewis Marr | | 6th | PoW |
| 14213158 | MILNE, WILLIAM ARMOND | N/a | 6th | DoW |
| 14515903 | MILNE, WILLIAM JOHN | N/a | 1LS | KIA |
| 2889498 | MILNER, NORMAN | N/a | 1LS | KIA |
| 2882491 | MILTON, FRANCIS | N/a | 6th | KIA |
| 14633837 | MILTON, JAMES | | 1LS | KIA |
| 2882161 | Milton, Robert | | 6th | W |
| 2820785 | Milton, William (Wally) | N/a | 6th | PoW |
| 2881302 | Mingo, Laurence | N/a | 6th | W |
| 2890727 | Minto, Ronald | N/a | 6th | W |
| 2889204 | Mitchell, Christopher | N/a | 1LS | PoW |

| Army Number | Name | Photo | Bn. | Fate |
|---|---|---|---|---|
| 6004756 | MITCHELL, DAVID | | 1LS | KIA |
| 2888287 | MITCHELL, FRANK | | 6th | KIA |
| 3252325 | MITCHELL, GEORGE ALLAN (VC) | | 1LS | KIA |
| 2885854 | Mitchell, Robert | N/a | 1LS | PoW |
| 3323858 | Mitchell, S.R. | N/a | 1LS | W |
| 2869152 | Mitchellson, James Thomas | | 6th | PoW |
| 2763628 | Mochrie, Archibald | N/a | 6th | PoW |
| 2881120 | MOCKFORD, DOUGLAS | N/a | 1LS | KIA |
| 14205449 | Moffatt, J.M. | N/a | 1LS | W |
| 3601880 | Moir, James (MM) | | 6th | W |
| 2886042 | Montgomery, Alexander | N/a | 6th | PoW |
| 3135476 | Montgomery, C.H | N/a | 1LS | W |
| 5348535 | Montgomery, William | N/a | 6th | PoW |
| 1517162 | Moodie, Albert George | N/a | 1LS | W |
| 2882981 | MOODIE, NORMAN | | 1LS | KIA |
| 5344666 | Moore, R. | N/a | 1LS | W |
| 2763629 | Moore, William | N/a | 6th | PoW |
| 1820225 | Moran, Finlay | N/a | 1LS | PoW |
| 2890730 | MORDAIN, STANLEY | N/a | 6th | KIA |
| 3252982 | Morris, Harrold | N/a | 6th | PoW |
| 2977263 | Morris, J. | N/a | 1LS | W |
| 2890305 | Morrison, Alexander | N/a | 6th | PoW |
| 2878131 | Morrison, Frank | N/a | 6th | PoW |

| Army Number | Name | Photo | Bn. | Fate |
|---|---|---|---|---|
| 2886256 | Morrison, Frank Gallacher | | 1LS | PoW |
| 1550356 | Morrison, John | N/a | 1LS | W |
| 2879547 | Morrison, Kenneth | N/a | 1LS | W |
| 2890731 | Morrison, Oswald | N/a | 6th | PoW |
| 2875703 | Morrison, Robert | N/a | 6th | N/a |
| 14201600 | Morriss, E. | N/a | 1LS | W |
| 14401484 | MOSS, FELIX | N/a | 1LS | KIA |
| 5848561 | Moss, S. | N/a | 1LS | W |
| 2755971 | Moug, J. | N/a | 1LS | W |
| 14648433 | Moule, Joseph | N/a | 1LS | W |
| 2889209 | Mowat, John | N/a | 6th | N/a |
| 2885277 | Mowat, Percy | N/a | 1LS | W |
| 2885635 | MUIR, MATTHEW | N/a | 6th | KIA |
| 3195326 | MUIRHEAD, WILLIAM | N/a | 1LS | KIA |
| 2889520 | Mullen, Michael | N/a | 1LS | W |
| 14201355 | Mullen, T. | N/a | 1LS | W |
| 3309327 | Mulligan, J. | N/a | 1LS | W |
| 2880534 | Mundy, Frederick | N/a | 1LS | W+W |
| 68138 | Munro, Charles (MBE, MM) | | 6th | N/a |
| 2881319 | Munro, David | N/a | 6th | W |
| 113006 | Munthe, Malcolm | | 6th | W |
| 7683046 | Murdoch, George | N/a | 6th | N/a |
| 2829532 | Murdoch, William | N/a | 1LS | W |
| 2889313 | Murdoch, William | N/a | 6th | PoW |
| 3242793 | Murphy, A.G. | N/a | 1LS | PoW |
| 14540404 | Murphy, Albert | N/a | 1LS | PoW |
| 2889435 | Murphy, Henry | N/a | 6th | PoW |
| 3248423 | MURPHY, JOHN | N/a | 6th | DoW |
| 7018981 | Murphy, Russell | N/a | 6th | PoW |
| 14595485 | MURPHY, THOMAS | N/a | 1LS | KIA |

| Army Number | Name | Photo | Bn. | Fate |
|---|---|---|---|---|
| 3247868 | Murphy, William | | 6th | PoW |
| 3239565 | MURRAY, ANDREW | N/a | 1LS | W + KIA |
| 2885407 | Murray, David | N/a | 1LS | W+W |
| 2879947 | Murray, Donald | N/a | 1LS | PoW |
| 1826705 | Murray, R. | N/a | 1LS | W |
| 14540405 | Murray, Sinclair | N/a | 1LS | W |
| 3247840 | MURRAY, WILLIAM | N/a | 6th | KIA |
| 2882725 | Musgrove, Ian | N/a | 6th | PoW |
| 14635957 | MUSKETT, REGINALD | N/a | 6th | KIA |
| 2889212 | Mutch, Arthur | | 6th | W |
| 2890352 | Mutch, Hugh | N/a | 1LS | W |
| 14629773 | Myers, Ralph | N/a | 6th | W |
| 14002719 | MYLCHREEST, JAMES | N/a | 1LS | KIA |
| 2763644 | Myles, James | N/a | 6th | W + PoW |
| 2763709 | Naismith, C. | N/a | 1LS | W |
| 2878463 | NAPIER, GEORGE | N/a | 1LS | W + KIA |
| 2760674 | Napier, J. | N/a | 6th | W |
| 14407377 | NEAL, STANLEY | N/a | 1LS | N/a |
| 14413924 | Neill, Dennis | N/a | 1LS | PoW |
| 2879218 | NEISH, WILLIAM | N/a | 6th | KIA |
| 2885456 | NESS, JAMES | N/a | 1LS | PoW + DoW |
| 2759565 | NEWLANDS, HUGHIE | N/a | 1LS | KIA |
| 14289640 | Newman, A. | N/a | 6th | W |
| 14200594 | NEWTON, FRANCIS | N/a | 1LS | DoW |
| 6297235 | Nicholson, Francis | N/a | 1LS | W |
| 2890259 | Nicholson, Fred Usher | | 6th | W |
| 2882151 | Nicoll, James | | 6th | PoW |

| Army Number | Name | Photo | Bn. | Fate |
|---|---|---|---|---|
| 2890695 | Nicolson, Alan | N/a | 6th | PoW |
| 109067 | Nimmo, T | | 6th | N/a |
| 2987193 | Nimmo, W | N/a | 1LS | W+W |
| 14559594 | Nitchen, L | N/a | 6th | W |
| 14291917 | NIXON, HARRY | N/a | 1LS | KIA |
| 2882819 | Noble, Andrew | N/a | 6th | W |
| 316441 | Nornable, Gordon (MC) | | GH | W |
| 14635385 | NOTT, ALDER | N/a | 6th | KIA |
| 1096143 | Nugent, James | N/a | 1LS | W |
| 3387173 | NUTTER, FRANK | N/a | 1LS | KIA |
| 2929496 | Oakes, Donald | N/a | 6th | PoW |
| 2889315 | Oates, Alexander | N/a | 1LS | W |
| 172402 | Oates, C | N/a | 1LS | W |
| 2993192 | O'Brien, Andrew (MM) | N/a | 1LS | W+W |
| 3459981 | O'Brien, J. | N/a | 6th | W |
| 14439277 | O'Conner, D. | N/a | 6th | W |
| 2885170 | O'Connor, Edwin | N/a | 6th | W |
| 2890169 | ODELL, THOMAS | N/a | 1LS | KIA |
| 14269991 | O'Donnell, A | N/a | 6th | W |
| 14641959 | Ogston, Albert | N/a | 6th | W |
| 14575239 | O'Hara, John | N/a | 6th | W |
| 3056428 | O'Hare, J. | N/a | 6th | W |
| 3324007 | O'MALLEY, DENNIS | N/a | 1LS | KIA |
| 2993300 | O'Neil, A. | N/a | 6th | PoW |
| 3323145 | O'Neill, E. | N/a | 1LS | W |
| 2884871 | Orchison, Robert | N/a | 1LS | W |
| 2888462 | ORFORD, CLIFFORD | N/a | 6th | KIA |
| 1527399 | ORMISHER, JOHN | N/a | 1LS | AK |
| 2882688 | Orr, John | N/a | 1LS | W |
| 3254634 | ORRICK, WILLIAM | N/a | 1LS | KIA |
| 5349836 | Ougham, Alfred | N/a | 6th | W |
| 14263571 | Outhwaite, A. | N/a | 6th | PoW |

| Army Number | Name | Photo | Bn. | Fate |
|---|---|---|---|---|
| 6619672 | OVERY, WILLIAM | N/a | 6th | KIA |
| 2826279 | Owen, G. | N/a | 1LS | W |
| 1799055 | Palmer, William | N/a | 1LS | W |
| 2766130 | Park, George | | 6th | PoW |
| 3195213 | Park, John | N/a | 1LS | W |
| 2823990 | Park, Robert | N/a | 1LS | PoW |
| 190768 | Parker, Harold (MC) | N/a | RA | N/a |
| 14341201 | Parker, J. | N/a | 6th | PoW |
| 3195259 | PARKER, JACK | N/a | 6th | KIA |
| 1795086 | Parker, Robert | N/a | 1LS | W |
| 5193893 | PARKER, THOMAS | N/a | 6th | N/a |
| 2883743 | PARKIN, GEORGE | N/a | 1LS | KIA |
| 3194114 | Parnaby, George | N/a | 6th | PoW |
| 14201974 | Parr, R. | N/a | 6th | W |
| 2883298 | Paterson, Alexander (MID) | | 6th | W |
| 2884145 | PATERSON, ALLAN | | 1LS | KIA |
| 2987916 | Paterson, David | N/a | 6th | PoW |
| 2882715 | Paterson, Downie | N/a | 6th | W |
| 2762111 | Paterson, G. | N/a | 1LS | W |
| 7962389 | Paterson, George | | 6th | PoW |
| 14209221 | Paterson, J. | N/a | 6th | W |
| 2882682 | PATERSON, PETER | N/a | 1LS | KIA |
| 14587761 | Paterson, Robert | N/a | 1LS | W |
| 14205465 | Paterson, W.G.W. | N/a | 6th | W |
| 2884253 | Paterson, William Alexander | N/a | 1LS | W |
| 2888476 | Paterson, William Graham (MID) | N/a | 1LS | N/a |
| 14642989 | PATON, MALCOLM | N/a | 6th | KIA |

| Army Number | Name | Photo | Bn. | Fate |
|---|---|---|---|---|
| 14653112 | PATON, WILLIAM | N/a | 1LS | KIA |
| 2889316 | Patrick, Daniel | N/a | 6th | PoW |
| 14205467 | PATRICK, THOMAS | N/a | 6th | KIA |
| 14530076 | Patterson, A. | N/a | 1LS | W |
| 2829292 | PATTERSON, JOHN | N/a | 1LS | KIA |
| 2890262 | Patterson, John | N/a | 6th | PoW |
| 2828265 | Paxton, J. | N/a | 1LS | PoW |
| 2822521 | PAYNE, MARTIN | N/a | 1LS | KIA |
| 14341184 | Payne, R. | N/a | 6th | PoW |
| 2889817 | Peacock, Roy | N/a | 1LS | PoW |
| 5961798 | Pearman, G. | N/a | 1LS | W |
| 14203077 | Pearson, E. | N/a | 1LS | W |
| 14217121 | Pearson, H. | N/a | 6th | PoW |
| 2890083 | PEARSON, WILLIAM | N/a | 1LS | KIA |
| 47259 | Peddie, James (DSO, MID) | | 6th | N/a |
| 4347353 | Peel, Harry | N/a | 6th | W |
| 88360 | Penman, Derek (MID) | | 1LS | N/a |
| 3254635 | Penman, Hugh | N/a | 1LS | PoW |
| 3061991 | Penman, W.H. | N/a | 1LS | W |
| 14209228 | Pennan, W. | N/a | 6th | PoW |
| 14201605 | Pepper, C. | N/a | 1LS | N/a |
| 14341179 | Perkins, Douglas | N/a | 6th | W + PoW |
| 14003008 | Perry, B. | N/a | 6th | PoW |
| 14341162 | PESTELL, CHARLES | N/a | 6th | KIA |
| 2890263 | PETRIE, ALEXANDER CASTLE | | 6th | KIA |
| 2877786 | Petrie, Andrew | | 6th | PoW |

| Army Number | Name | Photo | Bn. | Fate |
|---|---|---|---|---|
| 2890533 | Petrie, William | N/a | 6th | PoW |
| 3973917 | Phifer, John | N/a | 1LS | W |
| 2889446 | Philip, Alexander | | 6th | PoW |
| 2880313 | Philips, George | | 6th | PoW |
| 2880285 | Philips, Walter | | 6th | PoW |
| 14239874 | Pickard, William (MM) | N/a | 6th | W |
| 5955928 | PICKERILL, WILLIAM | N/a | 6th | KIA |
| 14204729 | Pickering, A. | N/a | 6th | PoW |
| 3313925 | Pickering, J. | N/a | 1LS | W |
| 14635964 | PICKLES, ERNEST | N/a | 6th | KIA |
| 2890696 | PICKMAN, DAVID HORACE | N/a | 6th | KIA |
| 14566154 | PIKE, EDGAR | N/a | 1LS | W + KIA |
| N/k | Pirie, Patrick Taldo (MC, MID) | | 6th | N/a |
| 5252526 | PITMAN, LAWRENCE | N/a | 1LS | KIA |
| 2879995 | Plain, William | N/a | 1LS | W |
| 1688319 | PLASTOW, JAMES HENRY | N/a | 1LS | KIA |
| 149076 | Pollock, Peter | N/a | 6th | PoW |
| 6406750 | Pollock, T. (MID) | N/a | 1LS | N/a |
| 2883057 | Porter, Alexander | N/a | 6th | W |
| 14217467 | Potter, David | N/a | 1LS | PoW |
| 3251323 | POTTER, WILLIAM | N/a | 1LS | N Italy |
| 13021367 | Pottle, Francis | N/a | 1LS | PoW |
| 2990481 | PoW, G. | N/a | 1LS | W |
| 2940008 | Power, Nicholas | N/a | 1LS | W |
| 2889679 | PRATT, FREDERICK | N/a | 1LS | KIA |
| 2763173 | Pratt, Henry | N/a | 1LS | W + PoW |

| Army Number | Name | Photo | Bn. | Fate |
|---|---|---|---|---|
| 3602386 | Price, Alfred | | 6th | W |
| 14383021 | Pringle, G. | N/a | 1LS | PoW |
| 3195875 | Pringle, John | | 6th | PoW |
| 14634181 | Prior, Peter | N/a | 1LS | W |
| 2940292 | Procter, Arthur (MM) | N/a | 1LS | W |
| 14111988 | Prosser, A. | | 6th | N/a |
| 2890698 | Prosser, Alister Colin | N/a | 6th | PoW |
| 2884755 | Prosser, Charles | N/a | 6th | W |
| 302171 | Provo, C.D.A. | N/a | 6th | W |
| 255459 | Prust, C (MID) | N/a | 1LS | W |
| 248065 | Pugh, James (MC) | N/a | RAMC | N/a |
| 14409981 | Pulford, Kenneth | N/a | 1LS | PoW |
| 2829241 | Purdie, H. | N/a | 1LS | PoW |
| 1632331 | QUIGLEY, JAMES | N/a | 1LS | KIA |
| 2940099 | Quigley, Thomas | N/a | 1LS | W |
| 14515812 | Quinn, J. | N/a | 1LS | W |
| 3237740 | Quinn, John | N/a | 1LS | W |
| 2991501 | Quirie, R. | N/a | 6th | W |
| 3601415 | Race, Thomas | N/a | 6th | PoW |
| 2886052 | RAE, GEORGE COLLIE | | 1LS | KIA |
| 88274 | Rae, Robert (MID) | | 6th | W |

| Army Number | Name | Photo | Bn. | Fate |
|---|---|---|---|---|
| 2889250 | Rae, John | | 6th | PoW |
| 14607633 | Raffan, R. | N/a | 6th | W+W |
| 1771486 | Rainbow, C. | N/a | 1LS | W |
| 5344445 | Rainbow, W. | N/a | 1LS | W |
| 2878834 | Rainnie, Jack (Jock) G. | | GH | W |
| 6297200 | RANDALL, ERNEST | N/a | 6th | KIA |
| 2885110 | RANKIN, DUNCAN (MID) | N/a | 6th | DoW |
| 2890176 | RANKIN, ROBERT | N/a | 6th | KIA |
| 14595576 | Rankine, David | N/a | 6th | W |
| 2881169 | Reace, George (DCM) | N/a | 1LS | W |
| 14207697 | Reay, J. | N/a | 6th | W |
| 2886695 | Reedy, Wilfred (MID) | N/a | 1LS | N/a |
| 2890700 | Reid, Alexander James | | 6th | N/a |
| 2879764 | Reid, Douglas | N/a | 1LS | W |
| 2886055 | Reid, George | N/a | 1LS | W |
| 2880224 | Reid, Gordon | N/a | 6th | PoW |
| 7043955 | Reid, J. | N/a | 6th | W |
| 2886178 | Reid, John | | 6th | W + PoW |
| 2890701 | Reid, John Knox | N/a | 6th | W + PoW |
| 14607637 | REID, THOMAS | | 6th | KIA |
| 14607639 | REILLY, FELIX | N/a | 1LS | KIA |
| 2976615 | Reilly, P. | N/a | 6th | PoW |
| 2889318 | REILLY, STEPHEN | N/a | 6th | DoW |
| 3250486 | Reilly, R. | N/a | 1LS | W+W |
| 14363548 | Renfrew, Daniel | N/a | 1LS | W |

| Army Number | Name | Photo | Bn. | Fate |
|---|---|---|---|---|
| 14621134 | RENNIE, ANDREW | N/a | 1LS | KIA |
| 2878127 | Rennie, David | N/a | 6th | PoW |
| 2879769 | Rennie, James (MM + Bar) | | 1LS | W+W |
| 2762832 | Revis, William | N/a | 1LS | W |
| 138957 | Reynolds-Payne, George (MC) | N/a | 6th | W+W |
| 4869130 | Rhodes, F. | N/a | 1LS | W |
| 2889145 | Rhodes, Richard | N/a | 1LS | W |
| 3715173 | Richards, Alfred | N/a | 6th | W |
| 14629904 | Richards, Donald | N/a | 6th | W |
| 7047719 | Richards, William | N/a | 1LS | PoW |
| 2567339 | Richardson, Joseph | N/a | 1LS | PoW |
| 6215626 | RICKETTS, RONALD | N/a | 1LS | KIA |
| 14209243 | Riddoch, John W | | 6th | PoW |
| 2877754 | Riddoch, William John | | 6th | W |
| 2881822 | Rigby, John | N/a | 6th | PoW |
| 2884922 | Ritchie, James (MID) | N/a | 1LS | N/a |
| 2877591 | Robb, James | N/a | 1LS | PoW |
| 2878501 | Robb, Richard | | 6th | PoW |
| 2879264 | Robb, William | N/a | 6th | W |
| 3196868 | Roberts, John | N/a | 1LS | W + PoW |
| 137923 | ROBERTSON, BRUCE | | 1LS | N/a |
| 2878041 | Robertson, Douglas | | 1LS | N/a |
| 2890704 | Robertson, George | N/a | 6th | PoW |

| Army Number | Name | Photo | Bn. | Fate |
|---|---|---|---|---|
| 2878334 | Robertson, Hector | | 1LS | N/a |
| 2889505 | Robertson, Henry | N/a | 1LS | PoW |
| 2879452 | Robertson, Hugh | N/a | 1LS | W+W |
| 6666223 | Robertson, J.E. | N/a | 1LS | W |
| 2760544 | Robertson, J.S. | N/a | 6th | W |
| 2884278 | ROBERTSON, JAMES | N/a | 1LS | KIA |
| 14350199 | Robertson, Richard | | 6th | PoW |
| 14563438 | ROBERTSON, THOMAS | N/a | 1LS | KIA |
| 2829358 | Robertson, W. | N/a | 1LS | W |
| 2871786 | Robertson, William | N/a | 6th | W |
| 2890733 | Robinson, Colin | N/a | 1LS | W |
| 3250167 | ROBINSON, ROBERT | N/a | 1LS | KIA |
| 14650184 | Robinson, Stanley | N/a | 1LS | W+W |
| 2829539 | ROBINSON, THOMAS | | 1LS | KIA |
| 14201309 | Robson, E. | N/a | 6th | PoW |
| 2879654 | ROBSON, THOMAS | N/a | 1LS | KIA |
| 3254771 | RODWELL, LEONARD | N/a | 1LS | KIA |
| 14203112 | RODWELL, PETER | N/a | 6th | KIA |
| 6985810 | Roe, Leslie | N/a | 1LS | W |
| 3184895 | Roebuck, George | N/a | 1LS | W+W |
| 14416231 | ROLFE, JULIAN | N/a | 1LS | KIA |
| 2886382 | ROLLINS, WILLIAM (MID) | N/a | 1LS | KIA |
| 2567514 | Rollo, David | N/a | 6th | PoW |
| 3316075 | Rollo, G. | N/a | 1LS | W |
| 2890269 | ROLLO, WILLIAM | N/a | 6th | KIA |
| 2886060 | Rose, Albert | N/a | 6th | PoW |
| 1264V | ROSE, George (MM) | N/a | 6th | KIA |
| 2877507 | ROSE, JOHN ROBERTSON | | 6th | N/a |

| Army Number | Name | Photo | Bn. | Fate |
|---|---|---|---|---|
| 2890175 | ROSE, JOHN STEWART | N/a | 1LS | KIA |
| 2882541 | Ross, George | N/a | 6th | W |
| 14212352 | Ross, H. | N/a | 1LS | W |
| 2888778 | Ross, James | N/a | 6th | PoW |
| 7962400 | Ross, Ronald | N/a | 6th | W |
| 6968685 | ROSS, STUART | N/a | 1LS | KIA |
| 14205483 | Ross, Vernon | | 6th | PoW |
| 195390 | Rowlands, Bryan | N/a | RAMC | W |
| 14642993 | Roy, James | N/a | 6th | W |
| 2058918 | ROY, JOHN BROWN | N/a | 6th | KIA |
| 14343444 | ROYALL, WILLIAM | N/a | 6th | KIA |
| 14563736 | Rubie, John (MM) | N/a | 1LS | N/a |
| 2827057 | RUDGE, ARTHUR | N/a | 1LS | KIA |
| 14291344 | Rumble, J. | N/a | 6th | PoW |
| 2880289 | Runcie, John (MID) | N/a | 6th | PoW |
| 14613259 | Rushton, Edward | N/a | 1LS | W |
| 2760549 | Rusk, Andrew | N/a | 6th | PoW |
| 2875678 | Russell, Alexander | N/a | 6th | W |
| 2875211 | RUSSELL, ALEXANDER GARIOCH | N/a | 1LS | KIA |
| 2886064 | Russell, Daniel | | 6th | PoW |
| 2879717 | RUSSELL, JAMES | N/a | 1LS | DoW |
| 229005 | RUSSELL, JOHN PATRICK (PAT) | N/a | 1LS | KIA |
| 2890369 | Samuel, George | N/a | 6th | PoW |
| 2884297 | Samuel, Robert | N/a | 1LS | W |
| 14390654 | Sanderson, L. | N/a | 1LS | W |
| 2885951 | Sandey, Alexander | N/a | 1LS | W |
| 897561 | SAVILLE, ARTHUR | N/a | 1LS | KIA |
| 4925811 | Sayer, Cyril | N/a | 1LS | W |
| 5347887 | Sayers, Leslie | N/a | 6th | N/a |
| 2766152 | Scobie, Andrew | N/a | 6th | PoW |

| Army Number | Name | Photo | Bn. | Fate |
|---|---|---|---|---|
| 2888780 | SCOTT, CHARLES | | 6th | KIA |
| 2878993 | Scott, Douglas (MM + MID) | N/a | 1LS | N/a |
| 3189632 | Scott, Eric | N/a | 1LS | W |
| 2890706 | Scott, George | | 1LS | W |
| 2880277 | Scott, James | | GH | W + PoWJ |
| 14212029 | SCOTT, JAMES | N/a | 1LS | KIA |
| 14554967 | SCOTT, JAMES | N/a | 1LS | KIA |
| 2890540 | Scott, John | N/a | 6th | PoW |
| 2990925 | Scott, M. | N/a | 1LS | W |
| 14595701 | SCOTT, WILLIAM | N/a | 6th | PoW + Died |
| 1802091 | SEAKINS, NORMAN | N/a | 1LS | KIA |
| 3253054 | SEAR, VINCENT | N/a | 1LS | DoW |
| 2753082 | Secker, N. | N/a | 1LS | PoW |
| 3603778 | SEDDON, WILLIAM | N/a | 1LS | KIA |
| 2940273 | SEGAL, JACK | N/a | 1LS | KIA |
| 2882287 | SEIVWRIGHT, WALTER | | 6th | KIA |
| 14621149 | SEMENITE, KARL | N/a | 1LS | KIA |
| 6216114 | Sevenoaks, W. | N/a | 1LS | W |
| 99735 | Shand, Harry | N/a | 6th | W + PoW |
| 2881377 | Shand, Peter (MM) | | 6th | N/a |
| 2881630 | Shand, Ronald | | 6th | N/a |
| 1465720 | SHAND, WILLIAM | | 6th | KIA |

| Army Number | Name | Photo | Bn. | Fate |
|---|---|---|---|---|
| 3197690 | SHANNON, ROBERT (Roy) | N/a | 6th | KIA |
| 2880440 | Sharp, James | N/a | 1LS | W |
| 2880040 | Sharp, Ronald | N/a | 6th | W |
| 996862 | Sharpe, E.K. | N/a | 6th | W |
| 2879565 | Shaw, David | N/a | 1LS | PoW |
| 4866304 | Shaw, G.W. | N/a | 1LS | PoW |
| 3194321 | Shaw, Gilbert | N/a | 6th | W |
| 2881619 | Shea, Arthur | N/a | 6th | W+W |
| 6981085 | SHEFFIELD, JOHN | N/a | 1LS | KIA |
| 2981802 | Shepherd, D. | N/a | 1LS | PoW |
| 91450 | SHEPHERD, DAVID (MC + MID) | | RA | PoW + DoW |
| 7047727 | Shepherd, Kenneth (MID) | N/a | 1LS | N/a |
| 5732479 | Sheppard, L. | N/a | 6th | PoW |
| 1545331 | Shevlin, J. | N/a | 1LS | W |
| 2989570 | Shields, Ross | N/a | 6th | PoW |
| 14201452 | Shilliam, R. | | 6th | W |
| 14633991 | Shipherd, William | N/a | 1LS | PoW |
| 6291093 | Sibbald, Thomas | N/a | 1LS | W |
| 14201530 | Silver, T. | N/a | 1LS | W |
| 2885152 | SIM, ANDREW | N/a | 6th | DoW |
| 5349677 | Simmonds, James | N/a | 6th | PoW |
| 2886638 | Simpson, Alexander | N/a | 6th | PoW |
| 2889455 | SIMPSON, ANDREW | N/a | 1LS | DoW |
| 3247811 | Simpson, C. | N/a | 6th | W |
| 2934299 | Simpson, G.R. | N/a | 1LS | PoW |
| 2883020 | Simpson, George Harold | | GH | N/a |
| 2879035 | Simpson, Henry | | GH | PoW J |
| 2884855 | SIMPSON, JOHN ANDERSON | N/a | 1LS | KIA |
| 2879737 | Simpson, Robert | N/a | 1LS | W+W |

| Army Number | Name | Photo | Bn. | Fate |
|---|---|---|---|---|
| 14210735 | Simpson, Thomas | N/a | 1LS | W |
| 2889457 | Simpson, William | | 1LS | PoW |
| 2890274 | Sinclair, Alexander | N/a | 6th | W + PoW |
| 45141 | Sinclair, James (MBE) | | 5th GH | PoW |
| 2881084 | Sinclair, John | N/a | 6th | W |
| 1820281 | Sinclair, L. | N/a | 1LS | PoW |
| 3066930 | Singleton, George | N/a | 1LS | PoW |
| 846964 | Sivewright, Alexander | | 6th | PoW |
| 14607809 | SKINNER, WILLIAM | N/a | 1LS | DoW |
| 2890170 | Slavin, James | N/a | 6th | PoW |
| 1528284 | Slobom, G. | N/a | 1LS | W |
| 3066652 | Small, Douglas | N/a | 1LS | W |
| 14201615 | Smith, A. | N/a | 1LS | W |
| 2890708 | Smith, Alexander | N/a | 1LS | W+W |
| 2886283 | Smith, Christopher | N/a | 1LS | PoW |
| 2884811 | Smith, Douglas | N/a | 1LS | W |
| 14602357 | Smith, E. | N/a | 1LS | W |
| 3325083 | Smith, J. | N/a | 6th | W |
| 6457004 | Smith, J.R. | N/a | 1LS | W |
| 3197766 | SMITH, JAMES | N/a | 1LS | DoW |
| 14552965 | SMITH, JOHN EDWARD | N/a | 1LS | KIA |
| 2890275 | Smith, John Morrison | N/a | 6th | PoW |
| 14522644 | Smith, Matthew | N/a | 6th | W |
| 2878111 | Smith, Raymond | N/a | 1LS | W |
| 1455413 | Smith, Robert | N/a | 1LS | W |
| 112974 | Smith, Robert W. | | 6th | W |
| 5956543 | SMITH, SYDNEY | N/a | 1LS | KIA |
| 14297907 | SMITH, THOMAS | N/a | 1LS | KIA |

| Army Number | Name | Photo | Bn. | Fate |
|---|---|---|---|---|
| 2874916 | Smith, Thomas | | 6th | N/a |
| 14205503 | SMITH, THOMAS WARD | N/a | 6th | DoW |
| 14587792 | Smith, W.G. | N/a | 6th | PoW |
| 4867515 | SMITH, WALTER | N/a | 6th | KIA |
| 2761845 | Smith, William | N/a | 6th | PoW |
| 1820289 | SNEDDON, WILLIAM | N/a | 1LS | KIA |
| 2829297 | Snell, Leslie | N/a | GH | W+W |
| 14582165 | SNELLING, FREDERICK | N/a | 6th | KIA |
| 14002865 | SNOOKS, ROYSTON | N/a | 1LS | KIA |
| 14643282 | Snow, Eric | N/a | 6th | W |
| 2883859 | Somerville, John | N/a | 6th | PoW |
| 14588271 | Souter, Gilbert | N/a | 1LS | W + PoW |
| 6666317 | Souter, Robert Louis | N/a | 1LS | PoW |
| 2885216 | Spalding, Robert | N/a | 6th | W |
| 2877540 | Spawforth, Arthur (MID) | | 1LS | W+W |
| 14209269 | Spence, D. | N/a | 6th | W |
| 2880674 | Spence, James | | 6th | N/a |
| 2882248 | SPENCE, JOHN | | 6th | DoW |
| 14613002 | SPIERS, CHRISPIN | N/a | 1LS | PoW + DoW |
| 2879576 | Spooner, Keith | | 1LS | N/a |
| 6985820 | Spray, William | N/a | 1LS | W |
| 3135347 | Sproule, Robert | N/a | 1LS | PoW |
| 2877665 | Stables, William | | 6th | PoW |
| 14649739 | Stanley, Walter | N/a | 1LS | PoW |

| Army Number | Name | Photo | Bn. | Fate |
|---|---|---|---|---|
| 14656817 | STARK, JOHN | N/a | 1LS | KIA |
| 5836887 | STEADMAN, J. | N/a | 1LS | DoW |
| 14205507 | Steel, G.F. | N/a | 1LS | W |
| 14573367 | STEELE, CLIFFORD | N/a | 6th | KIA |
| 2886074 | Steele, John Alexander | | 6th | PoW |
| 14644442 | Steele, Joseph | N/a | 1LS | W |
| 7917383 | Steele, Leslie | N/a | 1LS | W |
| 2879829 | Steele, Walter | N/a | 6th | W |
| 14629479 | STEELEY, JOHN | N/a | 6th | W + KIA |
| 13084670 | Steer, C. | N/a | 6th | W |
| 2890711 | Stephen, Stanley | N/a | 6th | PoW |
| 4619548 | Stephenson, J. | N/a | 1LS | W |
| 14201341 | Stephenson, W. | N/a | 1LS | W+W |
| 14559608 | Stevens, Clifford | N/a | 6th | W |
| N/k | Stevens, W. | N/a | 6th | N/a |
| 2882554 | Stevenson, John | N/a | 6th | PoW |
| 2383569 | Stewart, Alan | N/a | 1LS | W |
| 906684 | Stewart, Alfred | N/a | 1LS | W |
| 2760401 | Stewart, B. | N/a | 1LS | PoW |
| 2754278 | Stewart, Charles | N/a | 6th | N/a |
| 2816861 | Stewart, Francis | | 6th | N/a |
| 2889162 | Stewart, Henry | N/a | 6th | W |
| 3246973 | STEWART, JOHN | N/a | 1LS | KIA |
| 2880525 | Stewart, John | N/a | 6th | PoW |
| 1812001 | Stewart, John Pender | N/a | 1LS | W |
| 2760912 | Stewart, R. | N/a | 1LS | W |
| 1537278 | Stewart, R.B. | N/a | 1LS | W |
| 2880511 | STEWART, WILLIAM | N/a | 6th | AK |
| 2884828 | Stewart, William Mitchell | N/a | 1LS | PoW |
| 5343718 | Still, Ernest | | 6th | PoW |

| Army Number | Name | Photo | Bn. | Fate |
|---|---|---|---|---|
| 5051775 | Stimpson, B. | N/a | 1LS | W |
| 14633888 | Stirling, James | N/a | 1LS | PoW |
| 239424 | Stirton, D. | | 1LS | W |
| 5350711 | Stock, Ronald | N/a | 6th | PoW |
| 2886730 | Stockdale, John | N/a | 1LS | PoW |
| 14435635 | Stockton, S. | N/a | 1LS | W |
| 181906 | Stone, J. (MID) | N/a | 1LS | N/a |
| 1574394 | Stone, William | N/a | 1LS | W |
| 3197336 | Storm, Robert | N/a | 6th | PoW |
| 2883120 | Storrie, Alexander | N/a | 6th | PoW |
| 2890546 | Stott, James | N/a | 6th | W |
| 3193218 | Stott, Wilfred | N/a | 1LS | PoW |
| 3185098 | Strachan, John | N/a | 1LS | W |
| 14214370 | Strachan, William | N/a | 1LS | PoW |
| 2940125 | Stratham-Wild, George | N/a | 1LS | PoW |
| 2875937 | Strathdee, Stewart | | 6th | PoW |
| 5350344 | Street, P. | N/a | 1LS | W |
| 2880259 | Stronach, John | N/a | 6th | N/a |
| 14263582 | Sturgess, G. | N/a | 6th | W + PoW |
| 14410375 | Sudderick, Leslie | | 1LS | W+W |
| 14208287 | Sullivan, F. | N/a | 6th | PoW |
| 2886076 | Summers, James | N/a | 1LS | W |
| 3719174 | Sumner, J. | N/a | 1LS | PoW |
| 2884794 | SUTHERLAND, ADAM | N/a | 1LS | KIA |
| 14540488 | SUTHERLAND, ADAM M. | N/a | 1LS | KIA |
| 2880550 | Sutherland, Alexander | N/a | 6th | W |
| 14555282 | Sutherland, D. | N/a | 1LS | W |
| 2874998 | SUTHERLAND, ROBERT | | 1LS | KIA |
| 1087049 | SWAIN, ALBERT | N/a | 6th | KIA |

| Army Number | Name | Photo | Bn. | Fate |
|---|---|---|---|---|
| 4545941 | SWALLOW, PHILIP | N/a | 1LS | KIA |
| 3325994 | Swan, J. | N/a | 1LS | W |
| 1545391 | Sweeney, Alexander | N/a | 1LS | W |
| 2889464 | Sweeney, Owen | N/a | 6th | PoW |
| 14650204 | Swift, Thomas | N/a | 1LS | W |
| 118672 | Swindlehurst, R. | N/a | GH | W+W |
| 14204832 | Swinfield, E. | N/a | 1LS | W + PoW |
| 14621253 | Swinley, Andrew | N/a | 1LS | W |
| 2888627 | Sykes, James | N/a | 1LS | W |
| 2767187 | Syme, Andrew | N/a | 1LS | PoW |
| 2884917 | Syme, George (MID) | N/a | 1LS | W+W |
| 2765888 | Tadden, R. | N/a | 1LS | W |
| 14304557 | Taffinier, K. | N/a | 1LS | W |
| 2886651 | Tait, Douglas | | 6th | N/a |
| 14357608 | Tait, Dugald | N/a | 1LS | PoW |
| 2883661 | TALBOT, WILLIAM | N/a | 6th | KIA |
| 14200686 | Tant, G. | N/a | 1LS | PoW |
| 2890180 | TAPSFIELD, DONALD | N/a | 1LS | KIA |
| 2888790 | Tasker, Duncan | N/a | 6th | PoW |
| 2937847 | Taylor, A. | N/a | 1LS | W |
| 2875343 | Taylor, Alexander | | 6th | W |
| 2879742 | TAYLOR, ALEXANDER | N/a | 1LS | PoW + DoW |
| 14209283 | TAYLOR, ARCHBALD | N/a | 1LS | KIA |
| 2766500 | Taylor, F. | N/a | 1LS | W |
| 2880338 | Taylor, George | N/a | 6th | PoW |
| 14633995 | Taylor, James | N/a | 1LS | PoW |
| 2760273 | TAYLOR, JAMES DUTHIE | | 1LS | KIA |
| 79592 | Taylor, James Lennel | | RAMC | N/a |

| Army Number | Name | Photo | Bn. | Fate |
|---|---|---|---|---|
| 2882550 | Taylor, Peter | | 6th | W + PoW J |
| 14562463 | Taylor, R. | N/a | 6th | PoW |
| 2889166 | Taylor, Raymond | N/a | 6th | W |
| 2883974 | TAYLOR, ROBERT | | 1LS | W + KIA |
| 2890281 | Taylor, Samuel | N/a | 6th | PoW |
| 14499312 | Taylor, W. | N/a | 1LS | W |
| 3318037 | Taylor, W.V. | N/a | 1LS | W |
| 3194763 | Teggart, Victor | N/a | 6th | PoW |
| 2884848 | Templeton, James | N/a | 1LS | W |
| 14383335 | Terris, J. | N/a | 1LS | W + PoW |
| 2890282 | Tervit, James | N/a | 6th | PoW |
| 14214098 | Tewkesbury, G. | N/a | 6th | PoW |
| 2878136 | Thain, Alexander | N/a | 6th | W |
| 14219756 | Thain, E. | N/a | 1LS | PoW |
| 2878291 | THAIN, JOHN (MID) | | 6th | KIA |
| 2890715 | Thain, John I. | N/a | 6th | W |
| 14422445 | THOM, JAMES | N/a | 6th | KIA |
| 2883476 | Thom, John Gordon (DCM) | | 1LS | W |
| 2883033 | THOM, ROBERT | | 6th | AK |
| 14201538 | Thomas, E. | N/a | 6th | PoW |
| 13086983 | Thomas, F. | N/a | 6th | W |
| 14632245 | Thomas, Harold | N/a | 6th | W |
| 2880111 | Thompson, Donald (Denis) | N/a | 1LS | W + PoW |
| 2886698 | Thompson, Leonard | N/a | 6th | PoW |
| 2884246 | THOMSON, ALASTAIR | | 1LS | DoW |

| Army Number | Name | Photo | Bn. | Fate |
|---|---|---|---|---|
| 14595531 | Thomson, David | N/a | 6th | W |
| 2879884 | Thomson, George | N/a | 1LS | W |
| 14620952 | Thomson, George A. | N/a | 1LS | W |
| 2878777 | Thomson, George Petrie | | 6th | PoW |
| 2884636 | Thomson, James Allan Moir | | 6th | PoW |
| 2882641 | Thomson, James Leask Inkster (MID) | N/a | 1LS | N/a |
| 3194542 | THOMSON, JAMES WEDDEL | N/a | 6th | KIA |
| 2890285 | Thomson, Robert | | 6th | W + PoW |
| 2890284 | Thomson, Robert | N/a | 6th | W |
| 3314545 | Thomson, William | N/a | 6th | PoW |
| 2877712 | Thomson, William Bett | N/a | 6th | PoW |
| 2879937 | THORNE, ALBERT | N/a | 1LS | KIA |
| 14607394 | Thornton, C. | N/a | 1LS | PoW |
| 2185270 | Thow, William | | 6th | PoW |
| 2882496 | Tocher, Alexander | N/a | 6th | W |
| 2879252 | Todd, George | N/a | 6th | PoW |
| 2890286 | Todd, Robert | N/a | 6th | W |
| 14205519 | TOGNERI, GEORGE | N/a | 6th | W + KIA |
| 5127657 | Tomkins, T. | N/a | 1LS | W |
| 14401274 | Topping, N. | N/a | 6th | PoW |
| 14363647 | Torbet, William | N/a | 1LS | W |
| 14283292 | Towart, A. | N/a | 6th | PoW |
| 2884921 | Townsley, Ferdinand | N/a | 1LS | PoW |
| 2888978 | Tracey, Daniel | N/a | 6th | PoW |
| 158881 | Tregellas, Thomas Symons Treloar | | 6th | W |

| Army Number | Name | Photo | Bn. | Fate |
|---|---|---|---|---|
| 2886079 | Tripney, David (MID) | | 6th | W |
| 14206161 | TROMANS, LESLIE | | 6th | DoW |
| 14401247 | Tullett, W. | N/a | 1LS | W |
| 2875411 | TULLY, RICHARD | N/a | 6th | KIA |
| 14629329 | Tunney, Leonard | N/a | 6th | W |
| 3195900 | Turnbull, Andrew | N/a | 6th | PoW |
| 2879831 | Turner, David | N/a | 1LS | W |
| 5345574 | Turner, F. (MID) | N/a | 1LS | N/a |
| 14204593 | Turner, K. | N/a | 1LS | W |
| 14407682 | TUXWORTH, ERIC | N/a | 1LS | KIA |
| 1420468 | Twigg, K. | N/a | 1LS | W |
| 6985827 | Twigge, Frederick | N/a | 1LS | W |
| 2888800 | Twivey, William | N/a | 6th | W |
| 2931852 | Underwood, Albert | N/a | 1LS | PoW |
| 3123438 | Underwood, John (MID) | N/a | 6th | N/a |
| 2890213 | Ure, Donald | N/a | 6th | PoW |
| 14597454 | Vale, Herbert | N/a | 6th | PoW |
| 14323925 | Valentine, W. | N/a | 1LS | W |
| 14415090 | VANN, ARTHUR | N/a | 1LS | KIA |
| 2760585 | Vannett, J. | N/a | 1LS | W |
| 3194801 | Veitch, John | N/a | 6th | W |
| 14413551 | Venner, J. | N/a | 1LS | W+W |
| 14626591 | Vickers, Arthur | N/a | 1LS | PoW |
| 3195283 | VOWLES, FREDERICK | N/a | 6th | KIA |
| 2879692 | VYNER, VINCENT | N/a | 1LS | AK |
| 302900 | WADDELL, JAMES | N/a | 6th | KIA |
| 3318454 | WADDELL, ROBERT | N/a | 6th | KIA |
| 4921716 | WAIN, WILLIAM | N/a | 1LS | KIA |
| 14650213 | Wakeman, J. | N/a | 6th | W |
| 3322223 | Walker, A. | N/a | 6th | W |
| 2880110 | Walker, Ian | N/a | 1LS | PoW |
| 14412982 | Walker, James F. | N/a | 1LS | W+W |

| Army Number | Name | Photo | Bn. | Fate |
|---|---|---|---|---|
| 2886477 | Walker, John | | 1LS | PoW |
| 5052161 | Walker, John | N/a | 6th | PoW |
| 2889813 | Walker, Keith | N/a | 1LS | PoW |
| 14390673 | Walker, R. | N/a | 1LS | W |
| 2888337 | Walker, William | N/a | 6th | W |
| 14626595 | Walker, William J. | N/a | 1LS | PoW |
| 2890216 | Wallace, James | N/a | 6th | PoW |
| 6411947 | Walsh, Stephen | N/a | 6th | PoW |
| 14343462 | Ward, H. | N/a | 6th | PoW |
| 2880394 | Wardle, John (MID) | N/a | 1LS | W |
| 2888802 | Wares, John | N/a | 6th | W |
| 2883740 | Warn, Albert | N/a | 6th | PoW |
| 7022638 | Warren, John. | N/a | 6th | PoW |
| 14595722 | Warson, J. | N/a | 6th | PoW |
| 2764624 | Waterson, Walter | N/a | 6th | PoW |
| 2940013 | Watkins, A. | N/a | 1LS | W |
| 14260319 | WATKINS, HAROLD | N/a | 6th | KIA |
| 14206178 | Watkiss, J. | | 6th | W |
| 14201345 | WATSON, ARTHUR | N/a | 1LS | DoW |
| 2884864 | Watson, Edward | N/a | 1LS | W+W |
| 2929902 | Watson, Eric | N/a | 6th | W |
| 2762736 | WATSON, PETER | N/a | 6th | KIA |
| 14207715 | Watson, W. | N/a | 6th | W + PoW |
| 2886313 | Watt, Alexander (MM) | | 1LS | W |
| 6666556 | Watt, J. | N/a | 1LS | W |
| 14205530 | Watt, Robert (Bert) | | 6th | PoW |
| 14203118 | Watts, A. | N/a | 1LS | W |
| 2878461 | WEBB, JAMES EDWARD | N/a | 1LS | W |
| 2880340 | WEBSTER, JAMES DUNCAN | N/a | 6th | DoW |

| Army Number | Name | Photo | Bn. | Fate |
|---|---|---|---|---|
| 2886667 | Webster, John | N/a | 1LS | W |
| 2886296 | WEBSTER, JOHN GREENLAW | N/a | 1LS | KIA |
| 2890483 | WEBSTER, WILLIAM | N/a | 6th | KIA |
| 1467030 | Weir, Daniel | N/a | 1LS | W |
| 1798901 | WEIR, ERIC | | 1LS | KIA |
| 2878050 | Weir, Thomas | N/a | 1LS | PoW |
| 14648076 | Wellings, Cecil | N/a | 6th | W |
| 5347465 | Wellings, H. | N/a | 6th | PoW |
| 2935415 | West, Archibald (MID) | N/a | 1LS | W |
| 2882544 | West, James | | 6th | N/a |
| 2756327 | West, W. | N/a | 1LS | W |
| 2879053 | Westwater, William (MID) | | 1LS | PoW |
| 2883662 | Weyers, Thomas | N/a | 6th | PoW |
| 14659810 | Whatley, S. | N/a | 1LS | W |
| 14568192 | Wheeldon, Ronald | N/a | 1LS | PoW |
| 2878060 | WHEELER, DOUGLAS | N/a | 1LS | KIA |
| 7015063 | Whelan, John | N/a | 6th | W + PoW |
| 2571236 | WHINCUP, FRANCIS | N/a | 1LS | KIA |
| 14621189 | Whisker, Edward | N/a | 1LS | W+W |
| 4865330 | WHITE, LEONARD | N/a | 6th | KIA |
| 2884913 | White, Robert | N/a | 1LS | W |
| 2884825 | WHITE, ROBERT (MID) | N/a | 1LS | KIA |
| 2886396 | WHITE, WILFRED | N/a | 1LS | W + KIA |
| 2868884 | Whitecross, John | N/a | 6th | N/a |
| 2885491 | WHITEHEAD, ALEXANDER | N/a | 1LS | DoW |
| 2889687 | Whitehead, Clifford | N/a | 1LS | W |
| 3601692 | Whitfield, J. | N/a | 6th | PoW |
| 14409388 | Whitwell, Albert (Arthur) | N/a | 1LS | PoW |
| 2875277 | WHYTE, ROBERT | N/a | 6th | DoW |
| 14424559 | Whyte, W. | N/a | 6th | PoW |

| Army Number | Name | Photo | Bn. | Fate |
|---|---|---|---|---|
| 2886177 | WHYTOCK, LAWRENCE | N/a | 1LS | KIA |
| 5052171 | WILD, EDWARD | N/a | 6th | PoW + KIA |
| 14356302 | Wild, William | N/a | 1LS | W |
| 2763110 | Wilkie, Edward | N/a | 1LS | PoW |
| 2886395 | Wilkin, John | N/a | 1LS | W |
| 3320206 | WILKINSON, GEORGE | N/a | 6th | Died |
| 3195371 | Wilkinson, George A. | N/a | 6th | PoW |
| 2829557 | WILKINSON, JAMES | N/a | 1LS | KIA |
| 96961 | Will, Ian (MC) | | 1LS | W |
| 153405 | Will, Neil (DSO) | | 1LS | W |
| 4194342 | Williams, Lorwerth | N/a | 1LS | W |
| 2824053 | WILLIAMS, THOMAS | N/a | 6th | DoW |
| 3247842 | Williamson, H.D. | N/a | 6th | W |
| 2890220 | Williamson, Hugh Ballantyne | N/a | 6th | PoW |
| 73257 | Williamson, James (MC) | | 6th | W |
| 1475714 | WILLIAMSON, WILLIAM | N/a | 1LS | KIA |
| 14649783 | Wills, George | N/a | 1LS | W |
| 3254642 | WILSON, DANIEL | N/a | 1LS | KIA |
| 2878130 | Wilson, George Reidford (MM) | | 6th | W |
| 14595545 | Wilson, Henry | N/a | 6th | W |
| 50167 | Wilson, Henry (OBE) | | 1LS | N/a |
| 2763114 | Wilson, J. | N/a | 1LS | W |
| 2885418 | Wilson, James Brown Hamish | N/a | 1LS | PoW |
| 3066783 | WILSON, JOHN | N/a | 1LS | KIA |
| 1509810 | Wilson, Peter | N/a | 1LS | W |

| Army Number | Name | Photo | Bn. | Fate |
|---|---|---|---|---|
| 10602037 | Wilson, T. | N/a | 6th | W |
| 14204755 | Wilson, W. | N/a | 6th | W |
| 14203862 | Wilson, W.C. | N/a | 1LS | W |
| 2885281 | Wilson, William | N/a | 1LS | W+W |
| 4206811 | Wilson, William Arthur | N/a | 1LS | W+W |
| 961324 | Windass, George | N/a | 1LS | W |
| 4698650 | Windle, Ernest | N/a | 6th | PoW |
| 5347227 | Winter, G.E. | N/a | 1LS | W |
| 2757788 | Winton, A. | N/a | 1LS | W |
| 3315028 | Wolfenden, David | N/a | 1LS | W |
| 2882160 | Wood, Albert | N/a | 1LS | PoW |
| 2766025 | Wood, W. | N/a | 1LS | W+W |
| 2876821 | Wood, William (Alias Todd, William) | | 6th | PoW |
| 3602372 | Woodhouse, A. | N/a | 6th | W |
| 5194185 | Worrall, E. | N/a | 1LS | W |
| 14201546 | Worrall, Ronald | N/a | 1LS | W+W |
| 2940102 | Worthington, Thomas | N/a | 1LS | W+W |
| 14656828 | Wright, David | N/a | 1LS | W |
| 6353576 | Wright, N. | N/a | 1LS | W |
| 14635989 | Wright, Thomas | N/a | 6th | W |
| 2886733 | Wright, William | N/a | 1LS | W |
| 3135373 | WYLIE, DAVID | N/a | 1LS | DoW |
| 2884986 | WYLLIE, ANDREW | N/a | 1LS | DoW |
| 3309370 | Wyllie, H. | N/a | 6th | W |
| 3247917 | Wyllie, J. | N/a | 6th | W |
| 4272355 | Yeats, W.A. | N/a | 6th | W+W |
| 2890718 | Yeats, William | N/a | 6th | PoW |
| 14201484 | Yeomans, E. | N/a | 6th | PoW |
| 2758822 | Young, Archibald | N/a | 1LS | PoW |
| 2890225 | YOUNG, JOHN | N/a | 6th | KIA |
| 2890226 | YOUNG, ROBERT | N/a | 6th | KIA |
| 3247778 | Young, Robert O. | N/a | 6th | W + PoW |
| 1837134 | Young, Thomas | N/a | 6th | W |
| 14370898 | Youngs, C. | N/a | 6th | W |

| Army Number | Name | Photo | Bn. | Fate |
|---|---|---|---|---|
| 2890227 | Yuill, George | N/a | 6th | PoW |
| 2886673 | Yule, John | N/a | 6th | PoW |
| 14563468 | YULE, JOHN INGLIS | N/a | 6th | KIA |
| 3323695 | ZACK, MORRIS (BENNIE) | N/a | 6th | KIA |

# Index